W9-CKQ-814

Abraham Lincoln and a New Birth of Freedom

The Union and Slavery

in the Diplomacy

of the Civil War

HOWARD JONES

University of Nebraska Press

Lincoln and London

First Bison Books printing: 2002
Library of Congress Cataloging-
in-Publication Data
Jones, Howard, 1940–
Abraham Lincoln and a new birth of freedom:
the Union and slavery in the diplomacy
of the Civil War / Howard Jones.
p. cm.
Includes bibliographical references and index.
ISBN 0-8032-2582-2 (cl: alk. paper)
ISBN 0-8032-7565-X (pa: alk. paper)
1. United States – foreign relations – 1861–1865.
2. Lincoln, Abraham, 1809–1865. 3. Slaves –
Emancipation – United States.
4. United States – Foreign relations –
Great Britain. 5. Great Britain – Foreign
relations – United States 6. United States –
Foreign relations – France. 7. France – Foreign
relations – United States. 8. Intervention
(International law) – History – 19th century.
I. Title.
E469.J56 1999
327.73'009'034 – DC21 99-11170
CIP

For Mary Ann, my dearest friend and partner in life

If the negro is a man, why then my ancient faith teaches me that
"all men are created equal."
Abraham Lincoln, October 16, 1854

Contents

Illustrations

Acknowledgments

As always, it has proved impossible for me to write a book without considerable assistance. I have been fortunate, again, to receive advice and encouragement from several students of the Civil War and of history itself. For more times than he and she may want to admit, my longtime friends Forrest and Ellie McDonald read one of my manuscripts in its initial stages, offering countless suggestions that made their way into the final product. Both Pete Maslowski and Robert E. May continue to demonstrate their uncanny ability to make constructive criticisms while skillfully maintaining our close friendship of more than two decades. Lawrence F. Kohl again read my work, willingly sharing his deep knowledge of the period and helping to refine my ideas on Lincoln. Norman B. Ferris and Brooks D. Simpson also deserve my gratitude for reading the manuscript and suggesting numerous improvements. I also thank Trudie Calvert for yet a third time in offering superb editorial advice. For doing everything possible to create an atmosphere in which to work, I thank Kay Branyon, Loretta Fuller, and Julie Moore. Finally, to those archivists both inside and outside the United States, I know I speak for all historians in expressing my heartfelt appreciation for your help.

This work proved especially challenging. It continues my efforts to highlight the importance of diplomacy to the Civil War. The international dimension of these events has not drawn deserved attention because of the heavy emphasis on battles and leaders, and yet the foreign aspects of this era helped to determine the outcome of the war as well as its ramifications for decades to come. But even more venturesome was my attempt to deal with Lincoln. So many writers have written so much about the man that it becomes almost presumptuous to think that there is anything more to say. I hope to have provided something useful for those who enjoy studying Lincoln and his times as much as I do.

Nothing I do in history would be worthwhile without the support of family. My parents, my daughters, their husbands, and my grandchildren, Timothy and Ashley, as always, remain sincere supporters of my work. To Mary

Ann, however, goes special thanks each day (if not always verbally) for sharing her life with me.

If the following pages have any value, I freely share this attribute with everyone mentioned above. The mistakes or faulty analyses I must claim as my own.

ABRAHAM LINCOLN AND A NEW BIRTH OF FREEDOM

Prologue: To Preserve the Union

Liberty and Union, now and forever, one and inseparable!
Daniel Webster, 1830
Abraham Lincoln, 1856

Why another book on Abraham Lincoln? Admittedly, numerous writers have discussed nearly every conceivable aspect of his life. Yet no one has fully examined his impact on Civil War diplomacy, particularly as it derived from his constantly evolving views toward slavery and the way these ideas fitted into his concept of the Union. In 1945 Jay Monaghan published his classic work, *A Diplomat in Carpet Slippers: Abraham Lincoln Deals with Foreign Affairs*, but it rested almost entirely on American sources and reflected both a Union and a Lincoln bias. Moreover, Monaghan brought insufficient focus to Lincoln's efforts to tie antislavery to the creation of a better Union. This gap in the historiography of the period provides the rationale for this book.

Lincoln realized early in his presidency that the slavery issue proved that domestic and foreign affairs were inseparable. He had always found slavery morally objectionable, but not until a year or so into his presidency did he regard the demise of that institution as integral not only to the preservation of the Union but to its betterment. Emancipation, Lincoln also insisted, became a crucial ingredient in Britain's deliberations on whether to intervene in the Civil War, thereby making slavery a vital element in U.S. foreign relations from 1861 to 1865. Only when the Emancipation Proclamation went into effect on January 1, 1863, did the Lincoln administration finally end southern hopes for a British intervention. The French threat, however, lingered throughout the remainder of the war. Even though the British decision seemed irrevocable, Emperor Napoleon III appeared ready to act on his own. At stake was his puppet regime in Mexico, which he intended to use as a magnet for reestablishing monarchical governments all over the Americas. Throughout this intricate and weblike series of events, President Lincoln sought above all else to save the Union by using the growing popular sentiment against slavery to block any form of foreign intervention in the war. The supreme irony is that in achieving emancipation he increased the chances for bringing about the very calamity he fought so hard to avert.

The unfortunate feature of an otherwise rich historiography on the Civil War is that most accounts dwell on battles and personalities, seldom mentioning the pivotal role of foreign affairs. The result is that few students of the war realize how integral the European response was to its outcome. The South's efforts to win diplomatic recognition; secure contracts with European companies to build a navy, float loans, and purchase war matériel; engage in commercial pursuits; perhaps even secure military alliances – all hinged on the foreign reaction to its overtures. British intervention, in particular, would have drastically altered the fate of the Confederacy, perhaps even ensuring its success. The cautiously pragmatic prime minister of England, Lord Palmerston, confronted constant pressure for an intervention that centered on mediation and rested on the premise of southern independence. The less careful and more visionary Napoleon III of France repeatedly pledged his support if the British took the first step. Ultimately, he became frustrated with British hesitation and seriously considered taking the lead. Fortunately for the Union and not so fortunately for the Confederacy, longstanding and intense rivalries between England and France repeatedly helped to obstruct any joint cooperation by the so-called concert. Anglo-French collaboration in any interventionist effort would have changed not only the direction of the American war but the course of history as well.

Interventionist foreign policies constituted a veritable theme of the nineteenth-century Old World, which raised Union fears of Britain and then France interceding in the American Civil War and perhaps even recognizing southern statehood. Europe had recently gone through a tumultuous period that emphasized the principles of monarchical rule, conservative opposition to change, and the acceptance of joint intervention as a standard procedure in putting down popular revolutions against established regimes. In 1815, at the Congress of Vienna following the Napoleonic Wars, the victorious powers sought to put an end to liberal revolutions by restoring stability based on conservative rule. Austrian foreign minister Prince Klemmens von Metternich pushed for squelching popular uprisings in Spain, Portugal, and other European countries that had led to the establishment of constitutional governments. During the late 1840s, nearly fifty revolutions rocked the European continent, leading to a conservative counterrevolution that resulted in a reassertion of aristocratic authority.

Interventionism particularly appealed to aggressive leaders such as Palmerston and Napoleon (elected president of France in 1848 as defender of order), who considered it their prerogative to influence affairs both inside and outside their countries. Europe had rarely intervened in the Americas after 1815, but if such a move might satisfy the interests of either Britain or France, it was not beyond possibility. Indeed, more than a few Americans believed that both European nations regarded a permanent division of the United States as in their best interests. Whether such a fear was justified, the impression became widespread that Palmerston and Napoleon considered themselves self-appointed keepers of Old World order and would support the American antagonist in the Civil War whose victory best fitted their ambitions. Aristocratic, antirevolutionary, and self-interested, whether economic or imperial, these two powerful European figures sought to restore the halcyon days when iron rule assured international order.

Had the Confederacy secured diplomatic recognition from Britain and France, the remainder of the European countries would surely have followed suit. Coming during the Union's most tenuous days in late 1862, this monumental move could have reversed the outcome of the war and reshaped international relations. Foreign recognition of the South would have legitimized secession, destroyed the prewar Union, and dramatically altered U.S. and international history. How bitterly ironic that the "more perfect Union" envisioned by President Abraham Lincoln – that resting on freedom and the natural rights principles underlying the Declaration of Independence – would have come into existence but on a much smaller scale because of the establishment of another American nation – the Confederate States of America, which supported the right of property in slaves. The British would have encountered a vastly weakened American resistance to their expansionist aims in North America, and, with French forces already entrenched in Mexico, the chances did not seem farfetched that Napoleon might strike a deal with Confederate leaders and fulfill his uncle's long-standing dream of establishing an empire in the New World. Indeed, at one critical point in the war, foreign leaders contemplated the possibility of a five-power intervention (England, France, Russia, Prussia, and Austria), using military force to bring the fighting to an end. The historian Allan Nevins keenly observed, "No battle, not Gettysburg, not the Wilderness, was more important than the contest waged in the diplomatic arena and the forum of public opinion." In fact, he concluded, "It is hardly too much to say that the future of the world as we know it was at stake."[1]

South Carolina's dramatic announcement of secession from the Union in December 1860 ultimately led to a war for southern independence. The Palmetto State's decision soon attracted the support of six other southern states, and shortly after they drove federal forces out of Fort Sumter in mid-April 1861, four more states joined the fledgling Confederate States of America. By that spring, eleven states with a population of 9 million people, including 4 million slaves and another quarter of a million free blacks, had challenged the Union, itself the offspring of another rebellion, the American Revolution of 1776. For too many years, southerners complained, the North had cavalierly dismissed their ideals and threatened their idyllic way of life. The election of Lincoln, who they misleadingly stereotyped as a "Black Republican" and abolitionist, had pushed the South out of the Union. In reality, the new president held a moderate stance on slavery, believing it morally reprehensible but legally protected.

Despite these clear-cut domestic issues, the verdict of this war rested as much on foreign affairs as it did on the battlefield. Indeed, the two considerations were inseparable. At two crucial junctures in the Civil War – after Confederate Gen. Robert E. Lee's victory at Second Bull Run in late August 1862 and in the aftermath of the deadly stalemate at Antietam the following September – the South came close to achieving a European intervention. Moreover, even after the Emancipation Proclamation eventually convinced a resentful British people that slavery was on the path toward extinction, the cruelest of ironies regarding French interest in the conflict suddenly became clear. Whereas the vast number of French observers had long opposed the Confederacy because of slavery, they concluded that Lincoln's proclamation had closed the issue, freeing them and their emperor from moral constraints to ponder intervention as a means for securing both cotton and Mexico. Not until the close of 1863 did Napoleon grasp the impact of the Union's July victories at Gettysburg and Vicksburg: southern independence remained a fiction.

During the first two years of the war, however, most foreign observers thought the Union's restoration impossible, thereby providing a possibility for diplomacy to determine the outcome. Southern forces had repulsed the Union in their first major battle, at Bull Run on July 21, 1861, and then, in the spring of 1862, the Army of the Potomac had failed in the Peninsula Campaign against Richmond, the Confederate capital in Virginia. Union troops successfully assaulted the South Carolina Sea Islands and Roanoke Island, and they halted the Confederate invasion of New Mexico. Most important, they won the battles at Forts Henry and Donelson and captured New Orleans, Nashville, and Memphis. Ironically, however, these Union conquests never received the credit they deserved. Europeans (and most Americans) had become obsessed with the Virginia theater of the war and gave relatively little attention to the accomplishments of Union land and naval forces elsewhere. In August 1862 Lincoln bitterly remarked to French Count

Agénor-Etienne de Gasparin that it seemed "unreasonable that a series of successes, extending through half-a-year, and clearing more than a hundred thousand square miles of country, should help us so little, while a single half-defeat should hurt us so much."[2] Despite the Union's efforts, observers both inside and outside the United States considered southern independence a fait accompli.

To those watching the conflict from afar, the issues seemed clear: the South justified in seeking independence, the North unrealistic in demanding a permanent "union." President Lincoln's belated stand against slavery revealed the hypocrisy of a people who had long condoned the institution by their indifference to it. Further, his antislavery crusade threatened to unleash a wave of slave insurrections that would destroy the southern economy and necessitate an international peacemaking effort. Europeans were dumbfounded by naïve northerners who expected to subdue an opponent whose territorial boundaries stretched from the Atlantic to beyond the Mississippi and from Tennessee and Virginia to Mexico. How could an army of mere thousands force several millions of people into submission? More important, how could it kill an idea whose time had come?

From the outset of the fighting, President Lincoln's central purpose was to save the Union by defeating the South on the battlefield; but no less important was his need to prevent a European intervention that would have opened the door to foreign assistance to the South and facilitated its move for independence. Whether intervention took the form of a mediation offer, a call for an armistice, or an outright recognition of nationhood, such foreign involvement would have raised the South's status, energized its followers, and helped determine the war's outcome. Foreign intervention proved especially perilous to the Union during the first eighteen months of the war, when the outcome hung in the balance.

But at this point in the war the stakes became even more substantial: Lincoln's intention to preserve the Union evolved into an effort to form a more perfect Union and hence encompassed a higher purpose than the defeat of the Confederacy. Changing circumstances in the war encouraged him to adopt a progressively harder stance against slavery that became integral to an improved Union and thereby essential to victory. Lincoln was a fatalist who held onto an intensely personal religion based on the eternal laws of necessity, and he came to believe in a divine plan in which he as president acted as God's instrument in effecting great social changes that ultimately rested on the abolition of slavery.[3] In his First Inaugural Address and the Gettysburg Address, he appealed for a mystical and permanent Union that grew out of the natural rights principle undergirding the Declaration of Independence.

The Civil War, Lincoln believed, must beget a spiritual rebirth of the republic. As a master of rhetoric, he often used biblical imagery in focusing on the "born again" concept found in the New Testament Gospel of John. During the 1850s Lincoln set out a belief that he adhered to throughout the ensuing war: "Our republican robe is soiled, and trailed in the dust," he declared. "Let us repurify it. Let us turn and wash it white, in the spirit, if not the blood, of the Revolution."[4] Thus the same synergy that drove the great document of 1776 was now moving the American nation closer to the ultimate goal of freedom for all. The Declaration of Independence had provided the spirit of the Constitution, which itself served as the first real attempt to manifest that ideal, to be shaped in accordance with the steady progression toward universal liberty. The end of slavery became morally inseparable from the sanctity of representative government through the preservation of the Union – both a "military necessity" and "an act of justice," as Lincoln declared in his Emancipation Proclamation.[5] By viewing the war for the Union as a moral crusade, he attempted to vindicate the massive suffering as crucial to the acceptance of profound social change and suggested that divine intervention would assure victory. Lincoln appealed to universal principles of right and wrong and concluded that the destruction of the southern government and way of life was necessary for the betterment of the republic.

Thus North and South engaged in an ideological conflict that, ironically, revolved around two markedly different interpretations of the same two sacred documents: the Declaration of Independence and the Constitution. According to northern nationalists, the longevity of the Union proved its legitimacy against anyone seeking its dissolution. Confederate patriots countered that their growing minority status had left them vulnerable to northern oppression and that the right to withdraw from the governing pact remained a fundamental precept of the Declaration. Had not the contract theory of seventeenth-century English philosopher John Locke provided justification for the American colonies' break with Mother England in 1776? Further, southerners refused to address the natural rights principles of the Declaration and argued instead for the constitutionality of secession by charging the North with interfering in their domestic concerns – particularly their right to property in slaves as guaranteed by the due-process clause in the Fifth Amendment of the Bill of Rights. Lincoln responded that the promises of freedom contained in the Declaration of Independence were unfulfilled in the Constitution and that his objective as president was to redeem those ideals by forming a more perfect Union.

Lincoln recognized that a central problem remained unresolved during the first eighty-five years of the Union's existence: the eternal struggle between human and property rights. Indeed, he believed that the ideals of the Declaration of Independence provided the moral and intellectual framework of the war. Liberty was available to only some Americans. Black people in the United States did not enjoy the natural rights guaranteed by the Declaration's underlying philosophy, and Lincoln firmly believed that the present conflict rested primarily on the differences between North and South over slavery and thereby constituted an integral part of the larger problem of assuring freedom to all Americans. The most profound complication in freeing the blacks was the property right protected by the Constitution. Lincoln thought that human rights held priority over all else and soon considered it his responsibility as president to kill slavery by using its protector – the Constitution – as its executioner. Only by constitutional amendment could the peculiar institution finally be abolished. By mid-1862 Lincoln had decided to incorporate antislavery into the moral dimension of his war for the Union and, in so doing, drive home the point that the Union based on the Declaration of Independence could not coexist with a Constitution that safeguarded human bondage. Freedom and slavery could not live together. Union and freedom had at last become inseparable.

Most capable leaders waging lengthy wars recognize that their people need ideals as a motivating force. Lincoln grasped this basic truth in the early and most crucial stages of the Union's tribulations, when morale had plunged in the North after a series of failures in battle and the breakup of the Union seemed irreversible. Consequently, he wove ideals into the tattered fabric of the Union, giving it strength at its weakest point – the spiritual fiber of its being. Cynics both above and below the Mason-Dixon Line, as well as those self-appointed experts from across the Atlantic who followed the war through newspapers, travelers' accounts, and sheer rumor, openly scoffed at the tall, rail-like hick from Illinois. How could such a rube grasp such far-reaching ideas that lay well beyond his limited intellect? Regardless of their unfounded criticism, Lincoln had seized on ideals that cemented the very foundation of the republican experiment in government and skillfully used them in a manner that convinced many of his contemporaries and most of those in the years afterward of the moral and intellectual rightness of the Union cause.

The Confederacy capitalized on international interest in the struggle by relying on "King Cotton diplomacy" in an effort to win European recognition of its independence. In 1855 South Carolina senator James H. Hammond had painted a dire picture for Europeans deprived of southern cotton for three years or more. "England," he dramatically declared in Congress, "would topple headlong and carry the whole civilized world with her, save

7

the South. No, you dare not make war on cotton. No power on earth dares to make war upon it. Cotton is King!" Now, on the eve of the war, the *Charleston Mercury* boasted, "The cards are in our hands, and we intend to play them out to the bankruptcy of every cotton factory in Great Britain and France or the acknowledgment of our independence." Jefferson Davis and his advisers, according to the Confederate president's wife, thought the leverage of cotton so great "that foreign recognition was looked forward to as an assumed fact."[6]

Confederate strategy became quickly apparent to northerners and Europeans. Charles Francis Adams Jr., son of the Union's minister to London, noted Davis's misguided faith that if England did not get cotton it "would in less than six months be starved into subjection." The British, Davis further believed, "must raise the blockade to preserve . . . internal peace if not prevent revolution." The British foreign secretary, Lord John Russell, sarcastically remarked that southerners considered themselves "masters of the destiny of the world." Cotton was "not alone king, but czar."[7]

Unfortunately for the South, its bountiful cotton harvests in 1859 and 1860 had permitted both the British and the French to fill their warehouses. Indeed, the cotton surplus had created such a problem for manufacturers that the diminished imports resulting from the Civil War constituted a blessing for the owners if also a curse for the workers. With most Old World markets overflowing with cotton and the American market retracted by war, economic distress hit both England and France by late 1862 as many small operatives shut down, causing widespread destitution. In even the larger factories, management laid off large throngs of workers and put many others on short time, creating what numerous contemporaries and latter-day writers have called a "cotton famine" but which was in reality a cotton glut that owners sought to alleviate by reducing their workforce and selling their excess stores.[8]

The South never formally enacted an embargo on cotton to place further pressure on European consumers, but it instituted other measures intended to force compliance with its goal of recognition. Confederate leaders in Richmond, although under pressure from their public to enact an embargo, feared that such a move would push England and France into the Union's camp. Various state and local agencies, however, enforced an embargo before the first year of the war had passed, making it unnecessary for the government to take formal action. Further, the South had exported most of its prewar harvests before the fighting began and in 1862 focused its agricultural production on food. On May 10, 1861, the Confederate Congress passed a bill that prohibited trade with the Union, leaving the impression that since the legislators in that same session were discussing an embargo, the new measure was part of a concerted effort to halt southern commerce with anyone not friendly to its war aims. Almost a year later, on March 17, 1862, the Richmond Congress authorized the destruction of all cotton and other products that might come under Union control. Southerners torched hundreds of thousands of bales of cotton by the following summer and two and one-half million bales by the end of the war in 1865.[9]

Thus Lincoln encountered great difficulty in defining the conflict as a domestic insurrection. Not only were too many foreign economic interests involved in the struggle (northern wheat as well as southern cotton, along with investments of British banking houses), but the British and French also appeared to have imperialist or expansionist designs in mind. Many Americans believed that the British favored the breakup of the Union as a major step toward gaining advantages in North America. This argument was made more convincing by the American perception of the aggressive and saber-rattling Lord Palmerston in London, who had long been a staunch and bitter critic of America. Other Americans warned of the reckless nature of Napoleon III, who seemed bent on reestablishing French power in the New World. The conflict raging in America had a wavelike effect that hit European shores thousands of miles away.

Still other complications arose. The presence of slaves in the South at first posed problems for the antislavery British and French, but President Lincoln unintentionally relieved them of that dilemma by denying any relationship between slavery and the war and arguing that his sole purpose was to preserve the Union. As a result, many observers in England and France regarded the fighting in America as a southern struggle for independence against the northern oppressor. What is more, British and French intervention seemed imminent because of the widely expressed feeling in those countries – including among their leaders – that southern separation was a fait accompli. Union leaders considered the intervention question so dangerous that they warned British officials of war if they extended recognition to the South.

Before the outbreak of the Civil War, both the British and the French press overwhelmingly opposed southern secession largely because of slavery, only to reverse their stand when both North and South denied that slavery had caused the crisis. The London *Times* remarked that Lincoln's election in 1860 meant "that the march of slavery and the domineering tone which its advocates were beginning to assume . . . has been at length arrested and silenced." The North had "right" on its side. The *Economist* and *Edinburgh Review* agreed with this assessment, as did the *Saturday Review*, which criticized the South for attempting to spread slavery across the continent. The London *Chronicle, Dublin News*, and London *Review* blasted the South for its willingness to destroy the Union to protect slavery. In France, the *Moniteur, Patrie,* and *Pays*, all government spokesmen, agreed with the British view. The *Pays* claimed that "abolition of slavery is a noble cause to defend and bring to a triumphant conclusion." The *Constitutionnel* asserted that the South had seceded to "safeguard that dear peculiar institution," whereas the *Journal des d'débats* equated the North with freedom and the South with slavery. It was "a war against slavery," according to the *Revue des deux mondes*. But by the spring of 1861 the French press had become convinced that the North could not win. By what right "does the North desire to impose its government upon the South who do not desire it?" asked the *Constitutionnel*. The South had a legal and moral right to secession, according to the *Moniteur, Patrie*, and *Pays*.[10]

As the war passed through 1862 and into 1863, however, British and French views toward these explosive events underwent a transformation. The British gradually reversed their initial hostilities toward the Emancipation Proclamation of January 1, 1863, to realize that, regardless of the president's motives in taking a stand against slavery, the ultimate result would be its collapse. Consequently, the chances for British intervention ended by the early part of 1863, both because the ministry in London had secured enough cotton from alternative sources to rule out the economic imperative and because the possibility of war with the Union outweighed the humanitarian arguments for entering the conflict. Self-interest continued to guide British foreign policy – this time dictating *against* intervention.

Napoleon, however, held a different view of American events and maintained an interest in intervention until the end of 1863. The central reason lay in his dream of a New World empire that hinged on building a monarchy in Mexico strong enough to resist the so-called scourge of republicanism. A resurgence of monarchical rule in Latin America would not only restore what he believed to be the only legitimate form of government, but it would encourage French commercial activity in the New World, thereby bringing civilization and industry with the assistance of skilled immigrants while curbing further U.S. expansion in the Western Hemisphere. His "Grand Design for the Americas" welcomed a permanently divided America in which the newly independent Confederacy served as a buffer between the Union and a French-sponsored monarchical government in Mexico.[11] When the Union's victories at Gettysburg and Vicksburg in July 1863 raised severe doubts about southern separation, Napoleon changed direction and assured the Union that if it extended recognition to the new monarchy in Mexico, the French would no longer consider recognizing the Confederacy. Finally, when the Union emphasized that both the French and their monarchy must depart Mexico, he agreed to do so in 1867, thereby ending a five-year imperial effort in total defeat.

The most striking aspect of Napoleon's plan was his cavalier dismissal of slavery as a core issue in international relations. Indeed, Napoleon found a way to support the South without condoning slavery. The institution, he argued, would gradually come to an end as progressive ideas took hold. Mexico had abolished slavery some years earlier, perhaps encouraging the French emperor to believe that with time and modernization, the South would follow suit. And yet his attitude further demonstrates the ostrich-like attitude of Europeans in general – that slavery was *not* the central issue behind the American conflict and that economic or even imperialist designs by the Union had forced the South to arms. Just as the French people (along with most other observers, including northerners loyal to the Union) gave little thought to the importance of slavery, so did Napoleon's shallow solution fit the tenor of the times. The problem would go away with time, permitting him to negotiate an alliance with the Confederacy that would promote French imperialist objectives in the New World that were unencumbered by moral questions over slavery. For this reason and all the others associated with Napoleon's Grand Design for the Americas, the Union confronted still another threat.

Thus another irony became evident in America's diplomacy that stemmed from the constantly changing status of slavery: during the first part of the Civil War, the threat of British intervention posed the chief foreign challenge to the Union, whereas in the second part of the war France emerged as the Union's greatest peril. Until late 1862 the Lincoln administration advocated a moderate antislavery policy; afterward, the Emancipation Proclamation moved the nation into a stand against slavery that culminated in its abolition by the Thirteenth Amendment to the Constitution in January 1865. Once the Union made slavery the central issue in the war, the British found it difficult to consider intervention – particularly when the Union made clear that such a step meant war. But with slavery no longer a live issue in international relations because of the Emancipation Proclamation, Napoleon felt free to step up his interest in intervention as a means for promoting his imperial ambitions in the hemisphere.

Lincoln's steadily evolving position on slavery further complicated the interventionist issue. By the spring of 1865, he had undergone a profound change in perspective on its meaning and place within the grand scheme of history. Lincoln had always regarded slavery as the basic cause of this national cataclysm, but not until midway into the war did he grasp its critical relationship to the concept of Union and the related advance toward freedom for all people. The Gettysburg Address of November 1863 serves as the pivotal point in his growing understanding of the moral and intellectual impact of the war on both the United States and the universal principles of liberty.

As the historian James M. McPherson pointed out, Lincoln at the outset of the fighting emphasized the importance of "Union" as perceived before 1861, whereas by the time of the Gettysburg Address he focused on "nation" in calling for a new birth of freedom that required the death of slavery. No longer did Lincoln consider slavery a purely distinctive political question; by 1862 emancipation had become a weapon for attracting slave support, undermining the Confederacy from within, winning the war, and assuring a plan for reconstruction of the postwar nation. During the following year the end of slavery became the central issue in determining whether Americans preferred a Union more perfect than the one Confederate guns fired upon at Fort Sumter in April 1861.[12]

By 1863 Lincoln viewed the destruction of slavery and the establishment of an improved Union as inseparable. A republic, he had said before the war, could not endure half slave and half free. Americans had the choice of moving forward to the creation of a society resting on the principle of universal freedom or looking backward to the maintenance of a divided country that rested on archaic racial practices and arbitrary social distinctions based on color. The Union, as Lincoln conceived its metamorphosis during the war, must strive for the natural rights advocated by the Founding Fathers. To mold a better Union that encompassed this great moral end, slavery must cease to exist.

Despite Lincoln's moral condemnation of slavery, he maintained a pragmatic outlook on what objectives were attainable at a given time. Societal conditions must be receptive to change before reform-minded leaders could introduce liberal programs that the majority of Americans found acceptable. As a strong supporter of the Constitution, he respected the legal right of slaveholders in their property; but as an even stronger advocate of the Declaration of Independence, he opposed the extension of slavery into free territories. And yet as a realist he refused to alienate moderates by attempting to specify the measures necessary to kill slavery once it was contained. Before the Confederate siege of Fort Sumter, he suggested that only time and a progressively changing national mood could bring about the ultimate extinction of the institution without bloodshed. Afterward, when war had come, he realized that even though morality dictated an immediate implementation of freedom, reality necessitated a gradual approach. The struggle toward that ideal must come one step at a time, not by sacrificing achievement in the name of protecting principle but by accomplishing whatever was feasible while holding on to principle and allowing Americans time to adjust to revolutionary change at a slow and deliberate pace.[13]

Lincoln used the natural rights precepts of the Declaration of Independence as his guide to a better Union. The Constitution, he believed, had fleshed out many of the uplifting ideas of the celebrated document of 1776, but it had not yet instituted the actual freedom that must characterize a republic. Life, liberty, and the pursuit of happiness – those "self-evident" and "inalienable rights" expounded by Thomas Jefferson (whom Lincoln considered "the most distinguished politician in our history") – had not yet reached fruition. The democratic process, as Lincoln saw it, constituted a lengthy and difficult struggle toward social and political improvements that could come only when a substantial number of Americans appeared ready to accept them.[14] The existence of slavery graphically depicted the profound dilemma confronting a republic that professed liberty while condoning the enslavement of human beings. Morality and the law had diverged so sharply that the gulf between them had split the nation. Only the harsh crucible of civil war could cleanse the Union of its undemocratic past, alter deeply ingrained racial attitudes among Americans, and push them toward true nationhood.

Lincoln did not assume the presidency with these idealistic aims in mind. As a young lawyer from the Illinois prairie, he had never seen war in all its hideous dimensions. Nor had he taken the time or had the occasion to dwell on the morality of slavery and see its destruction as an integral part of a better nation. The Union of the pre–Civil War period remained a loose conglomeration of competing interests and states, held tenuously together in the face of ever-growing sectional differences. The congressional repeal of the Missouri Compromise in 1854 had forced him to contemplate these great moral and intellectual principles related to personal liberty, and then, as president, the threat of war between the sections forced him to confront the paradoxical relationship of slavery to a Union founded on individual freedoms.

Lincoln remained essentially a politician (albeit with a strong strain of morality) throughout his public career.[15] To accomplish any objectives, he realized, one must first win office. After that, one must be willing to compromise on issues without losing sight of moral principles. Like most Americans of his day, he initially failed to comprehend the profound importance of slavery to the southern psyche and therefore considered the question to be primarily political in nature. Most of the great issues before 1861 – including the Compromise of 1850, the Kansas-Nebraska Act, and the Dred Scott decision by the U.S. Supreme Court – merely demonstrated shrewd political maneuvering by expert politicians who capitalized on slavery as one of several variables intended to help them retain office. Surely southerners found it good politics to dodge the slavery question by evoking the doctrine of states' rights as the chief defense against continued encroachments by the northern majority.

Only a narrowly based group of abolitionists had raised searching questions about the morality of a nation that condoned human bondage. Immediate emancipation without compensation was their fervent cry. A more moderate approach came from a wide array of antislavery groups, who – Lincoln included – rejected the abolitionists' hurried demands as injurious to societal order and instead advocated gradual emancipation with compensation to slave owners. The Christian abolitionists, in turn, staunchly opposed this position as a compromise on slavery and hence a compromise with sin. Indeed, slavery itself was a sin and anyone who supported that institution, whether actively or passively, was necessarily a sinner. But most Americans regarded the abolitionists as a wild-eyed minority of fanatics who had irresponsibly applied the spiritual principles of evangelical Christianity to temporal matters. They dismissed the abolitionists as radical troublemakers who threatened law and order by exploiting Christianity as a means for seeking massive social, political, and economic upheaval. More than a few abolitionists had suffered persecution, instilling in them a sense of martyrdom that fed their fervor. Since the 1830s they had bequeathed a legacy of violence that made them the object of widespread condemnation.

Like most of his contemporaries during the Civil War era, Lincoln rejected abolition, but unlike many of those same Americans, he developed a moral and intellectual commitment to broader considerations that necessarily included abolition. Lincoln came to realize that the peculiar institution had permeated every aspect of southern life, touching the very fiber of the South's existence. Most important, slavery raised the explosive question of race by forcing an exploration of the future relationship between whites and blacks in the postwar South. Indeed, the outcome of the slavery issue promised to have a disruptive effect on the North as well. What would be the status of free blacks after the war – on *both* sides of the Mason-Dixon Line?

To Lincoln, the purpose of the war grew into more than suppressing a rebellion by southerners and saving the Union as he found it on taking office; it became necessary to destroy their antebellum world as the chief step toward ending slavery and constructing an improved Union. At first he regarded the conflict as primarily constitutional in origin. Like two of his favorites in history – Daniel Webster and Henry Clay – Lincoln considered the Union to be permanent and therefore not susceptible to secession. Southerners, he asserted, had exploited states'-rights principles to promote selfish interests that endangered the republic. Preservation of the Union as it existed in 1861 became his initial guiding principle.

But as the conflict intensified, Lincoln expanded his perspective of the

Union to bring it more in line with the ideals of the Founding Fathers. He agreed with Webster's famous reply to South Carolina senator Robert Hayne's defense of states' rights and nullification in 1830: "Liberty and Union, now and forever, one and inseparable!" To reach that lofty goal, however, the United States had to undergo a time of severe trial and tribulation that made its people come to grips with the wrongs of slavery and hence more receptive to change. Lincoln surmised that God had used "the awful calamity of civil war" as "a punishment, inflicted upon us, for our presumptuous sins, to the needful end of our national reformation on a whole People."[16] The war became an instrument for reshaping the Union of the Constitution into the more perfect Union envisioned by signers of the Declaration of Independence.

 Lincoln realized that to win this epochal war, he had to take a path that cut not only through the battlefield but into the diplomatic arena as well. Domestic policy, he learned, was inseparable from foreign affairs. Had England intervened on the Confederacy's side, France would have followed and the chances of southern independence would have immeasurably increased. With the formerly great republic drastically reduced in size and staggering from defeat, its principles would have stood vulnerable not only to new foreign neighbors on all sides but to opportunists at home who argued for massive governmental changes in the wake of democracy's failure. Lincoln correctly recognized at the war's outset that foreign intervention posed as great a crisis to the Union as did the building of an effective fighting force.

Political considerations at first compelled Lincoln to pronounce the purpose of the war to be preservation of the Union rather than the destruction of slavery. The border states of Missouri, Kentucky, Maryland, and Delaware teetered so dangerously close to following their slave-state brethren into the Confederacy that a wartime declaration against slavery would surely drive them into secession. In addition, Lincoln held the belief, however mistaken, that a huge and hitherto reticent groundswell of Union sentiment in the South would soon force the secessionists from power and permit a negotiated settlement. Finally, he realized that racism knew no sectional boundaries and that only the abolitionists and perhaps some of the antislavery moderates would support a war to end slavery.

Foreign problems immediately surfaced when Lincoln erroneously assumed that the British and other Europeans would automatically understand that slavery lay at the root of the American conflict. Southern emissaries in London and Paris, of course, ignored the references to slavery contained in the South Carolina ordinance of secession and insisted to their hosts that the peculiar institution had nothing to do with their declaration of independence. Northern oppression, they complained, had threatened their God-given right of self-government – states' rights – and forced the South into secession. Thus the issues in America became deeply confusing to observers thousands of miles across the Atlantic. In an ironic use of history, the British compared the South to the American colonists and the North to the monarchy of King George III. After nearly a century of soul-searching in England, it now seemed just for the American colonists to have broken their bond with the Crown during the eighteenth century, and it thereby followed that southerners had the same inherent right to sever their ties with the Union. Indeed, individuals and groups in England became active southern sympathizers in what they regarded as a defensive campaign against a tyrannical northern majority.

What becomes especially clear is that Civil War diplomacy is replete with ironies – that things rarely were what they seemed to be. At first glance, both the British and the French appeared either incredibly naïve or very disingenuous in their stated views of the war, for they were wrong about nearly every premise on which they acted. They never professed to understand that the conflict was about slavery, that southern independence was not a fait accompli, that the Union might win the war, and that, in one of their most dreaded premonitions, a race war growing out of emancipation was highly unlikely. In truth, however, both nations interpreted the war in accordance with their own desires to achieve whatever they could in promoting their own national interests. Napoleon's imperial motives were unmistakable: disruption of the Union provided him the best opportunity for securing a foothold in Mexico as the first step in implementing his Grand Design. Russell's interest in intervention was more subtle, yet it remained constant, even as the fortunes of the war shifted. Whatever justification he stated over the course of the war, he sought the policy that best suited his country's interests.

A close study of Russell's persistent push for intervention reveals that self-interest provided the most likely determinant for British policymakers, even when they espoused humanitarian rationales. Whether the Union or the Confederacy won military victories or whether slavery was a moral issue, he supported intervention and, ipso facto, southern independence. Despite the continually changing circumstances of the war, Russell justified intervention on either humanitarian or economic grounds. And yet when the potato famine devastated Ireland during the mid-1840s, he had refused to extend aid out of fealty to the economic dictates of a laissez-faire philosophy and a rigid faith in a grossly inadequate Poor Law system of aid. When the Irish called for national determination in 1848, Russell likewise rejected their plea, raising questions about his altruistic motives in calling for an independent southern republic as the solution to the American war. The Union's dissolution, he realized, would slow down America's commercial and military gains on Britain, secure southern cotton, protect Canada from the United States, and contain further American expansion in the New World. Given all these undeniable results from the Union's destruction, and combined with Russell's cold policies toward the Irish, it is difficult to believe his rhetoric that intervention in the American war was integral to his stand as defender of freedom.[17]

Lincoln was dubious about European motives. From his perspective, both England and France were bound by their own histories of imperialist behavior to exploit any opportunity to foster a breakup of the Union. This fear became so rampant in his administration that his fiery, gruff, and self-righteous secretary of state, William H. Seward, overcame his initial personal and political animosity for his superior to emerge as the Union's most outspoken and eloquent opponent of outside intervention and the president's most loyal supporter. Their risky strategy rested on Seward's heated warnings of instant war against any nation that dared extend diplomatic recognition to the Confederacy. A hollow threat perhaps, but Palmerston and other government leaders in London had too many times experienced the anger and often irresponsible behavior of frontier Americans afflicted with the disease of democracy and never could be sure what rash action they might take. Throughout the war, but most especially in the period before the interventionist crisis of autumn 1862, the Lincoln administration regarded foreign involvement in the American conflict as a mortal threat to the Union.[18]

An analysis of President Lincoln's role as wartime leader is not complete unless it encompasses foreign as well as domestic affairs. His most important objective on the eve of the war, as stated in his First Inaugural Address, was, in the words of the Constitution, "to form a more perfect union." That objective never changed, although it acquired a deeper and more fervent meaning with the passage of time. As the war began and took its murderous path to Appomattox Courthouse four years later, his goal became ideological: to forge a better Union by ridding the nation of slavery and instituting the natural rights principles contained in the Declaration of Independence. To succeed in this great endeavor, he had to block foreign intervention in the war.

The historian Garry Wills was only partially accurate in praising Lincoln's Gettysburg Address as a mere 272 words that miraculously remade the American nation. Wills correctly noted the absence of slavery in the president's address, but he mistakenly suggested that Lincoln had downplayed its importance in the overall path of progress toward a more perfect Union. In a practical sense, Lincoln recognized the impossibility of implementing great reforms unless the American people proved receptive. As the war relentlessly pounded on, however, he discerned a steadily changing mood among his people that encouraged them to believe that more was at stake than the present conflict. The eradication of slavery became an essential step toward transforming the United States into a better nation. Lincoln knew that only through "a new birth of freedom" could the republic's government evolve into what he thought the Founding Fathers had intended it to be: one "of the people, by the people, and for the people."[19]

Lincoln thus fitted the Civil War within a long historical process in America whose central strand was the continuing experiment in liberty. Recognizing that the Constitution was a living organism, he sought to revise it in conjunction with changing times in an effort to match more closely those natural rights principles underlying the Declaration of Independence. Wills pointed in the right direction by showing Lincoln's phenomenal moral and intellectual growth during a most wrenching war. Such a development justifies an examination of his leadership in remaking the American nation.

This book, of course, deals with the multitude of other issues essential to understanding the diplomacy of the Civil War, but it focuses on the integral relationship of the Union and slavery to the crisis over foreign intervention and the certain postwar troubles at home over race and liberty. Indeed, nearly all the explosive matters that arose in foreign relations revolved around slavery and the interventionist question, demonstrating the inseparability of domestic and foreign affairs and thereby posing one of the greatest perils the republic ever faced. The following pages also throw light on the long-debated issue of whether the South was victimized by its own inept diplomacy or by realistic considerations beyond its control. Through this study runs one consistent theme: Lincoln's desire to eradicate slavery as an essential ingredient in winning the war and, by implementing the principles of the Declaration of Independence, develop a more perfect Union based on a new birth of freedom.

CHAPTER ONE

Lincoln on Slavery: A Constitutional Right and a Moral Wrong

[The Founding Fathers] meant simply to declare the *right* [of universal freedom], so that the *enforcement* of it might follow as fast as circumstances should permit.　　Abraham Lincoln, June 26, 1857

[The black person is] as much entitled to . . . the right to life, liberty, and the pursuit of happiness . . . as the white man.
Abraham Lincoln, August 21, 1858

Abraham Lincoln revered the Constitution and the law and therefore viewed slavery as a political-constitutional issue rather than a question of morality.[1] As a politician and a pragmatist, he opposed any measure that forced a confrontation over the matter and preferred the indirect remedies of gradual emancipation with compensation, followed by the colonization of free blacks in areas outside the United States. He knew that Article IV, Section 2, of the Constitution gave Congress the "Power to . . . make all needed Rules and Regulations respecting the territory . . . belonging to the United States." And yet he also understood that endless debates would result over the meaning of "all needed Rules and Regulations" when it came to the question of extending slavery into free territory. He consistently opposed its extension, making clear his dilemma: the Constitution and the laws of the land protected slave owners in their property, but the natural rights principles found in the Declaration of Independence prohibited the spread of slavery.

Until the 1850s, Lincoln joined many of his contemporaries in accepting slavery as an unavoidable evil that would eventually fade away if left alone. Those who owned slaves, he declared in the early part of the decade, were not necessarily bad people; rather, they had adopted slavery as a labor system because of the practical demands of climate and economics. Lincoln found southerners no better or worse than northerners: "If we were situated as they are, we should act and feel as they do; and if they were situated as we are, they should act and feel as we do; and we never ought to lose sight of this fact in discussing the subject."[2] As more than a few slaveholders worked through their own dilemma of owning human beings while professing to live in a republic based on Christian principles, they vehemently opposed anyone who agitated the question by introducing it into either the political or moral arena. In that regard, Lincoln assumed the same stand: he considered slavery a moral and social wrong but a political and constitutional right, and he tried to avert a North-South confrontation over these irreconcilable differences.

More than any other single event, the passage of the Kansas-Nebraska Act in 1854 pushed Lincoln into taking a strong public stance on slavery that adhered to these principles and guided his behavior well into the early stages of the Civil War. Indeed, these same views on slavery profoundly influenced his diplomacy with Europe during the opening months of that conflict. Only the growing magnitude of the war dislodged him from this restrained position.

The Kansas-Nebraska Act embodied Lincoln's worst fears regarding slavery and serves as the pivotal point in refining his moral and intellectual views toward the institution. The Missouri Compromise of 1820 had drawn a line at the 36° 30′ parallel in those parts of the Louisiana Purchase of 1803 not yet admitted to nationhood, forbidding slavery above the demarcation while approving its existence below. Political considerations, however, had led Illinois senator Stephen A. Douglas and his Democratic party to secure a law that erased the Missouri Compromise line by authorizing the principle of "popular sovereignty": people in Kansas and Nebraska now had the right to determine whether slavery could exist in their newly established territories. Thus slavery could grow with the territorial expansion of the United States. Douglas had attempted to evade all moral considerations regarding slavery by making it a purely political proposition. While the Kansas-Nebraska Act encouraged northerners to continue treating slavery in an indifferent manner, its defenders could further safeguard its spread through use of the legal system. Passage of the act, Lincoln declared, "took us by surprise – astounded us. . . . We were thunderstruck and stunned."[3] That single move opened all the social, political, and moral arguments that he had preferred to keep closed.

Although Lincoln considered slavery a moral wrong, he accepted it as a legal right. Slavery was "the real issue" dividing the nation, he proclaimed in one of a series of Illinois Senate debates with Douglas, this one at Alton. It was a vital part of "the eternal struggle between these two principles – right and wrong – throughout the world." At stake was the outcome of a conflict

Abraham Lincoln in the 1850s. Courtesy the Gilder Lehrman Collection, on deposit at the Pierpont Morgan Library, New York. GLC 590. 1858.

that had raged since the beginning of time – that between "the common right of humanity" and "the divine right of kings." Lincoln realized, however, that his fellow Americans (and he also) were not yet ready to implement all the natural rights doctrines of the Declaration of Independence. He also knew that the Constitution guaranteed due process to property owners and that slaves were defined as property. Rather than see the Union endangered by a fight over slavery, he wished to leave the institution alone where it already existed while opposing its extension. Over the course of time, according to theory, cotton would deplete the nutrients in the soil and undermine the chief argument for slavery as a profitable source of labor. To take a stand against slavery itself would threaten the Union and sacrifice the only real chance of instituting genuine freedom. Like Daniel Webster and Henry Clay, Lincoln regarded the Union as the chief guarantor of liberty.[4]

In the prewar period, as well as into the first months of the war itself, Lincoln fought to keep the slavery issue out of the growing political maelstrom by calling for gradual change. Compromise was the essence of good politics, he knew, and this principle dictated that slavery must not become a moral issue and hence impervious to concessions. In a stand patterned after Clay's approach to the subject, Lincoln believed it prudent to administer a slow death to slavery through gradual emancipation and voluntary colonization rather than to follow the abolitionists in demanding an immediate end to slavery without compensation to owners, followed by racial equality. The removal of freed blacks to Africa had attracted interest for some time. Indeed, in 1817 the American Colonization Society came into being, drawing a membership list that included such luminaries as Clay, John Marshall, James Madison, and James Monroe. Five years later the group founded the Republic of Liberia on the West African coast, which became the home for about fifteen thousand freed blacks over the next forty years, many settling in the capital of Monrovia, named after President Monroe. Although by 1860 nearly all southern slaves had been born in the United States, the idea of colonization still drew the support of Lincoln and others. Only violence could result from outright abolition, Lincoln insisted, disrupting the Union and causing the collapse of the experiment in republicanism. Time might remedy the nation's sectional ills by removing the need for slavery and permitting a gradual change in public sentiment toward the institution.[5]

Lincoln's antislavery views had developed early in his life and remained eminently practical in application throughout his political career. His distaste for slavery became evident after he and a friend from Kentucky witnessed the slave trade on the Mississippi River in 1841. A slave owner had bought twelve blacks in Kentucky for his farm in the lower South. According to Lincoln's graphic account, the captives "were chained six and six together. A small iron clevis was around the left wrist of each, and this fastened to the main chain by a shorter one at a convenient distance from the others; so that the negroes were strung together precisely like so many fish upon a trot-line." The slaves, he observed, would never see their families again and were about to enter a harder world in the Deep South than they had experienced in the upper region. Despite their dismal future, they exhibited a surprisingly cheerful disposition. How true it was, Lincoln wrote a friend, that "God tempers the wind to the shorn lamb." The worst of conditions He made "tolerable" to human beings, while permitting the best "to be nothing better than tolerable."[6]

Like many Americans of his time, the young Lincoln showed no lasting concern over the slaves' plight but, unlike so many of these same Americans, gravitated in that direction as he examined the institution more carefully. Over a decade later, his perspective on slavery changed after several lengthy discussions with his outspoken antislavery colleagues in Congress, Joshua F.

Giddings and Horace Mann. Little evidence exists that the slaves' harsh situation had raised questions of morality in Lincoln's mind in 1841, and it may be that the strong feelings he claimed to have experienced as a young congressman cast a different shade on his memory of that event on the river of fourteen years earlier. In any event, he expressed concern about slave owners who feared that he intended to challenge their legal right to own slaves. To his southern companion on the trip down the Mississippi, Lincoln wrote that the sight of shackled slaves was "a continual torment to me." And yet he confessed that "I bite my lip and keep quiet" because the law protected the slave owner in his property. Indeed, Lincoln noted, he and "the great body of the Northern people do crucify their feelings, in order to maintain their loyalty to the constitution and the Union."[7]

Lincoln abhorred slavery, but he just as clearly understood the constitutional legalities and political wisdom of accepting its existence and hoping that changing popular attitudes could eventually encourage its demise. As early as the 1830s he took a public stand against slavery on moral grounds while finding it impossible to declare it illegal. In the Illinois legislature he signed a protest proclaiming that slavery was "founded on both injustice and bad policy" but nevertheless asserting that "the promulgation of abolition doctrines tends rather to increase than to abate its evils." In a statement he adhered to well into the Civil War, he declared that Congress had no constitutional power to interfere with slavery in the states permitting its existence.[8]

Lincoln's position on the fugitive slave issue also revealed his hesitancy about taking a strong public stand against slavery. He at first concurred with two legislative resolutions, the first condemning the governor of Maine – and hence any state executive – for refusing to surrender two Americans accused of kidnapping a slave in Georgia, and the second declaring that citizens of nonslaveholding states should not interfere with domestic matters between slaveholding states. He later wished to reconsider his position and offered a motion to postpone the matter for an indefinite period. Critics have argued that this shifting stand established Lincoln as a Machiavellian, prepared to maneuver in any direction that proved politically profitable.[9] But it is more convincing to assert that his altered position demonstrated a consistency that lingered until the outbreak of war in April 1861: avert a confrontation between North and South by opposing only the extension of slavery.

Lincoln hoped to kill slavery by preventing its spread. He chastised the Liberty party for its involvement in the election of 1844; the few votes garnered by its candidate, James G. Birney, cost Clay the presidency and the chance to stop the extension of slavery. Lincoln believed that despite America's profession of liberty ("paradox though it may seem"), it must not disturb slavery in its present location. Americans must encourage slavery to die "a natural death" by blocking its establishment in new places. He became in-creasingly outspoken against the extension of slavery during the sectional controversy of the late 1840s caused by the acquisition of California and the present states of New Mexico, Arizona, Utah, and Nevada as part of the Treaty of Guadalupe Hidalgo ending the Mexican War. He believed that if war hero Gen. Zachary Taylor became president in 1848 he should oppose further territorial expansion southward because it might agitate the slavery question. In the House of Representatives in mid-1848, Lincoln reiterated his opposition to the spread of slavery into the recently acquired territories, both because of his political constituency's feelings and his own. The follow-ing September in Massachusetts, Lincoln branded slavery an evil but re-peated his legally based argument that the government could stop only its ex-tension. And in Illinois he repeated his call for the election of Taylor as a means for halting the spread of slavery.[10]

During the 1850s Lincoln advocated greater opportunity for blacks in so-ciety; at the same time, however, he did not support social and political equality at least in part out of deference to the prevailing national mood. The Declaration of Independence, he proclaimed in his famous debates with Douglas in Illinois, was not simply "the white-man's charter of freedom." The Founding Fathers included blacks in their reference to "men" in the Declaration and thus made this "the great fundamental principle upon which our free institutions rest." Slavery was "violative of that principle" because it denied black people "all the natural rights enumerated in the Declaration of Independence." The black man, Lincoln insisted, was "as much entitled to . . . the right to life, liberty, and the pursuit of happiness . . . as the white man." Although Lincoln did not promote social equality, he insisted that the black man was "the equal of every living man" and had "the right to eat the bread, without leave of anybody else, which his own hand earns."[11]

Lincoln's political career would have come to a halt during the 1850s had he bolted widespread American sentiment and called for racial equality. But he took a bold step forward in *claiming* for black people "all the rights enu-merated in the Declaration of Independence" rather than following the usual pattern of *denying* them these same rights. In the 1850s Lincoln aimed at re-solving the slavery issue by appealing to the inalienable rights of life, liberty, and the pursuit of happiness; during the wartime 1860s he began to under-stand the profound ramifications of such principles for racial practices in the postslavery era. The Declaration's assurances were open-ended, not confined to bringing slavery to a close. It was a timeless document whose application must include all Americans, black and white. Pragmatic realist that he was, however, he recognized that the time for racial equality had not yet come.[12]

In the early years of the republic, Lincoln declared, Americans universally regarded the Declaration of Independence as sacred in principle and broad enough in meaning to encompass all people. Indeed, the Founding Fathers in Philadelphia had not specifically referred to "slavery" or "slave" in the Constitution. "They expected and desired that the system would come to an end," he later insisted, "and meant that when it did, the Constitution should not show that there ever had been a slave in this good free country of ours!" When slavery ultimately came to an end, the Founders could say there was "nothing in the Constitution to remind them of it." But by the mid-nineteenth century, the Declaration of Independence had become the source of mockery and ridicule as rabid slaveholders twisted the meaning of the document in attempting to justify their enslavement of human beings. The once heralded principle of natural rights "is assailed, and sneered at, and construed, and hawked at, and torn, till, if its framers could rise from their graves, they could not at all recognize it."[13]

Although Lincoln was correct in regarding the Constitution as the chief protector of slavery, he would have been on shaky ground if he had argued that the Founding Fathers intended the Declaration of Independence to provide equality for all peoples. In writing the document of 1776, Thomas Jefferson expressed the oft-stated sentiment of his contemporaries in seeking a society based on natural rights. Given the widespread racial inequality that characterized the colonial experience, it is difficult to believe that he (a slaveholder himself) and others of the Revolutionary generation could have envisioned a society promising equality to all people. And yet perhaps Lincoln was correct in seeing that the genius of the Declaration of Independence lay more in its idealistic potential than in its present reality. Its philosophy was so open-ended that Lincoln (or anyone else) could interpret it in the manner best suited to his argument.

The Founding Fathers thought slavery was legally sanctioned by the Constitution as the sum total of the colonial experience. From the first arrival of Africans into the American colonies in 1619, they assumed a distinct place within a society that practiced racial inequality. Custom and tradition encouraged a de facto form of slavery that soon acquired a de jure or legal basis. To make slavery economically profitable, the colonists devised a legal status for blacks that eventually tied them to lifelong servitude and rested largely on distinctions of race and color.[14]

Lincoln was the product of this heritage and therefore came face to face with the great enigma of the American republic – how a people committed to human freedom could condone human slavery. At the founding of the new nation, a paradox came into being that laid the basis for a bitter conflict over slavery. The Declaration of Independence emphasized that the philosophical basis of the new republic rested on liberty, whereas the Constitution focused on the practical governmental aspects of property. Since the Constitution became the supreme law of the land, legality took precedence over liberty and, in practical terms, shut out blacks from enjoying the egalitarian precepts of the Revolution. Not until five decades afterward, however, did the Constitution come under attack for protecting slavery. The great contract, according to critics, rested on the legal sanctity of private property – including slavery – and federalism, which assigned residual powers to the states and hence provided a means for maintaining the racial inequities that characterized all thirteen colonies on the eve of the Revolution.[15]

If the Declaration of Independence offered the possibility of universal freedom in the hazily defined and distant future, the Constitution inadvertently delayed that development in its rigid defense of private property. Few Americans in 1857 disagreed with Chief Justice Roger Taney of the Supreme Court when he declared in the Dred Scott decision that "the enslaved African race were not intended to be included, and formed no part of the people who framed and adopted" the Declaration of Independence. In Philadelphia in 1787, the framers of the Constitution sought to build a strong republic based on the protection of private property that included slaves. Indeed, the Constitution reflected the predominant racial views of the colonial period and hence contradicted the natural rights principles underlying the Declaration of Independence.[16]

In truth, the African American slave held a dual status as human being and property that had resulted from colonial law and predictably provided a basic sinew of the Constitution. James Madison, a slaveholder himself, insisted that its framers viewed slaves "in the mixed character of persons and of property." Thus the Constitution made liberty and property inseparable by providing legal protection for the freedom to own property in slaves. Drawing on this principle, southerners would fervently argue for their constitutional liberty to own slaves and insisted that government's central role was to safeguard an individual's right to property. In this manner, America's central paradox arose in a society dedicated to the principles of freedom found in the Declaration of Independence while nonetheless pledged to protect slavery as property under the due-process guarantees of the Constitution. The Constitution itself emerged as a compromise between freedom and slavery.[17]

Lincoln must have grasped these contradictions in American thought and action, for shortly after Henry Clay's death in 1852 he delivered a eulogy in Illinois that noted his champion's opposition to slavery, both "on principle and in feeling," but clearly approved a nonconfrontational approach to the issue. For five decades, Clay supported the gradual emancipation of slaves in Kentucky along with colonization of free blacks into areas outside the United

States. Slavery was so deeply rooted in southern society that he saw no way to end it immediately without causing a violent upheaval that might threaten human liberty by ushering in tyrannical rule. Both sets of extremists were dangerous, Clay believed: those who would resort to any means to abolish slavery now and those who defended slavery to the point of ignoring the fundamental premise of the Declaration of Independence – that "all men are created free and equal."[18]

The Civil War encouraged Lincoln to advance beyond Clay's restricted thinking on slavery. Whereas Clay warned that a major assault on slavery would cause a war between North and South, Lincoln confronted that very war and soon realized that he no longer had to act so cautiously on the question. Further, he realized that even the horrors of a civil war were preferable to permitting a southern minority to rule and thereby subvert the majority principles underlying a democracy. And, he insisted, public leaders must abide by a code of ethics that remained unshakable, regardless of the ferocity of the political wars. "Important principles," he declared in his final speech before his death in 1865, "may, and must, be inflexible." Failure to destroy slavery, he came to believe, constituted a threat to freedom. To preserve the peace, Clay kept separate his concepts of slavery and Union; once the war broke out, Lincoln eventually considered them inseparable when he called for the death of slavery as an essential prerequisite to a more perfect Union. Clay feared that the abolition of slavery would cause a civil war; when the war came, Lincoln used it as a crucible for forging a new birth of freedom that he believed the Founding Fathers had originally intended to undergird the Union. Both Clay and Lincoln were realists and opportunists in moving the nation as far forward as present circumstances permitted.

The Kansas-Nebraska Act of May 1854 drove Lincoln into taking a strong political and moral stand against slavery. The new law violated everything he had stood for during the previous two decades: in repealing the Missouri Compromise of 1820, Congress authorized the extension of slavery into new territories and thereby underlined the irrelevance of morality to the question. Congress had already taken this step in the Utah and New Mexico enactments of 1850, but the new bill of 1854 abrogated a long-standing sectional bargain and involved Kansas and Nebraska, so close in proximity to midwestern farmers. As the political creation of Douglas, the Kansas-Nebraska Act unleashed a firestorm of criticism in the North that earned him the opprobrious reputation as "doughface" – a northerner whose sympathies lay with the South. Most important, the act drew the battle line between North and South, providing a dark prelude to the great storm about to engulf the Union.

In a series of speeches in Illinois, Lincoln blasted the act as the chief impetus to a deadly confrontation between North and South over slavery. Some writers contend that he did not comprehend how deeply embedded slavery was in southern civilization or how integral it was to the South's notion of republicanism and consequent effort to protect itself against an alien northern majority. This is not entirely so. Admittedly, Lincoln stood among the vast majority of Americans of his time who failed to realize that slavery had the potential of causing arguments so powerful that they could lead to civil war. But his own words attest to his belief that slavery was "an unqualified evil to the negro, to the white man, to the soil, and to the State." Indeed, Lincoln praised the American system for making it possible for all people to improve their lot in life. In the 175 speeches he delivered from 1854 to 1860, his primary focus remained consistent with his thinking that first took form during the 1830s and followed the precedent he thought had resulted from the Northwest Ordinance of 1787: prevent the spread of slavery into free territories as the first and most fundamental step toward ending its existence. In permitting the extension of slavery, the Kansas-Nebraska Act assured a confrontation between the sections that removed the possibility of compromise and pointed to civil war.[19]

Lincoln's opposition to the Kansas-Nebraska Act proved impassioned and unyielding. He repeatedly denounced the legislation for reopening the slavery issue to heated political debate. To a former state senator from Illinois who had shifted to the Republican party after the Kansas-Nebraska Act went into effect, Lincoln declared that the measure should be "rebuked and condemned every where." As a Republican, he held a Whiggish belief in progress and hoped that the movement of free farmers west would effectively block the spread of slavery. But his stand rested on more than these political grounds. Lincoln discerned a huge difference between permitting slavery to exist only in its present location and allowing it to spread into a free territory. The first principle sought to curtail slavery by legal and constitutional means, the second to support its growth by committing a great moral wrong.[20]

Lincoln supported the right of self-government as expressed in the principle of popular sovereignty but insisted that the Kansas-Nebraska Act violated that principle by allowing the expansion of slavery into free territories. Americans must not condone such "a moral, social and political evil." Lincoln later charged that slavery violated the self-governing principles found in the Declaration of Independence. "When the white man governs himself that is self-government; but when he governs himself, and also governs *another* man, that is more than self-government – that is despotism. If the negro is a *man*," Lincoln asserted, "why then my ancient faith teaches me that 'all men are created equal.'" No man had a "moral right" to enslave another. Nor was he "good enough to govern another man, *without that other's consent.*" This was the "leading principle – the sheet anchor of American republicanism" – as made clear in the Declaration of Independence.[21]

Lincoln soon raised his arguments against slavery from the political to the moral level. He called slavery, "in the abstract, a gross outrage on the law of nature" and found no "natural right" that opened Kansas and Nebraska or any other free land to slavery. The American government rested on the "Universal Freedom" found in the free and equal statement in the Declaration of Independence. Slavery's entrance into free areas constituted a violation of morality. Lincoln hated the Kansas-Nebraska Act because of "the monstrous injustice of slavery itself." Congressional approval of slavery's extension exposed Americans as hypocrites for advocating personal freedoms while enslaving human beings. What a "perfect liberty" the slaveholders "sigh for," he facetiously told a large audience in Illinois – "the liberty of making slaves of other people." No longer could the United States stand as a model of republicanism. The principles of self-government so eloquently endorsed in the Declaration of Independence had fallen victim to the powerful forces of self-interest.[22]

The new legislation, Lincoln asserted, provided slavery with new stature. "I object to it because it assumes that there CAN be MORAL RIGHT in the enslaving of one man by another." The law provided "sad evidence that, feeling prosperity we forget right – that liberty, as a principle, we have ceased to revere." The Founding Fathers in Philadelphia did not mention slavery in the Constitution because they recognized that the time was not right to deal with it. "Thus, the thing is hid away, in the constitution, just as an afflicted man hides away a wen or a cancer, which he dares not cut out at once, lest he bleed to death; with the promise, nevertheless, that the cutting may begin at the end of a given time." The enslavement of human beings, Lincoln proclaimed, was not a "sacred right of self-government."[23]

Lincoln urged a closer analysis of the potentially explosive situation. The Kansas-Nebraska Act, he argued, had reversed all progress against slavery by repealing the restrictive provisions in the Missouri Compromise. "The spirit of seventy-six and the spirit of Nebraska, are utter antagonisms." If we stand for liberty, we can find no "moral right" in slavery. "Let us re-adopt the Declaration of Independence" and all its fine qualities. "If we do this, we shall not only have saved the Union; but we shall have so saved it, that the succeeding millions of free happy people, the world over, shall rise up, and call us blessed, to the latest generations." Most of mankind considered slavery "a great moral wrong" that struck "at the very foundation of their sense of justice." America's leaders must stop its spread before the growing sectional crisis erupted in war.[24]

The quick pace of events had pushed Lincoln into adopting a stronger position against slavery. He maintained his belief that the institution was a constitutional right and a moral wrong, but the firmer tone of his public statements indicated that his moral emphasis had begun to raise serious questions in his mind about the validity of laws that strayed so far from the natural rights doctrine found in the Declaration of Independence. The Kansas-Nebraska Act had not only needlessly inflamed the American political scene, but it unraveled the political compromise of 1820 and constituted a blatant violation of basic morality.

Like others of his generation who opposed slavery, Lincoln remained perplexed about finding a rapid solution to the problem. "If all earthly power were given me, I should not know what to do, as to the existing institution." His first inclination was to free all the slaves and send them to Liberia. But this measure was impractical. "If they were all landed there in a day, they would all perish in the next ten days; and there are not surplus shipping and surplus money enough in the world to carry them there in many times ten days." The alternative was to free them and maintain them as "underlings." Yet there was no proof that this would improve their condition. Lincoln could not consider them political and social equals. "My own feelings will not admit of this; and if mine would, we well know that those of the great mass of white people will not." This was the central issue, not whether this feeling accorded with "justice and sound judgment." In another well-placed emphasis on practical considerations, he declared, "A universal feeling, whether well or ill-founded, can not be safely disregarded." It followed that the most feasible remedy to the slavery issue was gradual emancipation, an evolutionary program intended to provide time for the American people to learn to accept black people in society. Because of prevailing realities, Lincoln concluded, "We can not . . . make them equals."[25]

Lincoln's mental bouts with slavery also operated within the confines of his fervent belief that the sanctity of the Union was the top priority. Arguments over the extension of slavery posed the "Behemoth of danger," he declared in late 1854, so much so that he would change his position and permit its extension if the choice was dissolution of the Union. "I would consent to any GREAT evil, to avoid a GREATER one." As Webster and Clay sought to protect the Union above all else, so did Lincoln. Some months later, in May 1856, Lincoln clarified his views by emphasizing that "*the Union must be preserved in the purity of its principles as well as in the integrity of its territorial parts.*" Without the Union, he believed, there was no hope for an improved society.

In a statement that repeated Webster's words while providing a glimpse into the direction Lincoln would ultimately take, he asserted that the goal must be "Liberty and Union, now and forever, one and inseparable." The two concepts had begun to mesh in Lincoln's mind, as shown by his growing focus on the inability of slavery and freedom to coexist in the United States. "A house divided against itself cannot stand," Lincoln declared in June 1858. "I believe this government cannot endure, permanently half *slave* and half *free*." Slavery must enter the course of "ultimate extinction."[26]

Lincoln's pragmatic position on slavery became clear during the course of his debates with Douglas for the Illinois Senate seat in 1858. To a large throng of people in Chicago, he declared that the Savior of man once said, "As your Father in Heaven is perfect, be ye also perfect." This was the standard, and even though no one could reach it, those who tried to do so "attained the highest degree of moral perfection." Consequently, Lincoln alluded to this idea in the following revealing statement: "So I say in relation to the principle that all men are created equal, let it be as nearly reached as we can." The authors of the Declaration of Independence, he insisted on another occasion, "meant simply to declare the *right* [of universal freedom], so that the *enforcement* of it might follow as fast as circumstances should permit." Their purpose was to establish a "standard maxim" that a free society should constantly attempt to emulate but without ever expecting to reach that perfect state. In writing the Constitution, the Founding Fathers "were obliged to bow to the necessity. . . . They did what they could and yielded to the necessity for the rest. I also yield to all which follows from that necessity."[27] His overriding objective regarding slavery was to achieve all that proved practically possible given the prevailing public tenor. Such a realistic stance by no means constituted a concession of principle.

Despite the claims of critics, Lincoln's position on slavery remained remarkably consistent in a rapidly disintegrating political arena whose most notable characteristic was inconsistency. He never deviated from his efforts to preserve liberty *and* Union. To avert war, he advocated a long-term resolution of the slavery issue that called for barring the spread of the institution as a major step toward its ultimate extinction. When war erupted, however, he naturally sought to form a Union that, once cleansed of slavery, better exemplified the principles of liberty found in the Declaration of Independence.

Lincoln's rejection of the eleventh-hour Crittenden Compromise demonstrates that, contrary to the arguments of some writers, he had become aware of how serious the South was about slavery and secession.[28] Within two years of his debates with Douglas in Illinois, Lincoln as president-elect from the Republican party in 1860 had decided that the South would never accept any compromise that did not provide protection of slavery. And the Crittenden

Compromise was anything but a compromise. According to its terms, the incoming administration must refrain from interfering with slavery in present states, bar the institution in territories above the Missouri Compromise line of 36° 30', and protect it below that line in all territories "now held, or hereafter acquired."[29] Lincoln repeated his belief in the legal and constitutional sanctity of slavery where it already existed and reaffirmed his intention to leave it alone. But, predictably, he rejected the provision calling on him to approve the future extension of slavery. Such a condition required him to abandon his long-held moral opposition to the spread of slavery and to trample on the basic platform of the Republican party that had brought him the election victory.

To his political allies, Lincoln expressed adamant opposition to the Crittenden Compromise as an attempt to undermine the Republican party's progress against slavery. "Entertain no proposition for a compromise in regard to the extension of slavery," he told one Republican congressman. Such a concession would lead only to demands for more. "The tug has to come & better now than later." There was "no possible compromise" on the extension of slavery, he told another; to give in would reverse the party's gains in the election. To still another party supporter, Lincoln asserted that approval of slavery's extension "acknowledges that slavery has equal rights with liberty." To party stalwart William H. Seward, who had staunchly resisted the compromise, Lincoln wrote that he too was "inflexible" in opposing the spread of slavery: "I am for no compromise which assists or permits the extension of the institution on soil owned by the nation. And any trick by which the nation is to acquire territory, and then allow some local authority to spread slavery over it, is as obnoxious as any other." To yet another congressman, Lincoln warned that a concession to the South would lead to other demands "ad libitum." In no time, he added sardonically, southerners would demand Cuba "as a condition upon which they will stay in the Union." And this was no idle threat. Southerners had repeatedly tried during the 1850s to acquire Cuba, by force if necessary.[30]

In Independence Hall, Philadelphia, President-elect Lincoln praised the great document of 1776 as his political guide: "I have never had a feeling politically that did not spring from the sentiments embodied in the Declaration of Independence." It "gave promise that in due time the weights should be lifted from the shoulders of all men, and that all should have an equal chance." Lincoln then referred to the plot to kill him in Baltimore. The Union, he proclaimed, could not survive without liberty. "But, if this country cannot be saved without giving up that principle – I was about to say I would rather be assassinated on this spot than to surrender it." Lincoln's claim that "all men are created equal," in theory if not yet in reality, encompassed blacks as well as whites.[31]

In his First Inaugural Address, the new president called secession "the essence of anarchy" and alluded to the Founding Fathers' attempt to protect liberty against tyranny by establishing a mixed government based on checks and balances. In Lincoln's eyes, secession was both an act of treason and a sinister, devious tool for defending slavery. Unanimous agreement on all matters was impossible; minority rule was unacceptable. Compromise without loss of principle served as the only feasible guide to governmental behavior. Throughout history, the two chief dangers to personal liberty were despotism and anarchy, both of which endangered individual freedom. The basis of sound government was a system of constitutional restraints on the majority that maintained the necessary balance of powers. If Americans rejected this principle, the result would be either anarchy or despotism. This explosive issue, he said four months later, threatened the existence of "a constitutional republic, or a democracy – a government of the people, by the same people." Could a group of rebels insufficient in number to control the government "break up their Government, and thus practically put an end to free government upon the earth"? "Is there, in all republics, this inherent, and fatal weakness?" "Must a government, of necessity, be too strong for the liberties of its own people, or too weak to maintain its own existence?"[32]

Lincoln as president believed he had no choice but to exercise his war powers under the Constitution to preserve the liberties found in the Declaration of Independence and now safeguarded by the Union. In so doing, he identified the federal government's military power with freedom and the Union and thereby reshaped the constitutional development of the nation by granting the administration in Washington a positive role that many Americans had long assumed belonged to states and individuals. The Civil War provided the impetus for moving closer to the more perfect Union that Lincoln envisaged for the nation.[33]

Soon Lincoln also realized that his thoughts on the central American paradox of slavery and freedom affected foreign as well as domestic policy and that failure to resolve that issue on either front could undermine the republic itself. The Union and slavery were inseparable and, in turn, inextricably interwoven into the diplomacy of the war. The Civil War eventually became a crucible for destroying the peculiar institution as a critical step toward forging a more perfect Union based on a new birth of freedom.

CHAPTER TWO

Lincoln, Slavery, and Perpetual Union

I hold, that in contemplation of universal law, and of the Constitution, the Union of these States is perpetual. . . . Continue to execute all the express provisions of our national Constitution, and the Union will endure forever – it being impossible to destroy it.

President Abraham Lincoln, March 4, 1861

As the American people plunged into civil war, the issue of slavery and its relationship to the Union became profoundly complicated both at home and abroad. Slavery had been the main driving force behind the growing sectional division in the United States, despite the claims of southerners that they were defending self-government and states' rights against northern tyranny. Did not South Carolina's declaration of secession in December 1860 repeatedly emphasize the importance of protecting slavery? Did not the Confederate Constitution adopted in Montgomery establish an elaborate defense of slavery, even guaranteeing its existence in the territories?

Southerners denied that slavery played a role in bringing on the war, and yet they declared slavery the cornerstone of their society and white supremacy its mortar. How else can one explain the rabid reaction by southerners to Lincoln's election in 1860? Before his inauguration, Lincoln expressed the core issue best to his old friend Alexander Stephens, the spindly and sickly congressman from Georgia who became the Confederacy's vice president: "You think slavery is right and ought to be extended; while we think it is wrong and ought to be restricted. That I suppose is the rub."[1] The Republican party's platform would undermine the antebellum South by barring the expansion of slavery, despite its assurance of no interference in areas where it already existed. Thus Lincoln's election placed slavery – and the Old South – on the path of ultimate extinction.

Both President Davis and Vice-President Stephens recognized the threat to their entire way of life. Although neither man considered himself a fire-

Abraham Lincoln, president of the United States. National Archives.

eater, they saw no room for compromise on the great issues dividing the nation. Davis defended secession as an act of survival against Lincoln and the so-called Black Republicans, and Stephens termed the Republican threat to slavery as "the immediate cause of the late rupture and the present revolution" leading to southern independence. Shortly after Lincoln's inauguration, Stephens pointedly rejected the doctrine of racial equality and declared that the Confederacy was "founded upon exactly the opposite idea; its foundations are laid, its cornerstone rests, upon the great truth that the negro is not equal to the white man; that slavery, subordination to the superior race, is his natural and normal condition. This, our new government, is the first, in the history of the world, based on this great physical, philosophical, and moral truth."[2]

The chief spokesmen on both sides of the imminent sectional conflict privately admitted that slavery lay at the heart of their differences, and yet they publicly attributed the division to constitutional-legal matters that were not

Jefferson Davis, president of the Confederacy. National Archives.

subject to moral debate. Try as they did, however, they could not conceal the role of slavery in virtually every disruptive issue. The result was a state of confusion in which North and South ironically found agreement on the most emotional issue that divided them: slavery itself. In a move that astounded observers thousands of miles away in Europe, Lincoln echoed the Confederacy's cry that slavery had nothing to do with the American crisis. States'

Charles Francis Adams, Union minister to England. Courtesy Massachusetts Historical Society, Boston.

rights and self-government were at stake, according to Davis and Stephens. To counter the South's resort to secession, Lincoln appealed to the sanctity of the Union.

Thus slavery retreated from center stage to assume a public status barely secondary in nature. The Confederacy sought diplomatic recognition from England and other nonslaveholding nations and predictably tried to remove slavery from the international picture. The Lincoln administration surprised Europeans by likewise dismissing the importance of slavery. The president had legitimate political reasons for emphasizing the Union's preservation over all other issues, even though he never separated the future of slavery from the future of the Union. But those watching American events from distant shores failed to grasp Lincoln's tenuous position and understandably took the words of both North and South at face value: slavery was *not* the central issue in the war – or so both sets of American antagonists professed to believe.

For domestic reasons, the Lincoln administration emphasized to Europe that the American conflict did not stem from slavery. Seward's instructions to his newly appointed minister to London, Charles Francis Adams, focused on the sanctity of the Union while skirting any reference to slavery as a divisive point between North and South. President Lincoln, of course, was not an abolitionist though he found slavery repugnant and had been on public record since the 1850s as opposing its extension without wishing to disturb its present existence. Seward as well opposed slavery without supporting the immediate dictates of abolition. To him, as well as to Lincoln, morality was not the central concern. Seward feared that the sudden collapse of slavery could cause widespread social and economic upheaval in the South that, in turn, would disrupt the southern economy, endanger the entire republic, and have a negative effect on international stability. Only gradual emancipation could afford the South time to adjust to a free labor economy.[3]

The president also had to consider domestic political factors in regard to the slavery question. Even an emphasis on the more moderate stance of antislavery, Lincoln knew, would alienate large groups of Americans, both North and South. A substantial number of these same people fell into the antislavery camp, whose attitudes ranged from lukewarm to heated but nonetheless remained moderate in setting no timetable for success and condoning compensation to owners of emancipated slaves. The abolitionists, however, called slavery a sin, rejected compromise, and advocated equal rights for blacks. Only total and immediate emancipation without compensation was acceptable to them. Most northerners strongly opposed the abolitionists and staunchly rejected a war against slavery. Lincoln also believed that a move against slavery would push southern Unionists into the Confederate camp, undermining his slim hopes of their seizing control and negotiating an end to the conflict. Most important, he feared that antislavery as a wartime objective would drive the border slave states of Missouri, Kentucky, Maryland, and Delaware out of the Union. Already shaky in their Unionism, they might join the South and virtually assure its independence.[4]

Even when war seemed inescapable, Lincoln remained the premier politician and chief adherent to the Constitution regarding the slavery issue; but observers thousands of miles away lacked his keen understanding of these domestic political and legal realities and began to ponder the wisdom of intervention. He feared that any further erosion of domestic support for the Union would assure a Confederate victory, but he also recognized the crucial importance of keeping England and France out of the war. His realistic approach to this problem resulted in a series of European misinterpretations of American events that threatened the Union's security by increasing the possibility of foreign interference.

As a result of Lincoln's policy, most of the British and French press changed from their initial antipathy toward the South because of slavery to become convinced that freedom was not the issue in the war. If the Republican party and the U.S. government could be believed, the London *Times* declared, their only goal was to keep the South in the Union. "Every politician throughout the states had over and over again declared that he has no wish to meddle with the 'peculiar institution' of the South." The Confederacy, now said the *Times*, fought for "the sacred right of self government." The London *Economist, Herald, Post*, and nearly all major papers in England, along with *Blackwood's Review* and the *Edinburgh Review*, expressed similar views. In France the same conversion occurred. The semiofficial organs of Napoleon and the government, the *Constitutionnel, Moniteur*, and *Patrie*, all had earlier denounced secession and slavery. The *Pays*, also a spokesman of the regime, had asserted that the "abolition of slavery is a noble cause to defend and bring to a triumphant conclusion." French observers, however, soon became equally perplexed and angry because of Lincoln's emphasis on the Union. Adams in London put his finger on the problem by noting that the British people "do not comprehend the connection which slavery has with [the war], because we do not at once preach emancipation. Hence they go to the other extreme and argue that it is not an element of the struggle."[5]

Lincoln's politically sound attempt to play down slavery as a cause of the war had the unfortunate result for the Union of permitting these European peoples to assess events in America on other grounds. Whereas some observers accepted the southern argument of northern oppression, most of them suddenly felt free of moral constraints to consider the dire prospects of a shrinking cotton market or, even more ominous, an outbreak of slave rebellions that would destroy the southern economy. As one Englishman wrote, despite "all our virulent abuse of slavery and slave-owners, we are just as anxious for, and as much interested in, the prosperity of the slavery interest in the Southern States as the Carolinan and Georgia planters themselves, and all Lancashire would deplore a successful insurrection of the slaves, if such a thing were possible." The French staunchly opposed slavery and expressed intense dissatisfaction with Lincoln's focus on Union. Consequently, the question of who might triumph in an imminent war became irrelevant to French observers because neither American antagonist wished to promote human freedom by abolishing slavery. Southern separation, to the French as well as to the British, became an acceptable solution to the American crisis. As the focus of interest in the war turned from questions regarding the morality of slavery to those of an economic or political nature, a new danger developed: the increased chances of a foreign involvement that could benefit only the South.[6]

Lincoln had become entangled in a no-win situation. If he pronounced that the conflict was grounded in slavery, he would alienate a critical mass of

William H. Seward, U.S. secretary of state. National Archives.

political support at home. If he removed slavery from the picture, he could lose vital support from friends abroad. Weighing the two considerations, he predictably took the second route, expecting the British and French to see through the approaching fog of war that slavery was indeed the great issue dividing North and South. In this gamble he maintained the support of most Americans above the Mason-Dixon Line while losing those Europeans who failed to grasp the overbearing influence of slavery. Because of this lack of understanding in London and Paris, Lincoln spent the bulk of the war trying to convince embittered British and French observers that his growing public stand against slavery rested on a consistent philosophical base that had its roots in the prewar period.

In early April 1861 Seward tried to avert the coming war by fomenting trouble with other nations and thereby rallying all Americans – North and South – around the flag. He believed so firmly in Unionist sentiment through-out the South that in trying to dodge a confrontation over the issue of federal control over Forts Sumter and Pickens, he advocated a foreign war in a des-perate effort to unite Americans on both sides of the issue against a common enemy. Seward's reputation for hotheaded, irrational behavior reaped its reward in making his angry threats believable. To Rudolf Schleiden, Bre-men's representative in Washington, Seward declared, "If the Lord would only give to the United States an excuse for a war with England, France, or Spain, that would be the best means of reestablishing internal peace." With that objective in mind, the secretary of state handed the president a memo (appropriately enough on April Fool's Day) titled "Some Thoughts for the President's Consideration," which urged him to seek a war with ei-ther Spain or France, depending on which nation refused to halt its meddling in New World affairs. Lincoln wisely ignored the note, while making clear that such a policy, if adopted, would be his alone to implement and not that of the secretary.[7]

If Seward committed a gross error in judgment, he was nonetheless correct in gauging the immensity of the foreign threat – particularly that of England – to the Union. The British never were passive observers of the American scene. In an idea briefly considered in London, the prime minister expressed interest in a plan similar to Lincoln's: undermine slavery in North America by restricting its expansion. Shortly after South Carolina proclaimed seces-sion in late 1860, the longtime American adversary Lord Palmerston consid-ered extending recognition to the Confederacy in exchange for its agreement not to reopen the slave trade. But what made the prime minister's plan espe-cially dangerous to American interests was his willingness to invite both the Union and Emperor Napoleon III of France to cooperate in halting the spread of slavery by persuading Mexico to bar the entry of slaves from the South. Palmerston had been a perennial advocate of closing the slave trade, but this recommendation, made in the context of the growing sectional crisis, took on a sinister meaning as a blatant European intervention in North American affairs. He nonetheless held on to the plan until finally dropping it in the summer of 1861, perhaps in part because of the Confederate Constitu-tion's prohibition of the foreign slave trade.[8]

The British foreign secretary, Lord John Russell, likewise recognized the importance of slavery to the American war and, in fact, became convinced that southern separation was a fait accompli capable of resolving that great issue. Although diminutive in physical size, Russell cast a large shadow over the making of British policy. He was a Whig in philosophy and a Liberal in

Lord Palmerston, British prime minister. Courtesy Massachusetts Historical Society, Boston.

party and claimed to support a people's right to overthrow oppressive rule. Self-government or local rule lay at the heart of the South's demands, he declared; the crisis in Italy of October 1860 demonstrated that same admirable principle at work. In the midst of that tumult, Russell had referred to the eminent Swiss writer on international law Emmerich de Vattel in asserting the right of people in Naples and the Roman states to determine their own fate. Now, in a move consistent with his stance on Italy, Russell concluded that the Union should accept the Confederacy as a second American state: "One Republic to be constituted on the principle of freedom & personal liberty – the other on the principle of slavery & the mutual surrender of fugitives."[9]

If Palmerston did not just as openly agree with Russell's justification for southern separation, he certainly believed the action irrevocable. The prime minister was ever the realist who accepted the rules of power politics in deter-

Lord John Russell, British foreign secretary. Courtesy Massachusetts Historical Society, Boston.

mining the outcome in America. To him as well as to Russell, the South's charge of northern aggression seemed eminently defensible. After all, the Lincoln administration insisted that slavery had not caused the war and then had appealed to some vaguely defined and questionable sense of "Union" in justifying its move to put down what appeared to be a reasonable argument for secession. Surely, both British leaders thought, the North was incapable of occupying so much territory and subjugating so many people. As early as New Year's Day of 1861, Palmerston assured Queen Victoria that the Union had veered down a one-way path to destruction.[10]

The British press likewise considered southern independence a fact. The *Times* and the *Economist* in London drew support from the city's other papers, in addition to that of the *Spectator*, *Westminster Review*, and *Saturday Review*, in proclaiming the impossibility of a northern conquest of the South. "Every one knows and admits," asserted the *Economist* in mid-May 1861, "that the secession is an accomplished and irrevocable fact." A few days later the journal mused that Seward's recent call for the Union's preservation constituted "the most futile dream which ever passed over the excited brain of a rhetorical American." The Union could not prevail, the *Economist* concluded. Those Americans in the North "[were] fighting, not with savage Indians nor with feeble Mexicans but with Anglo Saxons as fierce, as obstinate and as untamable as themselves."[11]

The White House, of course, considered slavery the principal cause of the war and expected the British to realize this fact as well. Lincoln and the Republican party had focused on halting the spread of slavery into the new territories as the chief means for assuring its death. The president emphasized the Union's preservation in his public declarations, but he never separated the issue of slavery from his overarching objective in the war. How could anyone ignore the most wrenching issue separating North and South? How could the Union prevail without destroying the greatest threat to its existence? Most British, however, failed to grasp the intricate relationship between slavery and Union. Russell almost casually remarked in late December 1860 that he could not understand why the North had not rid the nation of slavery. But just as he had a superficial understanding of the depth of southern feeling, so did a group of American dignitaries display the same shallow thinking while gathered at a White House dinner in March 1861. Declaring that the North was about to lead a war for emancipation, they confidently noted that the South could expect no help from England because of its stand against slavery.[12]

England's perspective on the American conflict became even more confused when the South joined the North in denying the relevance of slavery to these events. For domestic political reasons, the Lincoln administration circumvented the slavery issue in dealing with the European powers; so did the Confederacy find it necessary to dodge the subject of slavery in discussions with European leaders and to emphasize instead what Confederate emissary William L. Yancey blithely termed the "justice of the cause." In a pattern of behavior that became consistent during the early war period, southerners continually alluded to justice and providence, rather than realpolitik, in seeking diplomatic recognition. The fiery secessionist and staunch slaveholder from Alabama had led the southern delegation to Europe, where he and his companions, Pierre A. Rost and Ambrose D. Mann, met unofficially with Russell in England two times in early May to attribute secession to northern oppression and not to a defense of slavery. Indeed, they regarded slavery as so far removed from the conflict that Yancey, in an adept diplomatic move, renounced his longtime interest in reopening the African slave trade and gave assurances against its revival.[13]

The cool reception Russell accorded the three southern commissioners drew a mixed reaction in Richmond as Confederate leaders in the southern capital (moved from Montgomery, Alabama, after Virginia's secession) pondered the relevance of slavery to British thinking. President Davis was not surprised by the British attitude; he had earlier told the London *Times* correspondent in America, William H. Russell, that the South's support of slavery might threaten its relationship with England. One of his cabinet members, Judah P. Benjamin, nonetheless felt confident that British need for southern cotton would remove "this coyness about acknowledging a slave power." Yancey agreed with Davis, however, and reported home that the British people were "entirely opposed" to the Confederacy "on the question of slavery, and that the sincerity and universality of this feeling embarrasses the [British] Government in dealing with the question of our recognition."[14]

That the Confederate commissioners even managed to meet with Russell infuriated the Lincoln administration. Regardless of the aloof and noncommittal tone of their reception (and no one in Washington could have known this), the fact remained that they had won two audiences with the foreign secretary and thereby gained at least a symbolic triumph. Seward became irate over Russell's behavior, insisting that he had condoned the insurrection and expressed favor to the traitors. "God damn them, I'll give them hell," exclaimed Seward to Charles Sumner, Massachusetts senator and chair of the Foreign Relations Committee. Did not the sacred nature of the Union mean anything to the so-called civilized world?[15]

Lincoln soon became so fervent regarding the importance of the Union that the very term assumed a mystical aura that inadvertently pushed slavery even farther into the background. For more than seven decades American leaders had carried the banner of republicanism, inching ever closer to a better Union. The Union of the mid-nineteenth century marked an improvement on that of the period before, but the American republic still did not encompass every human being. Lincoln's Inaugural Address had focused on preserving the Union as a moral cause and resolving every issue that endangered that effort. "I hold, that in contemplation of universal law, and of the Constitution, the Union of these States is perpetual. . . . Continue to execute all the express provisions of our national Constitution, and the Union will endure forever – it being impossible to destroy it."[16] Lincoln had interlaced democracy, law, and the Union with a sense of moral righteousness, only by implication posing a threat to slavery. His dilemma, as always, was how to kill that institution without violating the constitutional rights of slave owners.

Secession aimed at dissolving the Union dominated by the North and building a new southern nation that legitimized slavery; Lincoln's concept of the Union soon therefore progressed from its mere preservation to something considerably broader in scope and meaning. His vision of an improved Union necessitated the destruction of slavery and the Old South, which would leave an embittered aftermath that might include, warned Seward and others in the administration, an outbreak of race war.[17] The first shots fired on Fort Sumter on April 12, 1861, had unleashed a whirlwind of events – a veritable revolution – that made it impossible to restore prewar America.

Restoration of the Union appeared highly improbable when on May 13 – the day Adams arrived in England to assume his ministerial duties – the queen enraged Americans loyal to the Union by announcing a policy of neutrality that automatically bestowed belligerent status onto the South. At first glance, the move seemed a sinister act, carefully orchestrated to mock the Union by sending a warning that its efforts to subjugate the South were both unjust and impossible. How calculated the decision by Queen Victoria to greet Adams with a neutrality proclamation! Granting belligerent status to the Confederacy was barely a step from diplomatic recognition, or so Union supporters charged, and to do so without giving their emissary a chance to present his case heaped insult onto injury. Sumner denounced the proclamation as "the most hateful act of English history since the time of Charles 2nd." If Britain extended recognition to the Confederacy, Seward sternly wrote Adams, "we from that hour, shall cease to be friends and become once more, as we have twice before been forced to be, enemies of Great Britain." When France predictably followed England's path in June by also declaring neutrality, Seward hotly warned both nations of the possibility of war.[18]

Despite the appearance of underhanded behavior, England's pronouncement of neutrality did not stem from some diabolical scheme to destroy the Union; rather, it derived from the Palmerston ministry's erroneous reading of Lincoln's declaration of a blockade of southern ports in April. The president had declared it "advisable to set on foot a blockade," which meant that he had *decided* to blockade the South but had not yet put the measure into play. The usually calm and staid British minister to Washington, Lord Lyons, recognized this crucial distinction and accepted Seward's note on the presidential proclamation as "an announcement of an intention to set on foot a blockade, not as a notification of the actual commencement of one." Lincoln had given British leaders time to consider the dangerous ramifications of any policy not favorable to the Union. Yet the government in London ignored Lyons's astute observation in its haste to conform with international and municipal law and thereby prevent British subjects from committing some illegal action that forced their government into the American war. From the ministry's perspective, the law of nations defined the fighting in North America as a civil war that shared the same features of a war between nations. Countries affected by the American war must declare neutrality in order to enact rules of conduct toward the belligerents.[19]

British neutrality did not always prove impartial, however, for several important spokesmen of the government in London supported the stand because it benefited the Union more than the South. If no special advantages were accorded to either antagonist, it followed that the North would become the chief beneficiary of neutrality because of its overwhelming superiority in

Lord Lyons, British minister to the United States. From Lord Newton, Lord Lyons: A Record of British Diplomacy, *2 vols. (London: Edward Arnold, 1913), 1: frontispiece.*

matériel, people, and seagoing vessels. Further, international law made clear that recognition of belligerency in a civil war helped the parent government (the Union) more than its wayward offspring in a variety of ways. It relieved that government of responsibility for the South's actions; allowed both belligerents' cruisers (the Confederacy had none) to pursue visit-and-search tactics at sea and send contraband to prize courts; granted the right of a parent state to establish a blockade that commanded respect from other nations; and prohibited insurgents (the South) from engaging in hostile preparations while within the jurisdictional limits of a neutral nation.[20]

Many of these same British adherents to neutrality also regarded that policy as the best means for avoiding an involvement in the war on the side of the slaveholding South. The Duke of Argyll, who held a cabinet post as lord privy seal, was an outspoken advocate of the Union and expressed alarm over the possibility of his ministry's recognizing the South's independence before it had actually earned that status on the battlefield. In Parliament, William E. Forster from the Liberal party rigidly opposed recognition. The son of a Quaker missionary and nephew of well-known antislavery advocate Thomas Fowell Buxton, Forster had publicly praised Harriet Beecher Stowe's best-selling abolitionist novel, *Uncle Tom's Cabin*, and repeatedly criticized the South's treatment of black people. Not only would premature recognition of the South violate international law, Forster warned the seemingly overanx-ious Palmerston ministry, but it assured a war with the Union that would re-strict commercial access to cotton and place England on the side "fighting for slavery." In a desperate move to undercut the South, the Lincoln administra-tion would resort to emancipation, hoping to instigate a slave insurrection that destroyed the South from within. The problem, Forster warned, was that such tactics could incite a race war that spread beyond the present boundaries of America and dragged in other nations, including England. Forster refused to believe that Russell "would commit any such insanity."[21]

Forster's fears had conjured up a hideous image of racial strife that touched a British nerve. No one could adequately explain how a race war in America could affect other nations, but most observers seemed to believe it a foregone conclusion because it would release so much pent-up black anger and frustration over slavery. The specter of a race war ignited by slave rebel-lions reminded the British of the Haitian insurrections at the turn of the cen-tury. Had not these bloody events virtually devastated the island's sugar economy and thereby hurt other nations? Would not the same international economic disaster result from a cotton South torn apart by racial conflict? Whether or not a distinct possibility, the threat of a slave rebellion weighed heavily on British thoughts of intervention.[22]

The Lincoln administration meanwhile failed to discern the advantages af-forded by British neutrality and became incensed with the Palmerston minis-try for awarding credibility to the South as a belligerent. The Confederacy gained the right to float loans and buy war matériel from England, to bring prizes to its ports that resulted from privateering (a practice favoring small-navy nations and abolished by the European powers in the Declaration of Paris of 1856), to enlist manpower for any activity that did not violate neu-trality laws, to contract the building of ships in British yards, and, as long as the equipping and fitting for wartime actions did not take place in England, to employ these vessels in the new Confederate navy. From the perspectives of both North and South, British recognition of Confederate belligerency marked the first major step toward recognition of Confederate independence.[23]

The queen's neutrality proclamation was justifiable, although its issuance doubtless came easier because of the insistence by both Union and Confederacy that the war had not grown out of the slavery issue. In conjunction with the British Foreign Enlistment Act of 1819, the neutrality measure barred British subjects from foreign enlistments and from "fitting out or equipping" vessels in British possessions for wartime purposes without government approval. The British government offered no protection to any subject who joined the armed service or violated the lawful blockade of any nation at peace with England.[24] Had the two American antagonists focused on slavery as the central issue in the war, the British government might have had more difficulty in opting for neutrality, but the outcome would have been the same. The overriding factor in the British decision was to stay out of the American war – as long as that war posed no threat to Britain's vital interests.

Charles Francis Adams warned, however, that the Union's renunciation of slavery as a cause of the war imperiled its relationship with Britain. As the scholarly son of one president and grandson of another, he had always recognized the strange ambivalence that characterized the Atlantic nations' feelings for each other. Almost British in his demeanor, Adams grasped the importance of cultivating good relations with his host government – short of conceding anything detrimental to the Union, of course. The slavery issue, he quickly learned, made this task extremely difficult. Despite Lincoln's best efforts, slavery remained a powerful force in the Atlantic relationship. Now, with slavery officially removed from the picture, a surprising twist developed when the British could conceive of no other issue worth the price of blood and questioned the Union's motives. The London *Economist* warned the Lincoln administration that its refusal to accept secession assured a long and bitter war of conquest, followed, if victorious, by a long and bitter period of military occupation of the South. "Even if the North were sure of an easy and complete victory," the *Economist* continued, "the war which was to end in such a victory would still be . . . an objectless and unprofitable folly." England's refusal to guarantee against recognition, Adams complained, assured continuous trouble with the Union.[25]

In this context of growing doubt about the Union's cause, the threat of slave insurrections in the South emerged as a major factor encouraging British intervention in the war. Russell had shown interest in a mediation, if invited, even before the fighting had begun. A civil war, he and other British contemporaries knew, usually left the divided nation so vulnerable that outside powers often yielded to temptation and intervened out of self-interest. In the United States, the danger loomed as particularly real because of the war's racial underpinning. Not only would a servile war undermine the cotton economy for years, but it could develop into a racial conflict that shook the foundations of the entire republic and even spread beyond American borders to hurt other nations. The United States had become so integral to the international economy that the domestic conflict would disrupt trade with Europe and lead to massive political unrest among its own people. The Union's attempt to subjugate its adversary, Lyons warned, caused southerners to fear for "their safety in the midst of their slave population." The simplest solution, Russell believed, was for the Union to condone southern separation.[26]

Although some British observers welcomed a permanently divided United States as advantageous to their interests, Russell and other more responsible spokesmen recognized that widespread destruction in America would have dire international repercussions. Shouts of approval echoed throughout the House of Commons when Sir John Ramsden (formerly a Liberal who had joined the Conservative party) gleefully assured his colleagues that they "were now witnessing the bursting of the great republican bubble which had been so often held up to us as the model on which to recast our own English Constitution." Russell immediately chastised these members of the Commons by insisting that slavery had caused the war and that England itself had thrown "the poisoned garment" over its former colonies. It was wrong, he proclaimed, "that there should be among us anything like exultation at their discord, and still less that we should reproach them with an evil for the origin of which we are ourselves to blame." A large majority in the Commons repudiated Ramsden's remarks but, notably, revealed no support for Russell's stand.[27]

Adams realized that the British people had failed to grasp the intimate relationship between slavery and the war and that hardly anyone thought the North either capable of or justified in resisting southern independence. Neither the Liberals nor the Conservatives could support the South if slavery were the decisive issue. But he also knew that most of these same people had the erroneous conception that since the Lincoln administration had refused to support emancipation, it had eliminated slavery as an issue. Indeed, more than a few welcomed dissolution of the Union as a means for achieving abolition: a slaveholding Confederacy, they believed, could not exist for long because of the certain seepage of slaves into neighboring free territory. In a statement that revealed Adams's acute understanding of the war, he declared that preservation of the Union was the key to protecting "liberty against reaction."[28]

The Confederate victory at the Battle of Bull Run in July 1861 further convinced the British of the South's independence and led Richmond's commissioners in London to reiterate the irrelevance of slavery to the conflict. Confederate forces had routed the Union's army, leading many observers on both sides of the Atlantic to conclude that the Union debacle at Bull Run constituted the first and the last pitched contest of the war. The London *Times* asserted that from the battle "enough has been learnt to show us that the subjugation of the South is next to impossible." In a telling comment, it compared the South with the rebellious American colonies: "Let the Northern States accept the situation as we did 80 years ago upon their own soil." So euphoric over the news were Yancey, Rost, and Mann that they wrote Russell a note seeking a treaty of friendship, commerce, and navigation. They deemed it wise to postpone a request for recognition, however, until the total impact of Bull Run had registered in the collective British mind. Slavery was not an issue in the fight, they again emphasized. If Lincoln introduced a plan to free the slaves, he would expose himself as a hypocrite capable of doing anything to win British support. Indeed, the commissioners darkly warned, the Union's military situation had become so grave that he was prepared to incite a slave insurrection in an effort to bring down the South from within.[29]

But the South's victory at Bull Run did not convince the Union that the war was over, nor did it induce the British to ignore the slavery issue and extend recognition to the Confederacy. Instead, the battle awakened northerners to the realization that a long and bloody war lay ahead and actually hardened their resolve. Within high governing circles in London, Russell and others maintained their icy neutrality toward American events, lamenting the Union's stubborn rejection of reality while reiterating their refusal to recognize the Confederacy. The latter act would place the British in virtual alliance with the South against the North, assuring a wider war that would hurt England, no matter the outcome.

Whether slavery in the South stood as the key element in the Palmerston ministry's consideration remains problematical; but even when its spokesmen sympathized with the South's claim to self-government against northern oppression, they almost always tempered their feelings with expressions of discomfort about its peculiar institution. Not surprisingly, Russell simply responded to the South's entreaties for recognition that England would continue neutrality and await the war's verdict.[30]

During the summer of 1861, Russell expressed his growing frustrations over the American war and the slavery issue to his longtime acquaintance and the former U.S. minister to London, Edward Everett of Massachusetts. Several issues had gnawed at Russell's patience, including tangled legal arguments over recognition and the Union's policies toward the blockade, port closings, and privateering.[31] Now, as the war seemed certain to grind on almost endlessly, other matters came to the front, all threatening to cause a British intervention that inescapably served Confederate interests. The huge prewar cotton surplus in England had blunted the South's initial efforts to gain leverage through King Cotton diplomacy, but estimates were that by the autumn of 1862 British (and French) textile mills would have been drained of their supplies and in need of additional cotton to stay in operation. Closure of these mills might cause a wave of unrest at home that would pressure the Palmerston ministry into challenging the Union blockade and, in so doing, bring on a war with the North that helped the South. International law, Russell knew, justified efforts by neutral nations to encourage those peoples at war to resolve their differences. Intervention could take the form of humanitarian appeals based on mediation; or, he carefully warned, it could constitute a resort to force if the fighting had a damaging effect on outside nations.[32]

If only Lincoln had proclaimed the war for what it was, Russell complained – a war for abolition – the Union would have attracted widespread foreign sympathy at the outset and avoided this confusion. Russell hated slavery and had been a member of the cabinet that abolished the institution in the West Indies. Slavery, he declared, was the driving force behind the American war, and Lincoln's admission of this reality would compel England and other European nations to oppose the South.[33]

If Russell expected consolation from Everett, he was sorely disappointed. The former minister and later president of Harvard College temporarily put aside the fond memories of his long hours of whist and other amicable social gatherings with Russell to emphasize that the British had failed to comprehend the depth of Union bitterness over their neutrality. Most important, the usually mild-mannered Everett indignantly charged, Russell and his people had not grasped the integral relationship of slavery to the war for the Union. Everett had been the vice-presidential candidate of the Constitutional Union party in 1860, which had ignored the slavery issue in calling for the Union's preservation. But now he too noted the paramount importance of slavery in bringing on the sectional conflict. The Lincoln administration had assumed that the British could not sympathize with the slaveholding Confederacy. But they had proved extremely shortsighted in failing to go beyond the official words of the White House to discern the underlying reason for the war. Indeed, the Palmerston ministry had inexplicably found reasons to condone the South's drive for independence. Of course, Everett proclaimed, the war was about slavery. It followed that the war had a moral fiber that undermined Russell's argument for permitting the South to leave the Union in peace. To do so would have constituted a further compromise with slavery and a gross injustice to black people.[34]

Everett was correct in asserting that Russell had failed to comprehend the war's profound implications for slavery. Despite the Union's bitter suspicions, Russell was not a silent supporter of the South. He had, however, joined numerous other British colleagues in concluding that southern separation was a fait accompli. The Union's refusal to accept this fundamental truth, they warned, would unnecessarily prolong the war and endanger the welfare of other nations as well. Thus both British and Union advocates considered themselves the voice of reason and right, paradoxically assuring that two peoples who did not want to go to war with each other might nonetheless end up doing so.

Admittedly, Russell recognized the role of slavery in bringing on the war; but he did not go any farther than to assert that the establishment of two American republics – one slave, the other free – was the solution. In an argument that never aroused support from his associates but drew praise from Lord Robert Cecil and numerous other members of the Conservative party, Russell insisted that identification of the South as a nation would make it the only slaveholding country in North America. He agreed with Cecil and others, who asserted that the South would come under enormous domestic and foreign pressure to emancipate its slaves rather than see them escape into free countries. The *Bee-Hive* of London supported Confederate independence and insisted that it necessitated a repeal of the Fugitive Slave Law and a resultant southern acceptance of emancipation. The North's attempt to restore the Union would cost untold amounts of blood and treasure and was impossible to achieve anyway. "For this reason," Russell explained, "I wish for separation."[35]

Russell's argument won support from the London *Economist*, which likewise linked the breakup of the Union with the opportunity to end slavery in North America: "We admit that we do regard the disruption of the Union as a matter for rejoicing rather than for regret. . . . We avow the sentiment, and we are prepared to justify it as at once natural, statesmanlike, and righteous." Whereas Lincoln had argued that maintenance of the Union would restrict slavery to the South and eventually lead to its death, the *Economist* insisted that *dis*union offered the same results and at a lower cost: "We do not see why we should hesitate to declare our belief that the dissolution of the Union will prove a good to the world, to Great Britain and probably in the end to America herself." Besides, the paper snidely added, since the United States had become so arrogant, "can we be charged with selfishness or want of generosity because we rejoice that an excess of power which was menacing to others and noxious to themselves has been curtailed and curbed?"[36]

The expected need for cotton by the fall of 1862 also dictated much of British policy, although that objective always arose within the broader and more explosive discussion of challenging the Union blockade and therefore raising the risk of war. Russell had just learned of a meeting between Seward and the

French minister in Washington, Henri Mercier, in which the latter had emphasized Europe's dwindling supplies of cotton. Mercier's resulting call for intervention contained "much good sense," Russell asserted to Palmerston, but the opportune time had not yet arrived. "I am persuaded that if we do anything, it must be on a grand scale." England and France must not attempt to break the blockade simply to secure cotton. But they should urge the warring Americans to resolve their problems peacefully. "We propose to give terms of pacification which we think fair and equitable." If either of the belligerents rejected the offer, the intervening powers should declare to that recalcitrant that "mediation is at an end, and you may expect to see us your enemies." Palmerston agreed that intervention solely for cotton was not wise "unless, indeed, the distress . . . was far more serious than it is likely to be." The London *Economist* meanwhile made the stakes clear when it warned that "to insist upon the United States ceasing the blockade would be neither more nor less than to declare war against them."[37]

Russell had taken a major step toward intervention when he expressed a willingness to propose terms of settlement and, more important, to cooperate with France in threatening to use force to close the agreement. Like most European observers, he failed to comprehend the depth of feeling that separated the two American antagonists. What possible compromise was there over the slavery question? All talk of any agreement short of war had ceased when Confederate guns fired on Fort Sumter. The Battle of Bull Run had further underlined the impossibility of peacefully resolving these difficulties. Both American camps had invested too much human and material resources to stop fighting and walk away from the battlefield. It was the height of naïveté to think a mediation feasible. How else to implement terms other than the use of force and the ultimate outbreak of war on a broader scale?

If Russell did not grasp the intensity of feeling in America, he surely came to understand the perils of neutrality. He had tried to demonstrate his aloofness from the war by twice receiving the Confederate commissioners on an unofficial basis, thereby hoping to send a message to Washington that the London government had not taken a step toward recognition. The effect proved exactly the opposite. Seward had blasted Russell so roundly that he agreed not to meet with the commissioners again. Then, in a matter of days, the British government granted the Confederacy belligerent status. Recognition of southern independence, the Lincoln administration feared, seemed only a matter of time. And while the Union's leaders fumed, so did those of the Confederacy. When Russell's correspondence with Adams was published in the United States, Yancey became livid on learning that the British foreign secretary had promised not to meet with the Confederate commissioners again. To his superiors in Richmond, Yancey unleashed his fury: "What truckling to the arrogant demand of Mr. Seward, that England should forego her international privilege of hearing the case of a belligerent power. What a violation, in fact, of that impartial neutrality proclaimed – a neutrality indeed, which includes the equal hearing of both sides, although upon unequal terms, – official on one side, unofficial on the other."[38] Russell's plight suggested the double-edged dangers of neutrality.

To approve Russell's proposed remedy based on southern separation, Lincoln realized, was to condone slavery and accept secession. The two antagonists had gone to war over the very issues that Russell had attempted to reduce in significance. The North could not make peace based on southern independence and protection of slavery; the South could not give up the war without an assurance of nationhood and safeguards for slavery. To grant either set of demands constituted a total victory for one belligerent and, necessarily, a total defeat for the other. Most important from the White House perspective, the South's attempted departure from the Union followed by the outbreak of war had moved the Lincoln administration beyond the politically careful stand of seeking to contain slavery and force its ultimate extinction. The blood already shed in these first few months of the crisis had washed away all hopes for any compromise on slavery. The war had come, and with it had risen the need to grapple with slavery as a moral wrong that desecrated the concept of a more perfect Union envisioned by the Founding Fathers and now embraced by Lincoln and his most avid supporters. Russell did not understand the vital connection between the end of slavery and the forging of a better Union. He could not know that there was no room for compromise, leaving war as the final solution.

CHAPTER THREE

Southern Slavery, Northern Freedom: The Central Dilemma of the Republic

> I cannot imagine that any European power would dare to recognize and aid the Southern Confederacy if it became clear that the Confederacy stands for slavery and the Union for freedom.
>
> President Abraham Lincoln, September 1861

> [Emancipation is] a military necessity, absolutely essential to the preservation of the Union.
>
> President Abraham Lincoln, July 13, 1862

Despite the Lincoln administration's efforts to focus on Union as the central purpose in the war, slavery became a vital consideration in both British and French thoughts about intervention. Ironically, however, the role of slavery in these foreign deliberations proved far different than assumed in Washington. The peculiar institution, as the White House correctly observed, emerged as a formidable obstacle to British involvement in the war. But it also played another unexpected role. Many British observers feared that Lincoln was prepared to announce emancipation in an effort to instigate slave insurrections aimed at destroying the South from within. Most ominous, they believed, such uprisings would develop into a race war that crossed sectional boundaries and ultimately hurt those nations dependent on goods from both North and South. The French situation was likewise more complicated than depicted by contemporaries. The public opposed slavery and hence had an initial affinity for the Union, but Napoleon had more important objectives unrelated to that issue. He wanted to build a commercial empire in the Americas that started with his establishing control over Mexico and depended heavily on a friendly and independent Confederacy to contain U.S. expansion. Both Britain and France, however, found it impossible to ignore the influence of slavery in nearly all matters affecting the American war.

Regardless of the issue at almost any time in the diplomacy of the Civil War, slavery almost always wound itself into the mix. The reason was clear:

any British or French troubles with the Union necessarily proved advantageous to the Confederacy and hence left the impression that they were taking the side of slavery over freedom. Regardless of Lincoln's public emphasis on preserving the Union, the fact was that his government did not support human bondage, whereas his adversaries in Richmond did. To many observers, the image of the South was as the bastion of slavery, whereas that of the North was as the defender of freedom.

The threat of war between the United States and Britain over the *Trent* affair in late 1861 demonstrated the inseparability of slavery from any troubles between the Atlantic nations. At the height of this winter crisis, British spokesmen warned that war with the Union would automatically place their government in the Confederate camp and hence on the side of slaveholders. And the chances for war proved real over the Christmas holidays. A Union naval vessel captained by Charles Wilkes, the uss *San Jacinto*, had in early November intercepted a British mail steamer, the *Trent*, in the Old Bahama Channel three hundred miles east of Havana and, instead of correctly seizing the vessel as a prize, he acted without orders in forcibly removing Confederate emissaries James Mason (to London) and John Slidell (to Paris) as the "embodiment of dispatches."[1]

The British reacted with predictable outrage. Wilkes's unprecedented definition of "contraband" to include human beings infuriated the British as a violation of neutrality and an insult to national honor. Argyll tied his fear of an Atlantic war over the *Trent* to his concern over British intervention in the American Civil War and denounced the thought of allying with the South, whether directly through treaty or indirectly by war with the Union. Lyons in Washington, visibly shaken by the *Trent* war scare, recognized that an Anglo-American conflict would heighten Union desperation even more and repeated his earlier warning that Lincoln intended to stir up a slave insurrection by announcing emancipation. "British subjects," the British minister nervously declared, "may have their throats cut by the negroes in a servile insurrection."[2]

The French likewise opposed slavery but had other, more pressing matters that compelled them to consider recognizing the South in the midst of the *Trent* crisis. The Union's minister in Paris, William Dayton, reported the ominous news that Napoleon stood poised to take advantage of an Anglo-American war over the *Trent* to satisfy his lifelong ambition of establishing a foothold in the New World. France had recently entered a tripartite treaty with Britain and Spain in London that authorized the use of force in collect-

uss San Jacinto *firing on British mail steamer* Trent. *National Archives.*

Captain Charles Wilkes. Library of Congress.

ing payment on long-standing debts and claims from Mexico. The French emperor, however, had far more in mind – the establishment of a monarchy in Mexico that advanced his great vision of building a commercial empire in the Western Hemisphere. An independent Confederacy, of course, would provide a friendly buffer between the postwar Union and a refurbished Mexico under French control. French foreign minister Edouard Thouvenel was

James Mason, Confederate minister to England. National Archives.

not privy to all the imperial designs of his superior, but his nation's growing cotton shortage had already forced him to set aside his personal favor for the Union and support the South. He instructed Mercier in Washington to persuade Lyons to join France in an intervention that would encourage the chances for Confederate recognition.[3] To French observers, the decisive factor was the national interest, not southern slavery.

British anger over the *Trent* likewise rested on self-interest, but on more defensible grounds than those of the French. Wilkes's infringement of British honor was unquestionable; no self-respecting nation could allow such action to go uncontested. Also important, however, were British concerns about Lincoln's seeming willingness to instigate slave uprisings in a desperate effort to win the war. Had not the South already raised this dreaded appa-

John Slidell, Confederate minister to France. National Archives.

rition in accusing him of the most unscrupulous tactics known to man? Britain's dilemma became clear: sacrifice national esteem by doing nothing to atone for the *Trent* violations, or go to war to preserve honor. The second course meant not only a costly war with the Union but at the least an informal alliance with the Confederacy. Lincoln might proclaim emancipation in an attempt to incite slave revolts that undermined the South. The outcome could be a race war that spread beyond the South to disrupt not only the entire American economy but also the livelihood of those nations having commercial relations with the United States.

The *Trent* crisis indirectly revealed that British fears about Lincoln's intentions regarding emancipation were not misplaced. The danger of war over

the *Trent* lasted until mid-January 1862, when the Union finally acknowledged that Wilkes had acted without either authority or legal justification
and agreed to release Mason and Slidell. Still, the Lincoln administration
won some satisfaction from England's discomfiture and then even fabricated
a victory by making the specious claim that British acceptance of the Union's
compliance with their demands constituted their own implicit promise
against further maritime violations such as impressment. The White House
had achieved its most important objective, however, in averting a war with
England – especially while fighting the Confederacy. But the crisis had demonstrated to the president that more than an appeal to the sanctity of the
Union was necessary to ward off foreign involvement in the American conflict. Slavery itself might provide a potent weapon in his struggle against
intervention.

With that concern weighing heavily on his mind, Lincoln told Senators
Orville Browning of Illinois and Garrett Davis of Kentucky that to save the
Union he would take whatever steps were necessary, including the destruction of slavery. Perhaps it is only coincidental that just two days after this conversation, Lyons wrote Russell: "The question is rapidly tending towards the
issue either of peace and a recognition of the separation, or a Proclamation of
Emancipation and the raising of a servile insurrection." Russell found it particularly distressing that the president pondered "a war of emancipation." He
soon warned the House of Lords that British aid to the South might lead the
president to instigate a slave uprising conducive to a race war.[4] Lincoln's objective was to block intervention by making clear the distinction between the
southern supporters of slavery and the northern proponents of freedom. But
even if the London government misinterpreted his motives, the result would
have been the same: a strong reason not to intervene.

British reaction to the American war proved increasingly exasperating to
the Union, forcing it to edge closer to an antislavery position. Seward found
it difficult to believe that the British failed to realize that the war had pitted
the constitutionally established Union government against what he considered to be a mob of fanatical slaveholding insurgents. But regardless of the
Union's fortunes both on and off the battlefield, Britain remained such a
seemingly hostile neutral that more desperate measures became necessary
that related to slavery. The Union consul in Bristol assured Lincoln in early
December, "The only antidote for their [secessionists'] mischief, would be in
the trusty anti-slavery men of the United States, dealing with the anti-slavery
men of England, and the anti-slavery sentiment, which seems to be universal." One American official in the legation in London, the outspoken and
fiercely antisouthern Benjamin Moran, bitterly remarked that it was ludi-
crous for the South to deny that black liberty was the chief issue in the war.

The Union's twin victories at Forts Henry and Donelson in mid-February, he thought, would finally cause England to "desert her slave-driving allies" and realize that the South was engaged in "an unholy war for slavery."[5]

The argument for emancipation took on increased importance when it became clear that no other action by the Union assured against a foreign intervention. On hearing of the fall of Forts Henry and Donelson, the London *Times* shocked northerners by expressing doubt that the victories had brought the Americans "any nearer than before to a reconstruction of the Union." The South's tenacity became increasingly evident to the British writer, who compared the collapse of Fort Donelson to "the first milestone from London toward Exeter."[6] Even battlefield conquests, usually the most reliable measure in determining the tide of war, had no impact on British observers who seemed convinced that the southern drive for independence was irreversible.

Lincoln recognized more and more the potential positive impact of emancipation on foreign affairs. In September 1861 the Union minister in Spain, Carl Schurz, assured Seward that a White House declaration against slavery would unite Europe against the South. Early the following year Schurz returned to the United States and talked with the president about using an antislavery pronouncement to block foreign intervention. After a moment of reflection, Lincoln responded: "You may be right. Probably you are. I have been thinking so myself. I cannot imagine that any European power would dare to recognize and aid the Southern Confederacy if it became clear that the Confederacy stands for slavery and the Union for freedom." In early February 1862 the son of former King Louis Philippe of France, the Prince de Joinville, urged Lincoln to push for emancipation before the South won recognition by assuring freedom for its slaves over a period of twenty to thirty years: "The anti-slavery party in Europe has been the only one there to sustain the cause of the Union. The feeling of repugnance to recognizing a slave confederacy has perhaps contributed more than anything to prevent Europe from interfering in your affairs." In addition, Napoleon's cousin Prince Jerome Napoleon assured Edward Everett that Europe considered emancipation the solution and could not understand why the Union held back. The president's known hostility to slavery had a favorable impact on England's abolitionists. On the morning of April 16, 1862, a large contingent of the Anti-Slavery Society, including a member of Parliament, met with Adams to praise the White House for its opposition to slavery.[7]

By the spring of 1862 the Lincoln administration had moved closer to making a public declaration clarifying the inseparability of slavery from Union in the war. Seward staunchly rejected Russell's remedy of two American republics and insisted that slavery and freedom could not coexist in harmony, either in the same country or next to each other as neighbors. But abolition, he knew, would harden the South's resolve. Adams had reported that the two Confederate ministers recently arrived in Europe, Mason in London and Slidell in Paris, had hinted at the South's willingness to approve gradual emancipation in exchange for British and French recognition. Adams thought the idea a deception intended to disarm slavery as an issue, but the story was serious enough "to demand the most active and immediate efforts at counteraction." The White House must announce its opposition to slavery. If it did, Russell would have to drop his argument that the main issue behind the war was northern empire versus southern liberty. Seward likewise considered gradual emancipation unlikely, for the measure would have the adverse effect of breaking the will of the rebellion. It was clear, however, that the Union could no longer ignore slavery. As he declared, "The time has probably come for the practical determination of the great issue which has thus been joined."[8]

By the summer of 1862 the government in Washington had adopted measures that helped to push slavery into the central maelstrom of the war. In early August 1861, Congress passed the Confiscation Act, which authorized the seizure of any property – including slaves – that aided the South's war effort. In February 1862 Congress debated a stronger confiscation bill that caused Lincoln considerable concern. To encourage slave owners to cease their resistance if they wanted to hold on to their slaves, the proposal stipulated that those slaves in areas still in rebellion who escaped to Union army camps become free in sixty days. Such a bill, the president believed, would alienate the border states by enticing their own slaves to leave the plantations. That same month he rejected a plan for commutation of the death sentence to Captain Nathaniel P. Gordon, who became the first American slave trader executed as a pirate. Finally, in early March, Lincoln asked Congress to approve gradual emancipation with compensation derived from federal funds granted to those states that voluntarily freed their slaves. This last action Adams termed the most important proposal in the war. Europe would react favorably, although he doubted that it would have the same positive impact in America. Russell, however, still feared a slave rebellion and remained skeptical about Lincoln's motives.[9]

Lincoln's call for gradual emancipation with compensation deserves special attention. On March 6, 1862, he asked Congress to appropriate "pecuniary aid" to "any state which may adopt gradual abolishment of slavery." The Confiscation Act of 1861 had aimed at removing slaves from southerners who used them to promote the rebellion, but Lincoln's emancipation proposal included all states containing slaves and would mean a gradual end to slavery itself. Most important, the new measure authorized action only within the legal confines of the Constitution. The federal government, he declared once again, "sets up no claim of a right, by federal authority, to interfere with slavery within state limits." The states should take the initiative in adopting a process leading to freedom and based on the principle that "gradual, and not sudden emancipation, is better for all." In a scarcely veiled warning to the South, he appropriated to himself all means that "may seem indispensable, or may obviously promise great efficiency towards ending the struggle."[10] Emancipation by choice, he implied, was preferable to emancipation by the sword.

Lincoln's proposal for gradual emancipation drew bitter criticism from the abolitionists, who either failed to understand or simply rejected the importance of the touchy situation in which the president found himself. No question exists about their claim that compensated emancipation based on the slave owners' consent violated the great moral principles of freedom on which rested the abolitionists' fierce opposition to human bondage. Further, in a legal sense the holders of slaves gained great advantages, both now and in some elusive postslavery period, in having the states determine the future of blacks, even if free. The abolitionist Wendell Phillips feverishly warned that no one could stop the onset of emancipation: "Abraham Lincoln may not wish it; he cannot prevent it; the nation may not will it; the nation can never prevent it. . . . I do not care what men may want or wish; the negro is the pebble in the cog wheel, and the machine cannot go until you get him out."[11]

While Americans on both sides of the slavery issue debated the wisdom of gradual emancipation, the administration's new antislavery thrust in the war became even more pronounced when, in Washington on April 7, the Union signed a treaty with England that provided for joint action against the African slave trade. The pact was primarily attributable to the White House effort to block British intervention on behalf of the South, but it also fitted nicely with the rapidly developing shift in the Union's policy toward slavery. In actuality, of course, Lincoln had already decided to focus on antislavery as the crucial ingredient in an improved Union, but, realist that he was, he recognized the need to move slowly by exhausting all other measures first. The British had long sought such a treaty from the United States, and now the moral basis of the projected move had meshed with the realistic needs of the war to necessitate a sharper definition of the Union's position on slavery. Hence Seward and Lyons signed a pact that authorized the mutual right to search ships off Africa and Cuba. Had the two nations agreed to this concept when they first took a stand against the slave trade in 1808, Seward asserted, "there would have been no sedition here, and no disagreement between the United States and foreign nations."[12]

Like most sound treaties, this one resulted from a combination of domestic and foreign considerations. Lyons thought the president's purpose was political – to maintain credibility with his party stalwarts in the event of his eventually having to make concessions to the South during postwar reconstruction. Seward emphasized the establishment of good Anglo-American relations as integral to his ongoing effort to keep the British out of the war. For Lincoln, the move against the slave trade had the potential of attracting British sentiment in the war and marked another step toward emancipation by drying up the African source of slavery. White House acceptance of a long-rejected mutual search policy with the British would publicize the Union's interest in undermining slavery and make it extremely difficult for the British to help the Confederacy. The treaty had pushed the Lincoln administration closer to an antislavery policy by placing the Union in the forefront of emancipation.[13]

The Lincoln administration's steady move toward emancipation became increasingly evident in the period following the Seward-Lyons Treaty. Just three days later, the president signed a bill authorizing gradual emancipation with compensation. Congress had given greater impetus to the confiscation approach by prohibiting army officers from facilitating the return of fugitive slaves to the South; but Lincoln preferred the more moderate program of gradual emancipation and urged the border states to approve and perhaps convince the South to accept the idea. Despite deep reservations expressed by the border states, Congress passed the gradual emancipation measure by a wide margin. Less than a week later Lincoln signed another bill that was bound to cause consternation among the slaves in neighboring Maryland and Virginia: it freed all the slaves in the District of Columbia but authorized compensation to owners and colonization for the blacks.[14]

Despite these efforts, the perceived threat of British intervention remained so intense that the Lincoln administration pointedly warned the Palmerston ministry that its involvement in American affairs could instigate a slave insurrection that could develop into a race war. Thus in a strange twist of events, the British thought the Union willing to resort to such a drastic measure, whereas the Union feared that further British flirtations with intervention might bring on the very calamity they had cautioned against. Before the Union's capture of New Orleans in late April, Seward wrote Adams (meant for Russell's perusal) that the Union army had become the slaves' chief avenue to freedom. If the Confederacy tried to stop this flow of runaways, Seward asked, who could prevent the present contest from "degenerating into a servile war?" A foreign intervention based on southern separation would assure such a war, wrecking the economies of both North and South and thereby destroying all European economic interests in America. When southern sympathizer William Lindsay in Parliament declared his intention to introduce a motion calling for diplomatic recognition of the Confederacy, Adams chose this time, June 20, to show Russell Seward's note of the previous May, warning of the probability of slave revolts if Britain interfered in American domestic affairs.[15]

Heightening French interest in intervention also threatened to spur the British into action. In late March Dayton talked with Napoleon, who expressed concern that the American war would undermine all hopes of securing southern cotton and ultimately destroy French industry. Thouvenel, in fact, had to travel through the manufacturing areas "incognito" because of the widespread economic distress. The following month Lindsay crossed the Channel to Paris and met with Napoleon on three occasions. In a startling statement, the emperor asserted his willingness to use force against the blockade if England joined him. Napoleon, according to Slidell's account (corroborated by Lindsay), declared that he "would at once dispatch a formidable fleet to the mouth of the Mississippi, if England would send an equal force." He "would demand free egress and ingress for their merchantmen with their cargoes of goods and supplies of cotton, which were essential to the world." Napoleon authorized Lindsay to inform the British ambassador in Paris of French willingness to cooperate with England in breaking the blockade.[16]

Despite the Lincoln administration's fears and despite Napoleon's assurances of support, the chances of a British intervention at this juncture in the war were remote at best. Russell admitted to pressure for mediation from the press and other British contemporaries, and he was appalled by the heightened ferocity of the war – particularly the ghastly two-day battle at Shiloh in early April – but he offered assurances against any involvement by the ministry. The *Economist* and the *Times* of London meanwhile angered the Union again when, just as in the aftermath of its victories at Forts Henry and Donelson, they blandly dismissed the importance of its conquests of New Orleans and Yorktown along with the high expectations coming from Union Gen. George B. McClellan's advance on Richmond. "The very victories . . . of the Northerners," the *Times* declared in a matter-of-fact tone, "have but brought to light the hopelessness of the case by revealing, in its true character and proportions, the spirit of the South."[17]

Americans denounced the *Economist* and *Times* as pro-Confederacy, but the truth is that the London papers joined government spokesmen and many others in England who considered a southern separation as the most feasible route to an early settlement of the war. The Union, they disgustedly declared, should accept this fundamental reality and stop the fighting. Even though the White House repeatedly asserted that support for separation automatically meant favor for the South, Palmerston insisted that he had not taken sides in the war and emphasized to Russell that "no intention at present exists to offer mediation." Such a move would be like asking two boxers to stop their bout after only "the third round." The war itself must convince northerners that reunion was impossible.[18]

By midsummer of 1862, however, the chances for blocking foreign intervention sustained a severe setback when Lincoln failed to win approval of gradual emancipation and felt compelled to act on his own. His repeated appeals to border-state congressmen to accept gradual emancipation aroused little support. In a move reflecting his longtime interest in colonization, and hence a plan for freedom without equality, he argued that South America could accommodate the freed blacks. At one point he warned that southerners' refusal to free their slaves on a voluntary basis would prolong the war and ultimately cost them their slaves without compensation. His plan, he insisted, "would come gently as the dews of heaven, not rending or wrecking anything. Will you not embrace it? . . . You can not, if you would, be blind to the signs of the times." Failure to approve gradual emancipation meant that slavery "will be extinguished by mere friction and abrasion – by the mere incidents of the war." But the border-state congressmen rejected his proposal by the decisive margin of twenty-nine to nine. The measure, they argued, would cost far more financially than the government could afford. Further, it would harden the South's resolve, encourage the secessionists in the border states to demand a departure from the Union, and increase the pressure on the president to issue a proclamation that violated the Constitution by freeing the slaves in the seceded states. That same evening, the president, still upset over the results, decided on a stronger measure – a proclamation of emancipation.[19]

Adoption of such a revolutionary program, of course, would place the presidency in front of Congress in determining the future of slavery. This bold step would establish a precedent drawing fierce resistance from more than southern states' rightists. Had not the president already aroused the ire of numerous Americans for suspending the writ of habeas corpus and engaging in other actions suggestive of dictatorial rule? In his own inimical way Lincoln started the wheels of revolution slowly by revoking the emancipation policies of two military officers and thereby sent an unmistakable signal of imminent strong presidential actions against slavery. In late August 1861 Gen. John C. Frémont issued an order freeing slaves belonging to rebels in Missouri. Lincoln revoked the order and, after Frémont continued his pattern of insubordination by opposing the president's action, recalled him. The following May of 1862 Gen. David Hunter freed all the slaves in Georgia, Florida, and South Carolina. Lincoln likewise revoked this order and declared that he alone would decide the question. Southern sympathizers cited these two actions as proof of Lincoln's reluctance to consider slavery an issue in the war; the truth was that the president had staked out a claim to being the supreme arbiter in these matters.

Lincoln's decision for emancipation had not come easily for several reasons. Foremost among his considerations was his respect for the Constitution, which led him to reject any measure that infringed on the sanctity of property rights – even in slaves. The border states, after all, still refused to free their slaves and remained a crucial part of his policy. And yet he was now engaged in a battle for national survival that threatened to force him into measures inconsistent with his long-standing beliefs. He must find a way to justify emancipation without violating his constitutional priorities. He succeeded in doing so by invoking his constitutional powers as commander in chief of America's armed forces in times of peril – both domestic and foreign. He therefore felt free to adopt any expedient deemed essential to preserving the Union – which included upending the South through emancipation.

On July 13, just moments after two-thirds of the border states turned down Lincoln's final appeal for compensated emancipation, he took the first step toward a more radical stance on slavery. He privately informed Seward and Secretary of the Navy Gideon Welles of his decision for emancipation while the three were bouncing noisily along in a carriage en route to the funeral of Secretary of War Edwin Stanton's baby boy. Slavery was "the heart of the rebellion," the president emphatically declared in his high-pitched voice above the clattering of hooves and irregular roll of wooden wheels. Emancipation would undercut the Confederacy by encouraging slaves to flee the plantations and seek safety behind advancing Union armies. Seward and Welles were both surprised in view of the president's past opposition to federal interference with slavery. They should not have been. The subject, according to Welles's own account of the conversation, had been on the president's mind for weeks. Emancipation, Lincoln insisted, was "a military necessity, absolutely essential to the preservation of the Union." The slaves were a source of strength to those they served, making it essential to win them to the Union's side. The existence of war, Lincoln argued, dismissed any legitimate protests over the constitutionality of emancipation. As commander in chief, he had the power to take whatever action was necessary to win the war. "The rebels," he asserted, "could not at the same time throw off the Constitution and invoke its aid. Having made war on the Government, they were subject to the incidents and calamities of war." The border states could not renounce slavery while it still existed in the South. "The Administration must set an example."[20]

Not by coincidence did the Lincoln administration's intensified move toward emancipation come at precisely the time that British and French recognition of the Confederacy appeared imminent. Parliamentary member Richard Cobden, no sympathizer with the South and ardently opposed to slavery, repeatedly warned his peers about the sharply diminishing supply of cotton in England and insisted that only a massive injection of the product could ward off intervention. Palmerston remained hesitant about intervention but confronted the growing problem of having to pacify irate textile workers with various relief efforts. Mason felt confident about British recognition, as did Slidell in Paris, who counted on France's following suit. Lyons had taken ill and returned to London, leaving the British embassy in Washington in the care of the British chargé, William Stuart, who believed the war had reached a turning point that he attributed to a fast approaching White House stand against slavery. According to Adams in London, General McClellan's recent rebuffs in the Peninsula Campaign had stimulated a renewed British interest in intervention that was similar to the sentiment following the Battle of Bull Run. Lindsay in Parliament had noted the expectant mood and decided to include both intervention and recognition in his motion for British action. Joint mediation with France and other interested powers, he declared, offered the best approach to ending the American war.[21]

The French intrusion in Mexico had meanwhile provided another serious problem for the Union because it involved the machinations of Napoleon III and threatened the hemispheric guarantees against the Old World made by the United States in the Monroe Doctrine. In the fall of 1861, when the Union's efforts to prevent European intervention in Mexico had failed, Seward tried to secure a pledge from the European powers that they sought only to collect on their debts. Toward this end, Dayton met with Thouvenel in Paris, authorized by the White House to offer a U.S. guarantee on the interest on the loan. But Thouvenel rejected this offer, saying that his government must have the principal. Neither France nor England, he declared, sought anything more from Mexico than payment of its debts. Dayton remained suspicious. "I cannot but feel," he wrote Seward, "that all these Governments are disposed to take advantage of the present distracted condition of the United States."[22]

Dayton was correct in his fears, and yet even he could not have imagined the scope of Napoleon's intentions. As early as November 1861 Prince Metternich, Austria's ambassador to Paris, was certain that the French emperor had already decided to place a monarch in power in Mexico and that it would be Austrian Archduke Ferdinand Maximilian. Indeed, Napoleon brazenly revealed to Metternich the procedure by which the new monarch would assume power and then create a new and more progressive state. Within a month rumors of Maximilian's ascension had become so rampant in Europe that Russell inquired of the Austrian ambassador in London whether the archduke had agreed to take the throne. The response was to the point: Maximilian was waiting for suitable conditions before deciding whether to accept the offer. He and his wife, Carlotta, were oblivious to the growing opposition in London and proudly proclaimed to Empress Eugénie in Austria that Providence had called on them to perform a "holy work" in the New World – a crusade to save the Mexicans from their backward state of existence. As the saviors of monarchy against the evils of republicanism, they would spread the new Mexican empire across Central America and, with the collaboration of Maximilian's cousin, the emperor of Brazil, divide Spanish South America between them.[23]

The three-power alliance began to disintegrate as both Britain and Spain became aware of Napoleon's hidden designs. President Ramón Castilla of Peru put it best when he complained that the Tripartite Pact was a ruse for a "war of the crowns against the Liberty Caps." The British, finally recognizing that Napoleon had duped them into a dangerous enterprise, promptly decided to withdraw from the tripartite pact. Spain likewise had prepared to distance itself from Napoleon. "A Monarchy under a European prince, if not guaranteed by Europe," the Spanish minister wrote Russell in London, "would not last a year."[24]

By the spring of 1862 the three European powers had occupied Veracruz, further convincing Seward that territorial control rather than debt collection was their central objective. All three U.S. ministries in London, Paris, and Madrid, along with other Union representatives on the Continent, affirmed this observation. Seward wrote Dayton in early March that the European actions against Mexico "are likely to be attended by a revolution in that country which will bring in a monarchical form of government there in which the crown will be assumed by some foreign prince." If any European power tried to implant a monarchy, it must send an army to secure its position, which would mark "the beginning of a permanent policy of armed European intervention, injurious and practically hostile to the most general system of government on the continent of America." In such event, Seward pointedly warned, "the permanent interests and sympathies of this country would be with the American republics." Lest there be doubt about the seriousness of the White House, Seward instructed Dayton to assure Thouvenel of war with the Union once it had defeated the Confederacy.[25]

In response to Dayton's warning, Thouvenel was less than candid in repeating his pledge against any territorial designs. Even as Seward's March 3 note was en route to Paris, Thouvenel wrote Mercier that the war in America meant that Napoleon's intervention in Mexico would probably not be the extent of his actions. Indeed, even the French foreign secretary recognized how his emperor's reach almost always exceeded his grasp. Less than three weeks later (and a day or so before renewing his assurances to Dayton), Thouvenel again wrote Mercier: "I have not received any information or any communication from Mr. Dayton concerning the Mexican affairs. Whatever it should be . . . you know already that it could not influence our conduct."[26]

The Lincoln administration had cause for alarm. As if privy to Thouvenel's confidential communications to Mercier, Seward even more adamantly warned of trouble if French intervention led to the installation of a monarchy. "We have more than once," he wrote Dayton, "informed all parties to the alliance that we cannot look with indifference upon an armed European intervention for political ends in a country situated so near and connected with us so closely as Mexico." Thouvenel immediately denied any wish to interfere with "the form of Government in Mexico." But he added a curious statement that strongly suggested an ominous change in attitude if not policy. All France wanted, the foreign minister declared, was "a *government*, not an anarchy with which other nations could have no relations." France would not object if the Mexican people decided to establish a republic. "If they chose to establish a monarchy, as that was the form of Government there, it would be charming, but they did not mean to do any thing to induce such action, that all the rumors that France intended to establish Archduke Maximilian on the throne of Mexico were utterly without foundation." Thouvenel had escalated French involvement to the point of noting his government's preference for a monarchy over a republic, even while he again guaranteed no interference with the form of government chosen by Mexico.[27]

Lincoln and Seward discerned the French danger in Mexico but could do nothing while the Union was at war with the Confederacy. Consequently, both men decided to ignore Thouvenel's well-designed assurances and instead praised France for maintaining its pledge against either interfering with the Mexican government or seeking Mexican territory. So did the president and secretary of state make the Union's position clear, just as England and Spain in April 1862 formally withdrew from the tripartite pact in the midst of the growing insistence by European observers that Napoleon intended to establish an empire under Maximilian. Both nations, however, assured approval of Maximilian as monarch if the Mexican people chose him for the position; neither nation, however, believed this outcome possible. The American press wasted no words in warning Napoleon against annexing Mexico and promising that once the Civil War came to a close, the United States would force his armies out of the Western Hemisphere.[28]

By July 1862 economic problems had combined with the dangerous Mexican situation to bear heavily on the interventionist issue. The cotton shortfall had hit England, the total available supply dropping to a bare two hundred thousand bales from 1.2 million in 1861. The London *Economist* feared that "the time when mills must stop and Lancashire must starve from an actual exhaustion of the whole supply of raw materials may be very near at hand." Most British textile industries operated at about half time. Of 1,678 mills in the Manchester district, only 497 were at full time, another 278 being closed and the other 903 open only two to five days a week. On July 4 nearly 80,000 workers were unemployed and 370,000 were at half time, the average total weekly wage dropping from £250,000 to £100,000. "These are the figures of the cotton famine," lamented the paper.[29]

Because slavery had initially been declared a nonissue, French popular interest in intervention grew in the context of the American war's damaging effects on the international economy. In March 1862 legislators in Paris expressed sympathy for the Union as "defender of the right and of humanity." Northern victory would surely seal the death of slavery, they declared, and yet they also knew that a lengthy war would undercut their own economy. Intervention in the name of peace became a powerful motivation, especially when Lincoln's antislavery measures in early 1862 (Confiscation Acts, Seward-Lyons Treaty, gradual emancipation bill, colonization for blacks freed in Washington DC) failed to draw much public support. French factories had already begun to close because of the rapidly diminishing supply of raw cotton. The reserve had dropped from 578,000 bales in 1861 to 311,000 in 1862, driving down the weekly average consumption from 11,114 bales in 1861 to 5,981 in 1862. Despite French opposition to slavery, Thouvenel thought the need for cotton a more important consideration in the debate over recognition of southern belligerency. As the war now seemed certain to last longer than expected, increasing numbers of French observers focused on challenging the blockade to secure that product.[30]

By mid-July 1862 Napoleon III had emerged as Europe's strongest champion of intervention. The emperor had long nursed a deep concern over the spread of republicanism, and some years earlier he had concocted a dream of building a canal connecting the Atlantic and Pacific oceans that would make Central America a vital center of world trade. In a private letter, Napoleon instructed his friend Maj. Gen. Elie Frédéric Forey, the officer in charge of French forces in Mexico, to inform the Mexican people that anyone cooperating with France would receive excellent treatment. "As for the prince who may mount the Mexican throne," Napoleon continued in a striking revelation of his intentions, "he will always be forced to act in the interests of France, not only by gratitude but especially because those of his new country will be in accordance with ours and he will not be able to sustain himself without our influence." The erection of a monarchy in Mexico would serve as

Napoleon III, emperor of France. Photograph from A. R. Tyrner-Tyrnauer, Lincoln and the Emperors *(New York: Harcourt Brace, 1962), opposite 96; copyright © 1962 and renewed 1990 by A. R. Tyrner-Tyrnauer, reproduced by permission of Harcourt Brace and Company.*

the initial step toward converting the other Spanish American republics into monarchies like that of the Second Empire of France. Not only would this process save the traditional rule of the throne, but it would block U.S. expansion in the Western Hemisphere and permit Mexico, after a massive influx of talented European immigrants, to exert new leadership in the region. Integral to Napoleon's so-called Grand Design for the Americas was an economic partnership with the Confederacy that would help contain the United States.[31]

Just before the British Parliament convened to consider Lindsay's motion for recognizing the Confederacy, the French emperor met with Slidell in Vichy in the afternoon of July 16 and expressed his growing inclination toward either joint mediation or joint recognition with England. The Union army's continued failures to take Richmond had caused Lincoln to seek three hundred thousand more soldiers, further proving how desperate the struggle had become. France, Napoleon admitted to Slidell, saw great advantages in having a strong United States to balance England's maritime strength, and yet the emperor conceded in an especially revealing statement: "My sympathies have always been with the South, whose people are struggling for the principle of self-government, of which I am a firm and consistent advocate." Disunion was unavoidable from the beginning of the conflict, but he had been unable to convince England to work with him in ending the war. "I have several times intimated my wish for action in your behalf," he assured Slidell, "but have met with no favorable response." In a statement that confirmed the rocky nature of the Anglo-French concert toward American affairs, Napoleon accused England of refusing to act but wanting the French "to draw the chestnuts from the fire for her benefit."[32]

Slidell warmly welcomed Napoleon's expression of sympathy with the southern cause and used the opening to criticize European compliance with the Union blockade as a violation of neutrality that hurt the South. Regardless of whether the Union blockade was effective, the emperor explained, he had earlier believed it in the interests of France to declare it so. If the Union had constructed a paper blockade, he would come under great pressure from business interests at home to continue commercial contacts with the South and thus challenge the Union's cruisers patrolling the Confederate coast. He preferred not to interfere with the blockade and had joined England in attesting to its effectiveness.[33]

Surprisingly now, however, the emperor suddenly agreed with Slidell's critical remarks about French policy toward the blockade. "I have committed a great error, which I now deeply regret. France should never have respected the blockade" and should have worked with other European powers in extending recognition to the Confederacy during the summer of 1861 while it held the southern ports and threatened the Union's capital in Washington. But that opportune time had passed. The key question now was what action to take. "To open the ports forcibly would be an act of war." Any action short of outright force likewise guaranteed trouble. The North would angrily refuse mediation, and "mere recognition" would be of "little advantage" to the South and "probably involve me in a war." Slidell countered, however, that the Union had failed to blockade much of the southern coast and that France could act within international law in entering these ports. Surely the French navy, Slidell later added, could clear the southern coasts of Union cruisers and pose a threat to New York and Boston that would prevent them from taking retaliatory action. As in the *Trent* crisis, the Union would complain but back down under pressure. Slidell insisted that such potential French actions came within the domain of international law. "I think you're right," Napoleon allowed. And Slidell might even have been correct in thinking that Napoleon likewise thought his navy sufficient to reopen the flow of cotton in exchange for tariff-free goods and war matériel from France. "I regret to say," the emperor pointedly observed, "that England has not properly appreciated my friendly action in the affair of the *Trent*."[34]

Slidell sought to exploit France's recent problems with England over the Mexican intervention by praising the French military action as beneficial to southern interests. France as a neighbor offered advantages to the Confederacy – at least for the duration of its war with the Union. Surely Slidell realized that Napoleon's rapacious appetite for a New World empire would not find fulfillment in Mexico alone. Texas, New Mexico – even Louisiana – would come within his reach once French forces were in Mexico. But the exigencies of the war forced Slidell to postpone these concerns until the South had won independence. Without instruction from his superiors in Richmond, he declared that his government sought only a "respectable, responsible, and stable government" in Mexico. Slidell blithely expressed confidence that Napoleon had no desire to impose a government onto the Mexicans that they did not want and assured him that since the Lincoln administration had sided with France's antagonist in the Mexican war, President Benito Juárez, the Confederacy had "no objection to make common cause with you against the common enemy."[35]

Despite the many subjects under discussion, the key issue remained intervention in the American war. Napoleon repeated that "simple recognition" would not help the South and that the North would reject mediation. By inference, he brought focus to necessary follow-up actions designed to assure southern independence that included, as a matter of course, commercial and military alliances intended to safeguard the fledgling Confederate nation. Slidell admitted that the Union would refuse mediation even as the South accepted it, and yet this outcome would benefit the Confederate cause by winning the sympathy of other civilized peoples and perhaps promoting an intervention aimed at ending the war on the basis of a southern separation. But mediation was not the South's objective, Slidell insisted. Recognition, although in the so-called simple stage indicated by the emperor, opened new avenues for success. In response to Napoleon's undoubted quizzical look, Slidell explained that the Lincoln administration's "reign of terror" had quieted the protests of a substantial number of northerners who wanted peace even at the cost of disunion. Recognition would provide such encouragement to those favoring peace that they might win the congressional elections and prevail on Europeans to end a war that threatened not only to devastate both North and South but to undermine the international economy as well.[36]

England, Slidell indignantly insisted, had failed to meet its responsibilities as a civilized leader of the world and left the task to France. The Palmerston ministry had pursued "a tortuous, selfish, and time-serving policy, which has only served to make all nations either [its] bitter enemies or [its] fair-weather friends." It had approved a paper blockade that worked to its own advantage, established a monopoly on cotton for its colony of India, and purposely misinterpreted to its own benefit the 1856 Treaty of Paris prohibiting paper blockades. England was no friend of the South's.[37]

Clearly Napoleon was turning over in his mind the possibilities of intervention as he posed several leading questions to Slidell. He first agreed with Slidell on the blockade issue and the importance of southern cotton to France. "If you do not give it [cotton] to us, we cannot find it elsewhere." He then concurred that France and the Confederacy had common interests and close familial ties that drew them together. Sensing the opening, Slidell remarked that "in my own family . . . French is habitually spoken." The slave question then rose for the first and only time in their long conversation. "Do you anticipate no difficulty from your slaves?" asked Napoleon. In a response that the emperor surely anticipated, Slidell asserted, "They have never been more quiet and more respectful and no better evidence can be given of their being contented and happy." Then, to the point, the emperor raised the most penetrating issue. "Do you expect that England will agree to cooperate with me in your recognition?" Slidell assured him that the South's friends in England were more optimistic than at any other time and that even Mason for the first time seemed encouraged. In less than a week Lindsay intended to recommend to Parliament that it support recognition. Palmerston must then take a stand.[38]

At the end of this hour-long conversation, Napoleon referred to one of the most serious impediments to intervention which no one seemed capable of resolving: the terms for settlement. What would be the boundaries of the two new American republics? To which nation would go the border states of Kentucky, Maryland, Delaware, and Missouri? Slidell shrewdly played on Napoleon's support for self-determination by recommending plebiscites in those states to ascertain their allegiance. The southern commissioner felt confident that all four states would choose the Confederacy – even though he not so shrewdly delineated the probable boundaries as the natural configurations of the Chesapeake, Potomac, and Ohio Rivers, thereby leaving Maryland and Delaware to the Union. The failing went unnoticed by Napoleon, however, for he had no map on hand by which he could follow the line.[39]

The meeting came to an end with Slidell informing the emperor of a formal demand for recognition that he intended to present to Thouvenel on his return from England. "I see no objection to your presenting your demand," Napoleon responded.[40]

Slidell's meeting with Napoleon proved how strongly favorable the emperor was to intervention. Only England's refusal to take the lead provided the chief restraint on his actions. Even the likelihood of war with the Union over the blockade issue had surprisingly little impact on his thinking. Together, he seemed to believe, the French and the Confederacy could emerge triumphant. Cotton remained a prime need of his people, although Mexico furnished the major motive behind his policy. His Grand Design for the Americas brought together a host of reasons for supporting the South. He agreed with Slidell that international law justified an involvement because the Union's blockade was proving so porous. Indeed, Napoleon had already thought an intervention defensible on the ground that the war was inflicting irreparable damage on outside nations. Now his considerations had advanced to the point that he contemplated the specific terms necessary to settle the war. Most important, he searched for a way to dismiss slavery from the picture. Regardless of the French need for cotton, the existence of slavery in the South remained an obstacle to intervention. Satisfied by Slidell's assurances against slave unrest, Napoleon could now ponder the consequences of an intervention that rested on his country's economic interests in the South as well as his own imperial designs in Mexico.

Despite Napoleon's southern leanings, he continued to waver on his American policy largely because of the hesitation of both England and his own advisers. Three days after his conversation with Slidell, Napoleon learned of the impending debate in the House of Commons over recognition and telegraphed Thouvenel, who was then in England on an unrelated matter: "Ask the English government if they don't think the time has come to recognize the South." After some delay, the foreign minister told his ambassador in London that the time had not come to terminate neutrality. France was already experiencing financial problems along with the sputtering expedition in Mexico, which led Thouvenel to declare that "our haste in starting a conflict with the United States is unwise and dangerous."[41]

Napoleon, however, refused to drop the idea of intervention, even to the point of exploring the highly unlikely prospect of securing the cooperation of Russia, his recent antagonist in the Crimean War. Shortly after the meeting with Slidell, the emperor asked the Russian foreign minister, Prince Alexander Gorchakov, about the possibility of a joint Anglo-French-Russian mediation. Gorchakov affirmed his government's support for the Union along with his regret over the war's destruction, but he declared that he could never act with England, a country the northerners so roundly hated. Russia favored reunion, and such a cooperative effort with England and France would take on the appearance of an unfriendly move against the Lincoln administration. Russia had no great need for cotton and, by standing outside the European community of nations that the United States had for so long distrusted, felt a natural affinity with the Union. "Both of them being young nations in the life of the civilized world," Gorchakov observed, "Russia and America have a special regard for each other which is never adversely affected because they have no points of conflict."[42] As in the *Trent* crisis, Russia refused to alienate the Union. Such a stance came easier in view of its closeness to the Americans that had resulted from its war with France and England in the mid-1850s. Only the United States had made its good offices available to the Russians in that costly Crimean War.

On July 23, 1862, Slidell kept up the pressure on the French by securing an interview with Thouvenel about the South's call for recognition. The southern commissioner immediately informed Thouvenel of his and Mason's intention to make official requests for recognition from France and England. Thouvenel at first counseled against such action until the direction of the war had become clear, but when Slidell informed him that Napoleon had expressed interest in intervention, the foreign minister suddenly dropped his hesitation over recognition and admitted that no one in France thought reunion possible. Slidell presented the note seeking recognition and Thouvenel promised to send a copy to the emperor. Two days later, Slidell exuberantly wrote Benjamin, "I am more hopeful than I have been at any moment since my arrival in Europe."[43]

If Napoleon acted solely on his own volition, Slidell's excitement was justified; but that was not always the case. Thouvenel feared that premature recognition of the Confederacy would mean war with the Union, a warning that had also come from Mercier in America. To his ambassador in London, Count Charles de Flahault, Thouvenel emphasized the necessity of cautioning the emperor against acting as hastily as he had done in other matters. "I see with great satisfaction," Thouvenel wrote, "that, on this point as on others, we are in agreement, and I shall perhaps need your help in order to guard us from an adventure even more serious than the Mexican one." In London, Mason had presented his case for recognition and sought an interview with Russell; but the foreign secretary declined, again deferring to the fortunes of war as his guide. The southern commissioner nonetheless felt uplifted by Napoleon's attitude. If France called for recognition, Mason insisted, "it may yet be that they [the British] may be dragged into an ungraceful reversal of their decision."[44]

Thouvenel had already framed his wary thoughts on intervention. He had earlier instructed his staff in Paris to draft a detailed plan, which it submitted on July 4 under the title of "Note for the minister, the American question." The boundary between the two republics of North and South would rest on a compromise between free and slave areas and the location of the military demarcation at armistice time. The Union would retain northern Virginia and all the border states, slavery would continue to exist in the South, and the North would agree to return fugitive slaves. The wisest solution to the American crisis, Thouvenel later declared in a view reflecting that of Russell and others in England, was "the formation of two *federated confederations*." Such a plan included the establishment of "a small mixed senate" that would, by its very existence, demonstrate the feasibility of "a federation of two republics." Indeed, he urged Mercier to add ideas of his own. If the time for mediation ever came, "it would be helpful to have a sketch of an arrangement in my pocket."[45]

Adams meanwhile sensed the growing foreign threat and warned the administration in Washington of the need to clarify its higher objectives in the war as a vital part of the effort to undercut possible intervention. England, France, and perhaps other European powers had discussed the situation without yet settling on a solution. But all signs, he felt, pointed to mediation. Even if such an offer took "the most benevolent aspect possible, the effect would be to concentrate in a degree the moral sense of the civilized nations of Europe in its behalf." The Union must focus on freedom as its wartime objective. Palmerston's resistance to intervention could snap under the formidable pressure for a mediation coming from disgruntled cotton workers, the heavy influence of Russell and Chancellor of the Exchequer William Gladstone in his cabinet, the great numbers of British vocal observers who believed that McClellan's defeat signaled the end of the Union, and Lindsay's rabid supporters in Parliament – including southern sympathizer John Roebuck and the Conservative opposition leader in the Commons, Benjamin Disraeli. Such powerful forces could tip the delicate balance toward intervention, particularly since the gap between southern separation and southern nationhood appeared so small.[46]

In a highly charged and nearly chaotic atmosphere, Parliament assembled on the evening of July 18 to debate Lindsay's motion for recognition. Rumors raced throughout the chamber of the Commons – doubtless planted by southern sympathizers and soon shown to be false – that McClellan had surrendered in Virginia and that the war was virtually over. After some semblance of order returned, Lindsay took the floor and, while Palmerston sat with hat pulled over his eyes and seemingly asleep, spent an hour giving a poorly delivered and fact-twisting speech that pronounced the disunion irreparable and the southern cause justified. Mediation was necessary, he insisted, to end the war and assure the importation of cotton. Lindsay proclaimed that he "desired the disruption of the American Union, as every honest Englishman did, because it was too great a Power and England sh'd not let such a power exist on the American continent." According to Moran, who keenly watched these events unfold, "Old Mason spat tobacco more furiously at this than ever, and covered the carpet."[47]

Opponents of Lindsay's motion then rose to state their case. P. A. Taylor, a new member from Leicester, who belonged to the London Emancipation Society, tried to defend the Palmerston ministry over loud protests from the Conservative opposition. Taylor drew more jeers when he praised Lincoln and argued that the American conflict centered on the battle between slavery and freedom. The result was what Moran derisively called a "burst of horse-laughter and ridicule" that was a "disgrace to the age." Support for the South, Taylor shouted above the bedlam, placed England on the side of slavery. Lord Adolphus Vane-Tempest, son-in-law of the Duke of Newcastle, came to Lindsay's defense but was so inebriated that he swayed back and forth while slurring his speech and nearly fell over the back of the bench in front of him several times. William E. Forster, staunch supporter of the Union and close friend of Adams's, gave a short and spirited speech in behalf of the ministry, warning that intervention would instigate a slave insurrection injurious to everyone's interests.[48]

The decisive moment came in the early morning hours, when Palmerston at last arose from his feigned stupor to declare his opposition to intervention. In a scant three minutes, he made clear that his government's only interest in the American war was "that it should end." The ministry would make all foreign policy decisions, he emphasized, not the House of Commons. Only the ministry had the information necessary to deal responsibly with such an explosive matter "according to the varying circumstances of the moment." It could adopt no interventionist policy until the South had "firmly and permanently established" its independence. Premature recognition would not guarantee the rightness of such a decision unless the step "were followed by some direct active interference." And such a move, he reminded his listeners now in rapt attention, would lead to "greater evils, great sufferings, and greater privations." Neither North nor South was ready to give up the fight, which meant certain failure for mediation. Lindsay's motion assured trouble with the United States, Palmerston solemnly told his colleagues. The ministry must maintain the discretionary power to decide "what can be done, when it can be done, and how it can be done."[49]

A moment of stunned silence followed, which suddenly gave way to raucous applause. Lindsay withdrew his motion, bitterly proclaiming that he would "wait for king cotton to turn the screws still further." Mason, Moran gleefully observed, sat by himself, "looking sullen and dejected." He was soon joined by southern supporter William Gregory, and they slowly left the chamber. The morning's press temporarily quieted the call for intervention by reporting that the stories of McClellan's surrender were untrue and praised Parliament for rejecting Lindsay's motion.[50]

The threat of British (and French) intervention lay dormant for only a brief time. Adams again warned the White House that only a firm Union stand against slavery would keep England out of the war. Mediation had growing appeal to numerous and diverse groups. Humanitarians believed the war a senseless bloodbath that civilized nations bore responsibility to terminate. Businessmen favored an end to the war as the major step toward reopening the flow of southern cotton and northern grain. Antislavery proponents emphasized the necessity of establishing two American republics as the most sensible way to bring an ultimate end to slavery. Both Russell in London and Thouvenel in Paris had reached the same conclusion. In the meantime the French, and particularly Napoleon, continued to goad the British into taking the initial step toward intervention while offering assurances that he would be closely behind. The lingering danger of foreign intervention left the Lincoln administration little alternative to continuing its rapidly escalating move toward emancipation.[51]

CHAPTER FOUR

Emancipation by the Sword?
Race War and Antietam as
Catalysts to Intervention

This government cannot much longer play a game in which it stakes all, and its enemies stake nothing. Those enemies must understand that they cannot experiment for ten years trying to destroy the government, and if they fail still come back into the Union unhurt.

President Abraham Lincoln, July 31, 1862

I concede that emancipation would help us in Europe, and convince them that we are incited by something more than ambition.

President Abraham Lincoln, September 13, 1862

About a week after Lincoln broached the subject of emancipation to Seward and Welles, the British chargé in Washington, William Stuart, informed his home office that the White House had changed its wartime objective to abolition and was now ready to instigate a slave insurrection in a desperate effort to win the war. Stuart was wrong about the administration's new direction in the war and wrong in his interpretations of Lincoln's method and purpose. Lincoln had not joined the abolitionist camp, nor had he decided to incite slave rebellions. Stuart did not grasp that the president's antislavery stand had become crucial to his paramount goal of preserving the Union. And Stuart had mistakenly equated emancipation with abolition, failing to realize that Lincoln's view of emancipation entailed the establishment of black freedom in areas dominated by rebels and the continued existence of slavery in regions under loyalist control. These fundamental and all-important distinctions eluded Stuart's thinking, leading him to send exaggerated, emotional responses to London that encouraged Russell and fellow interventionists to fear the worst. The president, Stuart asserted, intended to use emancipation in a final, apocalyptic campaign aimed at stirring up the slaves and destroying the South from within.[1]

In fairness to Stuart, his interpretation of Lincoln's intentions had not totally distorted the truth: the president recognized that even his limited form of emancipation guaranteed slave unrest, although he hoped the measure would merely encourage the slaves to abandon the plantations. The Union, Stuart correctly observed, had already moved closer to emancipation by implementing its confiscation measures and preparing to arm the slaves. But whereas he denounced these measures as carefully designed incitements to rebellion, Lincoln was convinced that these expedients would compel some Confederate soldiers to desert the ranks and return home to protect their families from vengeful slaves. And yet the president must also have realized that once such freedom was in motion, it had the potential of causing domestic instability and perhaps even sporadic outbreaks of racial violence.

Whatever Lincoln's innermost feelings, impressions spoke louder than truth, and in this instance they left the image of great danger not only to the South but to anyone – foreign as well as domestic – touched by the ensuing social disorder. The British emissary's inflated warnings of slave revolts and race war greatly alarmed Russell and drove him even more toward intervention. Like Stuart, the foreign secretary failed to realize that the British themselves had encouraged such a frightening outcome by their flirtations with intervention, and he argued instead that the White House fully intended to set off an uprising in a frantic effort to win the war. So deep were Russell's anxieties that Stuart read aloud his response from London to Seward and, for added impact, gave him a copy of the dispatch. The specter of race war, Russell declared in an obvious allusion to impending intervention, would "only make other nations more desirous to see an end of this desolating and destructive conflict."[2]

The Battles of Second Bull Run and Antietam served as a further catalyst to intervention. Lee achieved a clear-cut victory at Bull Run in late August 1862 that appeared to confirm the South's capacity to stand as a nation and led the British to inch closer to a mediation premised on a permanent division of the United States. Then, contrary to traditional historical accounts, the Union's narrow victory at Antietam the following month actually increased British interest in entering the war before the fighting spun completely out of control. The carnage of the battle had raised the cry for intervention that rested on an armistice followed by a negotiated end to the war.

In an ironic twist of fate, Lincoln's decision for emancipation so angered the British that it threatened to cause the very intervention that the White House sought to prevent. Morality had nothing to do with the president's sudden conversion to antislavery, the British charged with contempt. At the outset of the war, Lincoln had proclaimed slavery a nonissue and thereby continued

his nation's long-standing policy of tacitly condoning the institution by refusing to take a stand against it. Emancipation at this stage of the war could
be nothing but pure hypocrisy – a last-ditch attempt by a dying Union to incite a slave uprising aimed at snatching victory from the jaws of defeat by
forcing the collapse of the South. The only way to blunt this fiendish act,
accordng to irate British observers, was to intervene in the war and reach a
settlement based on the reality of southern separation.

The White House, in turn, became infuriated with the British for accepting the South's argument about northern oppression and failing to understand the tactics of emancipation. The "slaveholding insurgents," Seward
disgustedly wrote Adams, had sought foreign assistance in overthrowing the
duly established government in Washington and then, to encourage this aid,
had resorted to the economic pressures of King Cotton diplomacy. Their in-
sidious strategy aimed at securing help from England with one hand while
stabbing it in the back with the other. The South stood guilty of both treason
and waging a war against humanity, Seward hotly charged. How could the
Palmerston ministry ignore these fundamental truths? If the British were not
pro-Confederacy, Seward complained, they certainly did not look kindly on
the Union. No White House action found favor in Europe. Victory "does
not satisfy our enemies abroad. Defeats in their eyes prove our national inca-
pacity." Even emancipation, he wrote with growing exasperation, drew only
derision – and, in all places, England itself. "At first the [Union] government
was considered as unfaithful to humanity in not proclaiming emancipation."
Now, "when it appeared that slavery, by being thus forced into the contest,
must suffer, and perhaps perish in the conflict . . . the war had become an in-
tolerable propagandism of emancipation by the sword."[3]

Lincoln believed, however mistakenly, that his move toward emancipation offered a further guarantee against foreign intervention. Instead, it had
given the British a stronger incentive to step into the conflict. The ministry in
London, it seemed to many Americans, had ulterior motives that lay hidden
behind stated and defensible humanitarian concerns. Regardless of the war's
direction, British observers justified an intervention that would have encouraged the chances of southern independence while opening the way to British
commercial and military gains at the expense of the United States. Not only
would the British secure southern cotton, but they would encase the Union
with a stronger Canada to the north and a Confederate friend to the south. It
is impossible to determine the real motives behind British interest in intervention, but it is difficult to believe that altruism alone guided everyone's behavior. Despite the Union's repeated warnings that British involvement
would set off a slave rebellion, the British insisted that failure to intervene
would permit the Union to stir up that horrific event in a frenzied effort to

salvage a victory in the war. In either case, the surety of increased bloodshed elevated the stakes of intervention by conjuring up the dark apparition of a racial war that would disrupt the southern economy and inflict great damage on those nations tied to its welfare.

The president proceeded with his antislavery policy, oblivious to the danger quietly developing between the Union and England. At Stanton's urging, Lincoln met with the prominent New York attorney and Democrat Francis B. Cutting, who had undergone a conversion from a proslavery stand to favor destruction of the institution as a major part of the war effort. Emancipation, Cutting assured the president, would appease antislavery groups on both sides of the Atlantic and undercut any chance for recognition of the South. Bolstered by this two-hour conversation, Lincoln informed his cabinet later that same day of July 22 that he intended to issue a proclamation of emancipation. It was a "necessary military measure" for winning the war, he insisted to stunned advisers as he read from his draft without having first sought their opinion about the wisdom of this monumental decision. In an effort to combine gradual, compensated emancipation with his new move against slavery, he declared that in sixty days the Second Confiscation Act would take effect unless the rebellion stopped. To encourage southerners to lay down their arms, he promised monetary assistance to all states that agreed to gradual emancipation. But the day of reckoning was nigh. As of January 1, 1863, Lincoln asserted, all slaves in states still in rebellion would become free.[4]

The cabinet's reaction was generally favorable, although its members' ensuing remarks contained a note of caution regarding the timing of the announcement. The only opposition came from a border-state representative from Maryland, Postmaster General Montgomery Blair, who had always resisted abolition and now warned that emancipation would alienate great numbers of Americans and lead to Democratic control of Congress following the fall elections. The next day, however, he admitted that the step might thwart foreign intervention. Secretary of the Treasury Salmon P. Chase welcomed emancipation as a step toward his longtime goal of abolition and even urged the president to authorize his generals to arm the slaves. Stanton agreed and implored the president to move immediately. Seward, however, favored emancipation but thought the time not yet right. He opposed any effort "to proselyte with the sword" and clearly took to heart British suspicions of American motives. A proclamation of emancipation should come only after a Union victory on the battlefield; otherwise, the announcement would appear to be "the last measure of an exhausted government, a cry for help . . . our last shriek, on the retreat." Indeed, the step could actually *provoke* a British intervention by appearing to be an effort to incite a slave uprising. Lin-

First Reading of the Emancipation Proclamation, July 22, 1862.
*Painting by Francis B. Carpenter presented to Congress in 1878. Left to
right: Edwin M. Stanton, secretary of war; Salmon P. Chase, secretary of
treasury; President Lincoln; Gideon Welles, secretary of the navy; Caleb
B. Smith, secretary of the interior; William H. Seward, secretary of state;
Montgomery Blair, postmaster general; and (beyond photo) Edward
Bates, attorney general. National Archives.*

coln saw the reasoning and agreed to delay the proclamation until Union
forces won a battle.[5]

For Lincoln, emancipation had become attractive for reasons that again
demonstrated his pragmatic approach to events. The war, he insisted, had
necessitated the move. But it came easier because it also mollified his antislavery feelings, provided a higher purpose in the war that might yield victory by
raising Union morale, and worked toward discouraging foreign intervention. "I must save this government if possible," he declared to War Democrat
Reverdy Johnson of Maryland. "What I *cannot* do, of course, I *will* not do;
but it may as well be understood, once for all, that I shall not surrender this
game leaving any available card unplayed." Ever the realist, Lincoln seized
the moment as particularly auspicious for emancipation in rebel territories.
Indeed, the Union could no longer continue its forbearance toward the

South. To the New York financier and Democrat August Belmont, the president wrote: "This government cannot much longer play a game in which it stakes all, and its enemies stake nothing. Those enemies must understand that they cannot experiment for ten years trying to destroy the government, and if they fail still come back into the Union unhurt." He added, emphatically, "Now is the time."[6]

Belmont agreed with the president's increasingly hard-line position but cautioned him to soften the blow as much as possible. Confederate leaders had already accused the Union of seeking "conquest and subjugation" and had thereby hurt any chances for awakening a dormant Unionist sentiment in the South. But Lincoln thought otherwise. To a Union advocate in the South, he crisply remarked that the insistence by slaveholders in the loyal states "that the government shall not strike its open enemies, lest they be struck by accident," had caused the "paralysis – the dead palsy – of the government in this whole struggle." Lincoln refused to wait any longer: "The truth is, that what is done, and omitted, about slaves, is done and omitted on . . . military necessity."[7]

Lincoln's embracing of emancipation elicited favorable responses in many quarters. In the American embassy in London, Charles Francis Adams's son Henry defended the Union's right to destroy the South if such a measure proved necessary to prevent foreign intervention in the war. Peace, the younger Adams indignantly noted, remained unreachable "so long as the southern people exist." To his brother he wrote: "I don't much care whether they are destroyed by emancipation, or in other words a vigorous system of guerilla war carried on by negroes on our side, or by the slower and more doubtful measures of choaking [*sic*] them with their own cotton." The Union "must exterminate them in the end, be it long or be it short, for it is a battle between us and slavery."[8]

Lincoln's decision became the subject of much discussion in Europe. Seward had recently given Lincoln a letter from French Count Agénor-Etienne de Gasparin, who noted the heightening concern on the Continent and opposed a European involvement as an impetus to a longer and wider war. The Union, Gasparin insisted, must curtail the interventionists by emphasizing the end of slavery as essential to universal freedom.[9]

Approval of the administration's new antislavery policy also came from the western theater in the war, where Gen. Ulysses S. Grant, just triumphant at Forts Henry and Donelson and Shiloh, praised confiscation as essential to victory. A Union officer put it bluntly: "The policy is to be terrible on the enemy. I am using Negroes all the time for my work as teamsters, and have 1,000 employed." Grant wrote his family that his sole purpose was "to put down the rebellion. . . . I don't know what is to become of these poor people in the end, but it weakens the enemy to take them from them."[10]

Lincoln's move toward emancipation received further impetus from his skepticism over the Second Confiscation Act of July 17, 1862, designed by the Radical Republicans to seize the property of rebels, including their slaves. According to the act, all slaves in areas still in rebellion "shall be forever free." General McClellan had indignantly opposed the act as a violation of "the highest principles known to Christian civilization." The president must conduct war on these principles, he wrote Lincoln. "Neither confiscation of property . . . [n]or forcible abolition of slavery should be contemplated for a moment." Lincoln's deepest concern, however, was that Congress had taken the lead in emancipation. "It is startling to say that congress can free a slave within a state," he noted, for it violated the Republican platform and the principles of the Constitution."Congress has no power over slavery in the states," he told his friend and Illinois senator Orville Browning; "so much of it as remains after the war is over . . . must be left to the exclusive control of the states where it may exist." The only acceptable federal power over slavery lay in the war power clause, but he chose not to battle Congress on the matter. Instead, he approved the confiscation bill (after making sure its use applied only to the individual accused of rebellion and not to the family) while taking the first step toward emancipation.[11]

The Second Confiscation Act proved misleading in scope. Although the appearance was that of an army gloriously awarding blacks freedom as it won battles, the reality was of emancipation taking place on a tedious case-by-case basis, with the federal court deciding in each instance whether the owner in question was indeed a rebel. Such a requirement meant that, with perhaps 350,000 slave owners in the South, these cases would clog the courts for years. Two months after the law went into effect, Lincoln caustically observed that "I cannot learn that that law has caused a single slave to come over to us." But even though the law contained impractical procedures, it also encouraged blacks to leave the plantations and thereby further undercut the Confederacy. In a move that took the administration closer to Chase's long-standing plea to arm the freed blacks, the act authorized the president to welcome into the Union's military service – with pay – any blacks who contributed their labor.[12]

On the same day that Congress passed the Second Confiscation Act, it made a momentous move: it approved the use of black troops by sending the president the Militia Act. This measure permitted him to call three hundred thousand nine-month militiamen from the states into armed services, the figure in each state in proportion to population. The president could enlist "persons of African descent" as soldiers or for any other suitable positions in the war effort. Further, he had the power to emancipate any slaves (along with their families) who enlisted, if (in an attempt to spare the border states) their masters had supported the Confederacy. Later in the war, the Lincoln administration granted freedom to slave-soldiers from "loyal owners," who, in turn, received bounties for their losses. On August 25, 1862, Secretary of War Stanton made history by authorizing Gen. David Hunter in South Carolina to raise five thousand black troops.[13]

Despite the far-reaching implications for emancipation of both the Confiscation and Militia Acts, Congress had not burst ahead of Lincoln in formulating an antislavery policy. Neither act had freed any slaves; the term "confiscation" signified the seizure of "property." The Militia Act itself welcomed blacks as soldiers only after the president had emancipated them based on their enlistment. Thus Lincoln maintained the principle that he alone as president determined emancipation.

The pressure on Lincoln to resist emancipation appeared to be as intense as that coming from those in favor of the measure. Many white northerners had shown no interest in fighting a war against slavery, and they fervently condemned the abolitionists' cry for an immediate end of slavery with no compensation to owners. Even the moderates in the antislavery camp urged the president to act slowly and deliberately, being careful not to alienate the Union's supporters. If slavery became the overarching issue, they warned, the Peace Democrats would demand an end to the war at any price and take the border states with them. The War Democrats likewise opposed emancipation, the moderates warned. Both contingents within the northern-based party denounced the Republicans as fanatics whose liberal racial doctrines had brought on violence against blacks in several northern cities that summer. Union soldiers, the moderates insisted, would lay down their arms before shedding blood for black people. The time was not right for emancipation.[14]

In this heated atmosphere, Lincoln again considered a long-favored approach to the problem – voluntary colonization of freed blacks. Such an expedient might make emancipation more palatable to those Americans in both North and South who feared massive racial unrest in its aftermath. According to theory, freed blacks would leave the United States, thereby easing anticipated racial strains. During the 1850s Lincoln had been a leader in the Illinois Colonization Society and had advocated this idea during his debates with Stephen A. Douglas. As late as December 1862 Lincoln proposed a constitutional amendment authorizing payment to blacks willing to colonize elsewhere. "I cannot make it better known than it already is," he told Congress, "that I strongly favor colonization."[15]

The previous August of 1862 Lincoln assured a black delegation from the District of Columbia that colonization offered escape from the evils of racism. "We have between us," he declared, "a broader difference than exists between almost any other two races. Whether it is right or wrong I need not discuss, but this physical difference is a great disadvantage to us both, as I think your race suffers very greatly, many of them by living among us, while ours suffer from your presence. In a word we suffer on each side. If this is admitted, it affords a reason at least why we should be separated." Without the black presence, Lincoln insisted to his visitors, there would be no civil war. Slavery was "the greatest wrong inflicted on any people." But even when it came to an end, "you are yet far removed from being placed on an equality with the white race." He noted that "on this broad continent, not a single man of your race is made the equal of a single man of ours." He concluded that "it is better for us both, therefore, to be separated."[16]

Lincoln's argument generated great opposition. Besides the practical problems of expense and transportation, the very idea of colonization drew a fierce outcry from many groups, including the abolitionists, southerners, the foreign governments asked to receive those colonized, and, most important, the blacks themselves. A black Philadelphian indignantly told Lincoln in a letter that appeared in the press, "This is our country as much as it is yours, and we will not leave it." The famous black leader and former slave Frederick Douglass publicly castigated the president for "canting hypocrisy" and "contempt for negroes."[17]

Even while Lincoln advocated colonization, he realized that its probable rejection would have a great saving value. From a pragmatic viewpoint, the dismissal of colonization would further highlight emancipation as an end in itself, forcing supporters of the Union to realize that desperate measures had become mandatory and that they must fight for black freedom. That necessary period of adjustment to the death of slavery and all its social, political, and economic ramifications had already begun to transpire. Lincoln did not plan to touch the status of the slaves in the border states, meaning that there would be relatively little disturbance in the social setting. He must have realized, however, that the impetus given to such a revolutionary change would doubtless take on a momentum of its own that could lead only to the abolition of all slavery.[18]

The heightening ferocity of the war edged the British closer to a mediation offer in the early autumn of 1862, even while the Lincoln administration felt increasingly secure for having moved toward emancipation. In late August the president published a letter in response to Horace Greeley's editorial on behalf of emancipation that he addressed to Lincoln and printed in the *New York Tribune* under the title "The Prayer of Twenty Millions." The president's letter, dated August 22 and appearing in the same paper three days afterward, explained his eminently practical position on slavery and the war. "My paramount object in this struggle," Lincoln wrote, "*is* to save the Union, and is *not* either to save or to destroy slavery." He continued: "If I could save the Union without freeing *any* slave I would do it, and if I could save it by freeing *all* the slaves I would do it; and if I could save it by freeing some and leaving others alone I would also do that."[19]

Lincoln again demonstrated his political acumen in responding to Greeley's charges of failing to take a stand against slavery, as called for in the Second Confiscation Act, and of making the "preposterous and futile" attempt to end the rebellion without stamping out slavery. The president intended to assure the great number of concerned northerners that the war would not become a crusade against slavery, and yet he also wanted to mollify antislavery groups by suggesting that he was about to take another step against the institution. Lincoln had already decided that the war for the Union and the war against slavery had become one. His "paramount object" remained the preservation of the Union, but his care in the choice of words indicated that "paramount" meant "principal" and not "only." Virtually overlooked in his published letter was a reaffirmation of his "oft-expressed *personal* wish that all men every where could be free," along with his pragmatic assurance that he would "adopt new views so fast as they shall appear to be true views."[20]

Some British observers recognized the broad purpose of Lincoln's statement. Stuart remained fearful of a slave revolt but informed London that Sumner, an abolitionist, affirmed the nearly unanimous support within the president's cabinet for a proclamation of emancipation that aimed at uniting Americans at home while warding off intervention from abroad. Argyll in England, who remained a staunch supporter of the Union, did not discern Russell's bitterly negative attitude toward emancipation and noted with relief that the measure would discourage British involvement in the war. Even a mediation offer, Argyll warned Palmerston, would alienate the Union, which was engaged in a "Life or Death" struggle that left no room for compromise.[21]

But rather than stem the movement toward intervention, Lincoln's emancipation policy caused a widespread feeling of exasperation overseas that expressed itself in a growing desire to step into the American struggle, if only after the two sides had exhausted themselves. From Washington, Stuart disgustedly told Russell that only "another Bull Run" would encourage the North to give up the fight. At least one high-ranking British figure in the Foreign Office, however, revealed no sense of urgency to end the war. The more damage sustained by both sides in the war, Under Secretary for Foreign Affairs Edmund Hammond wryly declared, "the less likely will they be to court a quarrel with us or to prove formidable antagonists if they do so." From his post in Paris, Confederate minister Slidell detected a similar sentiment among the British. He wrote his superiors in Richmond that the French would only follow England's lead and that the Palmerston ministry refused to act until neither North nor South could fight anymore.[22]

Gladstone expressed the view of many contemporaries when, in the autumn of 1862, he supported a mediation to end a war that had escalated in savagery while beginning to have an adverse economic effect on other nations. He admitted that the North was not yet receptive to a negotiated settlement, but he also insisted that Europe could not "stand silent without limit of time and witness these horrors and absurdities, which will soon have consumed more men, and done ten times more mischief than the Crimean War." Gladstone insisted that the fighting should stop because the outcome was "certain in the opinion of the whole world except one of the parties." The Union's obstinate refusal to end this senseless fighting, he argued, had caused a near depletion of the cotton supply in Britain and now threatened to incite riots among its textile workers. By September the cotton stock had plunged to one hundred thousand bales from double that amount in July, with a weekly drain of thirty thousand to either industrial use or exportation. Much of the workforce was unemployed or on short time. Mediation was justified because of the "frightful misery which this civil conflict has brought upon other countries, and because of the unanimity with which it is condemned by the civilised world."[23]

In a shallow approach to the subject of intervention, Gladstone agreed with Stuart that recognition should follow a rejected mediation offer. "It is our absolute duty to recognise, when it has become sufficiently plain to mankind in general that Southern independence is established, i.e. that the South cannot be conquered." European intervention, he declared, would be "an act of charity." The powers did not have to warn the Union against "resorting in extremity to a proclamation of Emancipation for that I cannot think Lincoln would do."[24]

But Gladstone and others in England had underestimated the negative impact of southern slavery on any interventionist move that could only help the Confederacy. Admittedly, a third of England's textile mills had closed, and yet they were small in size and employed less than a third of the country's cotton workers. In addition, cotton would soon arrive from other sources, including that garnered by blockade runners and from producers in India, Egypt, China, and Brazil. Moreover, the Union provided a substantial supply by illicit trade with southerners and by taking over cotton plantations for freed blacks to work. Further, the British people and government worked to ease economic distress by extending both private and public charity to needy families in stricken districts. One of the South's chief propaganda agents in England, however, lamented that antislavery sentiment posed the greatest obstacle to foreign assistance. Henry Hotze asserted that the "Lancashire operatives" were the only "class which as a class continues actively inimical to us. . . . With them the unreasoning . . . aversion to our institutions is as firmly rooted as in any part of New England. . . . They look upon us, and . . . upon slavery as the author and source of their present miseries."[25]

It is indeed curious that British laborers had a better understanding of the wartime issues than did their governmental leaders in London. Slavery in the South, labor spokesmen asserted, made it obligatory to support the North. But slavery was not the issue, Russell and other interventionists insisted; both North and South had made this clear at the outset of the war. Northern oppression, Russell professed to believe, justified the South's move for independence in the name of national self-determination. The growing brutality of the war provided humanitarian grounds for observer nations to bring an end to the fighting. The loss of cotton had a negative effect on England and other industrialized nations so dependent on the product. To Russell and numerous others in England, the solution was simple: establish two republics in North America, one slave and one free. Such a proposal seemed disarming only at first because it rested on the principle of compromise. But to those many American loyalists who remained suspicious of British motives, the so-called compromise offered the British a host of advantages that came solely at the expense of the Union.

Hotze's firsthand observations suggest that many workers in England perceived the North as the proponent of democracy and the South as the defender of slavery. Lincoln had earlier discerned this reaction and promptly labeled the war "a People's contest." Appropriately, he had chosen July 4, 1861, as the day to tell Congress that the Union supported equal opportunity for all mankind. Karl Marx, arch advocate of the workers and, with the support of Friedrich Engels, founder of communist theory, triumphantly declared from his place of exile in England that Lincoln was "the single-minded son of the working class," who now headed a "world-transforming . . . revolutionary movement" against the "slave oligarchy." A world-shaking epoch was under way in America, Marx asserted. "As the American War of Independence initiated a new era of ascendancy for the middle class, so the American anti-slavery war will do for the working classes."[26]

Argyll typified the attitude of numerous British opponents of intervention who insisted that the American war centered on slavery and that the fighting alone should determine the outcome. The issues did not break down easily into "independence" versus "Empire," he declared to Gladstone. In an argument that reflected the teachings of his mother-in-law and famous opponent of slavery, the Duchess of Sutherland, Argyll asserted that the struggle had arisen from "one great cause, in respect to which both parties have been deeply guilty, but in respect to which, on the whole, the revolt of the South represents all that is bad, and wrong." Neither North nor South could escape blame for allowing human bondage to exist well into the nineteenth century. Southern separation did not provide the solution, despite Gladstone's insistence to the contrary. Slavery had not only corrupted southerners, but it was "rotting the very heart & conscience of the Whites – all over the Union – in direct proportion to their complicity with it." The system must not last any longer than the war. Consequently, the war itself must serve as the crucible for abolition. England must not intervene while the outcome remained uncertain. Once the fighting had resolved all the issues between North and South, "*then* I shd not object to *help* in the terms of peace."[27]

In the meantime, French interest in intervention had become more pronounced than that of England because of growing economic problems stemming from their own sharply diminishing supply of cotton. Both industrial production and shipping had decreased, causing workers to exert great pressure on the Paris government to take some action aimed at ending the American war. Foreign Minister Thouvenel made no attempt to hide his concern. At a reception in Paris in April 1862, he bluntly informed the Union's minister in Brussels, Henry Sanford, "We are nearly out of cotton, and cotton we *must have*." That same evening Thouvenel drove home the point by suggesting the possibility of intervening on a unilateral basis. "We are going to have cotton," he emphatically told his guest, "even if we are compelled to do something ourselves to obtain it." Autumn of that same year found thousands of French workers unemployed, marking the country's worst period of unemployment and deprivation. Despite French opposition to slavery, Thouvenel felt it more important to consider recognition of southern independence out of concern over cotton. As the war now seemed certain to last longer than expected, increasing numbers of French observers focused on the possibility of having to challenge the blockade to secure that product.[28]

In Washington the French minister, Henri Mercier, was not yet aware of the growing sentiment in Paris for a unilateral intervention and continued his efforts to persuade the British to act jointly with his government in securing southern independence. But Mercier likewise had attached a sense of urgency to the matter. He did not want to stop with a mediation offer; he preferred to grant recognition to the Confederacy, while leaving the ominous implication that the European powers should take further steps toward ensuring the safety of the fledgling nation. Mercier tried to convince Stuart that the government in London should join the French in postponing a mediation until after the congressional elections in November. If the Peace Democrats emerged victorious, the British and French should offer to mediate an end to the war. Indeed, Mercier was so certain that the war party would lose the elections that he wanted the two European governments to draft a "Manifesto" extending recognition to the Confederacy, which their two ministers in Washington could implement at the time they thought proper. Stuart likewise favored the extension of recognition, but he doubted the wisdom of allowing their governments' emissaries to make such a far-reaching decision. If either North or South rejected a mediation offer, Stuart argued, the home governments in London and Paris should decide on recognition. At that point, the intervention process would come to an end. Mercier strongly objected to this proposal as narrow, weak, and provocative. It would infuriate the Union while "playing away one of our best cards without doing us any good."[29]

Stuart's belief that diplomatic recognition constituted the final step in the intervention process was naïve at best. Recognition would have bestowed the rights of nationhood onto the Confederacy, permitting it to negotiate any type of treaty – including military and economic pacts aimed at winning the war against the Union. Those powers that sold goods to the Confederacy would have operated as neutrals and not as allies, which meant that the Union could have lodged no complaints under international law. To challenge such actions by the European powers would have placed the Union outside the pale of the community of nations, leaving it to stand alone against the so-called civilized peoples in the world. It is difficult to believe that neither Mercier nor Thouvenel grasped the full implications of their shift toward an intervention resting on recognition: the action would have set off a chain of events that ultimately could have destroyed the Union.

French interest in intervention posed a far more serious danger to the Union than did those proposals under consideration in London. Whereas the British had almost settled on a mediation that *might* lead to diplomatic recognition of the Confederacy (both initial steps in intervention justified by international law), the French stood prepared to use these two steps as a means for moving quickly and directly to the climactic measure of recognizing southern nationhood. From Paris in late August came an alarming report from John Bigelow, the Union's consul general and minister, who feared that Napoleon had lost nearly all confidence in Lincoln's capacity to defeat the South and was "now hovering over us, like the carrion crow over the body of the sinking traveler, waiting until we are too weak to resist his predatory instincts." Despite the antipathy of the French people to slavery and the South, their most important consideration was France's welfare, and even an inter-

vention that resulted in southern separation was preferable to continued neutrality if the intervention stopped the war and reopened the flow of cotton to
French textile mills.[30]

Perhaps it was only coincidental that Mercier made a strong call for unilateral action at precisely the time that Thouvenel seemed likewise ready to
act alone. The French minister again first urged his home government to seek
a joint mediation arrangement with Russell in London. The Peace Democrats in the Union might respond favorably and exert enough pressure on the
White House to accept the offer. But Mercier warned that the move must
take place on a public and disinterested basis. Otherwise, Seward would cynically blast the measure as the product of self-interest on the part of the interventionists and thereby unify Americans against so-called European imperialists. Mercier emphasized that the mediation offer must come on a friendly
basis but with the unmistakable message that if it was rejected by the Union,
diplomatic recognition of the Confederacy would automatically follow. The
timing was good: the Lincoln administration was faltering both on the battlefield and at the polls and could not hope to overcome the additional burden of foreign assistance to the South.[31]

Almost unbelievably, Stuart recommended that the ministry in London
cooperate with the French in making a mediation offer. He had not thought
through the implications of the proposal, nor had he read enough history to
recognize the danger of collaborating with the French on any foreign venture. It was alarmingly clear that Napoleon had more in mind in Mexico than
mere debt collection, and yet Stuart ignored the danger of working with the
emperor and supported Mercier's plan. Lyons had recovered his health and
intended to return to his post in Washington on the eve of the November
elections, and this seemed an opportune time to offer mediation. Russia supported the Union, Stuart added, and doubtless would privately encourage
the Lincoln administration to accept mediation but without itself participat-
ing publicly in any move leading to a southern separation. England would be
in an awkward position. If it refused to act, Stuart warned Russell, other nations would criticize the Palmerston ministry for having "some ulterior object in continuing to look quietly on."[32]

Thus while the government in London proposed mediation, the one in
Paris pushed for recognition. And yet both measures carried the same implications, regardless of label. British leaders realized that a failed mediation
would automatically lead to recognition, whereas the French preferred to by-
pass the intervening step and move directly to recognition. In either case, the
South would win international approval of its independence, leaving it free
to negotiate for additional help. Resistance by the Union would pit it against
England, France, and any other Old World governments siding with the in-

terventionist powers. Surely the Lincoln administration would retreat from its impossible stand.

But matters were not as simple as they seemed. Both the British and French had moved dangerously close to a policy that virtually assured what they were trying so desperately to prevent: a wider war than the one already under way in America.

Intervention became even more likely in mid-September 1862, when news arrived in Europe of the Union's second resounding defeat at Bull Run. Confederate armies under Gen. Robert E. Lee repelled the Union forces and prepared to take the war north – into Union territory. The elder Adams in London sank into despondency. He could not have known that matters were even worse than they appeared. The Union's leaders in Washington had learned that General McClellan had stood idly nearby with his forces during the battle, refusing to help the entrapped fellow soldiers falling in droves before the deadly Confederate assault. Stanton and Chase led other irate cabinet members in demanding that the president remove McClellan from command. Attorney General Edward Bates warned Lincoln of the imminent fall of the nation's capital. The president, according to Bates, "seemed wrung by the bitterest anguish," even stammering that he was "almost ready to hang himself." But he refused to relieve McClellan, declaring that "he excels in making others ready to fight."[33]

The Union's second disaster at Bull Run seemed to make European intervention nearly inescapable. Russell triumphantly assured Palmerston that McClellan's failure to deliver on his promise to conquer the South gave further justification for a British intervention. Indeed, the foreign secretary had become an earnest advocate of recognition. He asked Thouvenel about a joint suggestion of an armistice that, if rejected, would lead to British, French, Austrian, Prussian, and Italian recognition of the South as "Independent Confederate States." Such a drastic measure might "dispose the North to Peace."[34]

Both Mercier's dispatches and numerous press stories had reached Thouvenel by early September, confirming in his mind the hopelessness of northern efforts to subjugate the South. The foreign secretary conveyed these thoughts to Dayton but in a sympathetic fashion. The North should have let the South go at the outset of the sectional conflict, Thouvenel declared. In a year or so, he insisted, those states would have returned to the Union, albeit with suitable safeguards for slavery and states'-rights principles. But the Union's resort to force drastically changed the situation. "I think that the undertaking of conquering the South is almost superhuman . . . [and] to me the undertaking seems impossible." Thouvenel agreed with the British that the North was incapable of subjugating a region so large and a people so numerous.[35]

Thouvenel clearly had in mind a foreign mediation of the war. Russell's interest in the project was undeniable, as indicated by the British ambassador in Paris. In conversation with Thouvenel, Lord Cowley had suggested an armistice that, if rejected, would lead to a threat to recognize the South. Thouvenel remained dubious about the chances of the Union's accepting such an intervention. And yet he wanted the war to end before the cotton shortages caused irreparable damage to the French textile industry, and he desperately desired a postwar America strong enough to balance British maritime interests. Perhaps, Thouvenel almost wistfully wrote Mercier, Second Bull Run had finally convinced northerners to call off the war.[36]

But as was the case following the Union's first defeat at Bull Run in July 1861, the British and French erroneously expected the Union to admit to the futility of the war. Both times the European powers felt confident that the Union would come to its senses about the impossibility of subjugating the South; both times they were sorely disappointed. Instead of accepting southern separation, the Union rallied its soldiers to carry on the fight. Although fate had seemingly dealt a final, climactic blow at Second Bull Run (had not Stuart earlier assured London that only "another Bull Run" would convince the North to stop fighting?), it had instead injected an uplifting sense of martyrdom into the Union's cause – particularly as Lincoln increasingly raised his voice against slavery in an attempt to define the struggle as one of righteousness versus evil. Only through long-suffering and torment, he realized, could great changes take place in a society so set against change. Even while Russell and Thouvenel expressed the feelings of their people in denying the possibility of a Union victory, the Lincoln administration baffled and infuriated Europeans by speaking glowingly of inevitable triumph and hardening its resolve against foreign intervention.[37]

Mercier perhaps grasped the intensity of Union feeling when he talked with Seward about European intervention in the aftermath of Second Bull Run. The French minister first suggested mediation. Was not the secretary of state aware of the heightened foreign interest in ending the war? "I have noticed it," Seward roughly responded, "but as for us it would be a great misfortune if the powers should wish to intervene in our affairs." Mediation presupposed a disposition by the Union to make concessions that admitted to the legality of secession. "There is no possible compromise, tell Mr. Thouvenel, and at any price, we will not admit the division of the Union." In a hard-fought effort to reciprocate Mercier's assurances of goodwill, Seward grimly declared that "we do not doubt your sentiments but the best testimony that you are able to give us of it is that you will stay out of our affairs." The only feasible solution short of prolonged war, Mercier interjected, was to establish two "confederated Confederacies." But Seward abruptly cut off this line of thought by reemphasizing the impossibility of southern separation from the Union. "Do not believe for a moment," he exclaimed with mounting exasperation, "that either the Federal Congress, myself or any person connected with this government will in any case entertain any proposition or suggestion or arrangement or accommodation or adjustment from within or without upon the basis of a surrender of the Federal Union." Not until the South surrendered would the North cease to fight.[38]

In a bitter twist of fate, the British and French had become more determined to intervene in the war just as the Union became even more determined to prevent that disaster. Mediation, armistice, recognition – no form of foreign intervention appealed to the Union because the measure automatically bestowed, at the minimum, de facto nationhood status to the South. Emancipation, assumed by the Union to be the most decisive step intended to thwart that intervention, took on the appearance overseas of a maniacal effort to incite a slave insurrection conducive to a race war and now emerged, almost paradoxically, as an essential element in the European powers' deliberations for a direct involvement. Idealistic and realistic considerations had combined in separate and independent processes on both sides of the Atlantic to promote a foreign intervention that could profit only the South.

The Union's defeat at Second Bull Run had both national and international repercussions. On the domestic front, Confederate forces under Lee turned northward, wishing to take the war out of the South and perhaps deliver a knockout blow. The drive north might even persuade foreign powers to recognize the Confederacy. Indeed, the British became even more certain that southern independence was a fact that only the stubborn North refused to accept. The time had come to end the fighting on the basis of a separation, or so many British observers argued in the autumn of 1862. The *Times* and the *Morning Post*, both more often than not expressing the views of the Palmerston ministry, urged recognition of the South, whereas the London *Morning Herald* captured the feelings of many readers by making a broad humanitarian appeal: "Let us do something, as we are Christian men." Whether "arbitration, intervention, diplomatic action, recognition of the South, remonstrance with the North, friendly interference or forcible pressure of some sort . . . let us do something to stop this carnage."[39]

The popular clamor resulting from Second Bull Run appeared to be the last necessary ingredient in convincing the Palmerston ministry to intervene. The prime minister exulted in the news from abroad. "The Federals," he declared to Russell, "got a very complete smashing, and it seems not altogether unlikely that still greater disasters await them, and that even Washington or Baltimore may fall into the hands of the Confederates. If this should happen," he added with growing conviction, "would it not be time for us to consider whether . . . England and France might not address the contending parties and recommend an arrangement upon the basis of separation?" If either North or South rejected a mediation offer, England and France should "acknowledge the independence of the South as an established fact." Russell heartily agreed. If a mediation attempt failed, "we ought ourselves to recognise the Southern States as an independent State."[40]

The distinct British move toward intervention all but guaranteed a conflict with the Union, particularly since the approach under consideration included the French, who thought recognition the certain outcome of a failed mediation. The implication was clear: both Old World nations considered Confederate independence a foregone conclusion. And regardless of Anglo-French claims to altruistic intentions, the truth was that mediation rested on the premise of a divided United States and that recognition formally designated the South as a nation. The Union, with justification, would regard either action as hostile interference in American domestic affairs and accuse the interventionists of allying with the South. Whether or not a formal partnership, the mere act of intervention could in no way help the North, just as it could in no way hurt the South. Indeed, recognition would open southern commercial and military avenues with other nations and doubtless assure the Union's dissolution. The Lincoln administration would have no recourse other than a humiliating acceptance of European intervention or a war against England that might involve other nations on the European continent and hence prove disastrous to the Union.

But before the Palmerston ministry could initiate the procedure leading to a mediation offer, news reached London of Lee's daring raid into Maryland. Whitehall's diplomatic machinery came to an abrupt halt as government leaders took stock of the new situation and pondered the wisdom of waiting for additional Confederate victories that might, at long last, convince the Union of the impossibility of subjugating the South.

The news of Lee's bold action had a mixed effect on Palmerston. Although the prime minister already seemed prepared to give in to the pressure for intervention, he still preferred to wait for more Confederate victories because of his concern about a war with the Union. Lee's turn northward afforded the chance for these additional conquests and, as a matter of course, would further weaken the North in the postwar era. A sense of relief permeated Palmerston's note to Russell: "Though the time for making a communication to the United States is evidently coming, yet perhaps it is partly actually come." As the two huge armies neared each other above Washington, "another great

Robert E. Lee. Library of Congress.

conflict is about to take place," the outcome of which should place us "in a better State than we now are in, to determine as to our course." Lamentably, the "northern Fury has not as yet sufficiently spent itself," and another series of defeats might put the Union into "a more reasonable state of mind." Russell saw the wisdom in hesitation and signified his agreement with the queen's recommendation to consult Austria, Prussia, and Russia about taking interventionist action, although he urged prior talks with France because of its staunch support for the move. Stuart in Washington had just sent a dispatch highlighting Mercier's warning that if the two European powers did not act now, the whole world would have to undergo the lengthy agony of waiting for the Union's "complete exhaustion."[41]

The time spent waiting for further news from America allowed Palmerston to reassess the wisdom of intervention and, as an additional cautionary measure, to push for Russia's involvement. Even if both American antagonists agreed to mediation, the issue would doubtless arise of whether "the fact of our meddling would not of itself be tantamount to an acknowledgement of the Confedera[cy] as an independent State." But he also realized that as well intentioned as he claimed mediation to be, the odds were that the North would reject the offer and push the intervening powers into either backing off or taking more serious action. The only chance for winning northern support for a mediation was to invite Russia to participate in making the offer. Palmerston hoped that Russia would set aside its animosities toward its former wartime antagonists in the Crimea and realize that peace in America served the interests of all nations. Still, he realized that the odds for the Union's acceptance of mediation were slim at best, with or without Russian involvement, and that the possibility of Russian participation was highly unlikely.[42] Had not Palmerston himself admitted that any involvement in American affairs constituted a meddlesome act? Could a self-professed supporter of the Union agree to an action that necessarily undermined that support?

Once again wartime events dictated British policy by temporarily warding off intervention. Lee's movement into Union territory seemed to assure a major confrontation with federal forces that would, at last, convince them to lay down their arms and accept southern independence. Not only had the Union found it impossible to subjugate the South, but it had been unable to defend its borders against a southern invasion. "It is evident," Palmerston wrote Russell, "that a great conflict is taking place to the north-west of Washington, and its issue must have a great effect on the state of affairs. If the Federals sustain a great defeat they may be at once ready for mediation, and the Iron should be struck while it is hot. If, on the other hand, they should have the best of it, we may wait awhile and see what may follow."[43]

But even though the process of mediation had momentarily stalled until additional news arrived from the American battle front, the rapidly accelerating sentiment in England for intervention did not lose intensity. Rather, it posed an even greater danger to the Union because those in favor of mediation assumed that Lee's forces would win the climactic battle and, for the first time, began to formulate peace terms. On September 24 Palmerston informed Gladstone of Russell's support for a mediation proposal that included the participation of France and Russia. Whether or not they accepted the invitation to join, the settlement would rest on an armistice that required the Union to lift the blockade and enter negotiations based on southern separation. Russell wrote Gladstone shortly afterward that he favored an "offer of mediation to both parties in the first place, and in the case of refusal by the

North, to recognition of the South." To the British ambassador in Paris, Russell reiterated his intention to extend recognition to the South upon the Union's rejection of mediation. "Palmerston agrees entirely in this course," Russell insisted.[44]

Gladstone expressed great relief over the certainty of intervention. The two sides in the war had reached a near stalemate, making this the most propitious time to offer a mediation. Indeed, it seemed wise to do so before the Confederacy made such impressive military gains that it, too, might oppose a quick end to the fighting out of interest in securing more advantages. Another consideration bearing heavily on his mind was the fear of violence in his native Lancashire. To that moment, its textile workers had suffered "with a fortitude and patience exceeding all example, and almost all belief." But if they erupted in angry protest and the Palmerston ministry then moved toward an intervention in the American war, the act would appear motivated solely by cotton interests and the government would lose its claim to being an "influence for good." The Union could rally Americans against the British and French as Old World imperialists once again intervening in New World affairs out of raw self-interest. Thus Russian participation in the mediation effort would give it "moral authority."[45]

Russell had deluded himself into believing that this mediation plan posed no special danger to the Union and that he could alleviate all suspicion of British intentions by simply reaffirming neutrality. To Gladstone the foreign secretary attempted to relieve concern over possible danger by stipulating mediation "on the basis of separation and recognition accompanied by a [renewed] declaration of neutrality."[46] Somehow Russell had convinced Palmerston to join the interventionist camp, although the prime minister remained ever the realist, willing to take action only when he knew the outcome benefited his native country. And yet peace in America did just that, even if Russell's humanitarian arguments did not provide the basis for the hardened statesman's decision to intervene. Rarely do sweeping policies result from either idealistic or realistic considerations. Usually there is a mixture of both. Certainly Palmerston's interventionist stand derived from his concern that the American war would further hurt the international economy or even expand into a wider war. Russell likewise valued these arguments while adding the humanitarian dimension. How could anyone fault the British for taking the lead in proposing such an act of altruism? At bottom, however, was always the residual effect – whether or not intentional: a United States greatly disabled by such a debilitating war and the automatic economic, strategic, and military advantages accruing to the British.

But Russell failed to grasp the peril that a seemingly innocuous call for mediation posed to the Union. *Any* form of intervention enhanced the Confederacy's status and undermined the Lincoln administration's denial of the right of secession. The British proposal, however, was especially dangerous because it presumed the separate identity of the Confederacy and automatically extended recognition to it as an independent state. From the Union's vantage point, mediation marked the first step toward a virtual alliance between the interventionists and the rebels. Indeed, mediation constituted an act of war.

Russell had gotten swept up in the euphoria of the moment. Soon after Lee won the expected monumental battle in the North, the Peace Democrats, according to Stuart's exuberant predictions from Washington, would win the November congressional elections and work toward ending the war. At that pivotal point, the mediation process would begin. England would invite other nations – particularly the Union's supporter, Russia – to join the venture and thereby avert any charges of self-interest. World opinion would support the peacemakers, further isolating the Union and forcing it to capitulate to the realities of a major battle loss, an international humanitarian appeal, and the implied readiness of the interested nations to use force to bring the combatants to the peace table. Even if the Lincoln administration resisted the mediating powers, it would first have to wait through the fast-approaching winter months and doubtless reconsider the wisdom of resuming a fight that now involved not only the South but the intervening powers as well. Thus to Russell sitting three thousand miles away in London, it made eminently good sense to stand ready with a mediation and recognition plan that awaited good news from the American battle scene and then merely legitimized the established fact of southern statehood.[47]

On September 17 at Antietam Creek, located near the small hamlet of Sharpsburg in Maryland, Confederate and Union forces engaged in the bloodiest single day's fighting in the war. The South's attempt to move the fighting into the North resulted in a brutal and deadly climax as tens of thousands of American soldiers locked in mortal combat. When evening approached and the battle wound down, Union and Confederate casualties totaled more than twenty-four thousand. The following day Lee grasped the enormity of his losses and decided to retreat before McClellan could resume the battle. While the Union general's equally battered troops gathered their own dead and wounded, Lee's army staggered back toward Virginia that evening, leaving the Union in control of the battlefield and hence able to claim a narrow victory.[48]

The first news of Antietam reached London in late September and proved immensely disappointing to the ministry. The high hopes engendered by Lee's advance northward had dramatically died with the stark realization that the Confederacy had failed to deliver the predicted climactic victory. Rather than demonstrate the Union's futility in continuing the war, the outcome allowed the White House to claim victory at Antietam and refuse to call off the war. In truth, the battle confirmed the growing suspicion that the two armies had locked in a death grip, ensuring an extended war. Stuart in Washington correctly declared Antietam "as near a drawn Battle as could be, only that the Federals have since held the ground."[49]

But then, in an amazing twist of good fortune for the Confederacy, the British interest in intervention showed no signs of dissipating. Seward appeared correct: the British seemingly regarded southern independence as their primary step toward humbling the United States and intended to justify intervention on any grounds. Palmerston agreed with Stuart's assessment of the battle and, with no small sense of relief, told Russell that this was "just the case for the stepping in of friends." Both antagonists had satisfied honor and might now see the sense in ending the conflict. "One thing must be admitted and that is that both sides have fought like bull dogs." The Union and Confederacy were "pretty equally balanced," each incapable of subjugating the other.[50] Palmerston's support for mediation seemingly assured a British intervention. Indeed, it appears that his interest in such action had been stronger than usually assumed. He had almost approved mediation following the news of Second Bull Run, and he had taken another step closer to that decision on learning that Lee had ordered his forces into the North. Now, despite his earlier insistence on further Confederate conquests, he quickly altered that position to declare that the bloody stalemate at Antietam reported by Stuart had been sufficient to drive the Union into accepting a foreign mediation.

French pressure for mediation likewise grew. Less than a week after the battle, Mercier called on Lyons to join him in urging North and South to agree to an armistice aimed at encouraging a discussion of peace terms. Mercier and Lyons would stand ready to make their good offices available but with the freedom to act in their countries' own interests. To encourage northern compliance, Mercier added, the call for an armistice should avoid using the word "separation." He expressed optimism about the chances for an armistice, particularly after the gruesome details of the battle became known. Surely neither antagonist would favor the resumption of hostilities once the full impact of Antietam had registered. Stuart insisted that most northerners sought peace and thought the London ministry could pursue Mercier's proposal with "perfect safety."[51]

Stuart's alarmist analyses had proved less than dependable on more than one occasion, and this time was no exception. He had earlier assured London that a "second Bull Run" would finally convince the North that continuing the war was pointless. Then, in a startling example of déjà vu, the Union forces followed the pattern set in the aftermath of First Bull Run by rallying in the face of adversity to fight with renewed ferocity. Now, Stuart erroneously detected widespread northern sentiment for ending the war and informed the ministry at home that the time was propitious for intervention. Indeed, Stuart's consistent evaluations highlighting the certainty of southern statehood suggested either a dangerous naivete that guaranteed trouble with the Union or an equally perilous favoritism in the war that ministers in foreign countries should avoid. Determining Stuart's true sentiment is impossible, but the image his assessments portrayed quite naturally encouraged his superiors in London to believe intervention both timely and necessary.

The British reaction to Antietam suggested that their interest in intervention ran even deeper than it appeared. Russell and Gladstone had consistently bemoaned the growing intensity of the war, which the horrid details of Antietam only confirmed. Newspapers in London, if not always reliable, had repeatedly expressed the same sentiment. Gladstone, indeed, thought the southern defeat a godsend. "I am not sorry for the apparent ill success of the Confederates as invaders," he wrote Argyll. "They might have become intoxicated, & entangled, by good Fortune."[52] Gladstone's feelings perhaps touched the pulse of numerous close British observers of the American scene: it mattered not who won the war. To those making the humanitarian argument, the fighting must come to an end before it engulfed other nations. To others, however, the defense of intervention ranged from an effort to protect British industry by preventing the destruction of the South's cotton economy to reaping the myriad advantages of slowing the growth of the United States. In all cases, the solution was intervention.

Not everyone in the British cabinet supported the move. Argyll, who remained a staunch Union supporter, agreed with Earl Granville in discerning a humanitarian reason for mediation, but both feared a third Anglo-American war. Argyll assured Gladstone of support for mediation if it had a "reasonable chance" of acceptance. But the Union remained convinced that it could subjugate the South, and the Confederacy had not yet proved its right to independence. Granville, a former foreign minister who now sat in the House of Lords, had consistently opposed foreign entanglements, and he now perceptively warned that a mediator bore the related responsibility of suggesting the conditions for peace. Surely, he surmised, no one in England understood the American situation well enough to formulate terms satisfactory to both antagonists. Did not the outbreak of war prove their own inability to devise a settlement? Further, mere recognition of the Confederacy would not force the Union to lift its blockade and thereby permit the British textile mills to increase their dwindling supplies of cotton. Instead, recognition would infuriate northerners and instill greater support for the war. And the longer the war went on, the greater the chances for a direct British involvement that freed Napoleon III to pursue his imperialist designs in Europe. A change in the British policy of neutrality, Granville reminded Russell, would be "premature."[53]

But Granville failed to realize that the supporters of intervention could defend their action by calling it a natural outgrowth of neutrality. Outside powers had the right under international law to intervene in an ongoing war if it had a deleterious effect on their neutrality. Russell, Gladstone, and others had argued on humanitarian, economic, and political grounds that the American war posed a threat to disinterested neutral nations. The heightening level of the fighting – now further clarified by the Battle of Antietam – confirmed the certainty of a prolonged conflict that could force the Lincoln administration to adopt emancipation as a means for fomenting slave revolts. In the meantime, the steady drain on the cotton surplus would soon empty British coffers, thereby increasing the chances for protests by textile workers followed by demands to challenge the Union blockade. Events were fast spinning out of control, raising the likelihood of foreign intervention.

Given these developments, it seems significant that the Earl of Shaftesbury, who was Lady Palmerston's son-in-law and unquestionably under the prime minister's influence, spoke glowingly of imminent British intervention. On September 23 (*before* Europe had learned of Antietam) Shaftesbury visited Paris, where he, according to Slidell, offered assurances of British recognition within a few weeks. The British people, Shaftesbury told the Confederate minister, supported the South's drive for independence and self-government against the imperial Union. One week after this discussion, on September 30 (*after* Europeans had learned of Antietam), Shaftesbury assured Slidell that British sentiment remained constant: "There is every reason to believe that the event so strongly desired of which we talked when I had the pleasure of seeing you in Paris is very close at hand." Charles Francis Adams considered Shaftesbury a "good key" to gauging British policy. If this was a correct observation, the Battle of Antietam had further encouraged the movement for British intervention.[54]

The Union's victory at Antietam came heavily laden with ironies. Part of the reason for Lee's advance into the North was his desire to win a monumental battle and prove the Confederacy's right to recognition, and yet his decision to undertake the campaign at this time actually curtailed a certain British move for mediation that would have led inexorably to intervention. But surprisingly, instead of quieting the talk of intervention, Lee's narrow defeat came at the cost of so much bloodshed on both sides that it encouraged humanitarian concern for intervention. Others, however, had more selfish interests in mind but nonetheless also favored intervention. The ironies continued to appear when Adams in London agreed with Seward that the battle had happily undermined a British move to intervention. Lincoln, too, misread the international situation to mean that Antietam had dealt a stunning setback to the interventionists and that the time was now right to close the door on this threat by issuing a proclamation of emancipation.

Neither the American embassy in London nor the leaders in the White House realized that the longtime British fear of a racial war born of emancipation had combined with Lee's shocking defeat at Antietam to convince greater numbers of British observers that they owed it to civilization to intervene. But just as the Americans failed to interpret the British position accurately, so did the British continue to believe, also erroneously, that mediation posed no special threat to the Union – even if its rejection led to recognition. All this explosive situation needed was a spark to set it off – and that came with Lincoln's announcement of emancipation.[55]

CHAPTER FIVE

"Days of Grace": Emancipation the Prelude to Foreign Intervention?

The character of the war will be changed. It will be one of subjugation. . . . The [old] South is to be destroyed and replaced by new
propositions and ideas.

President Abraham Lincoln, September 25, 1862

The Battle of Antietam followed by the announcement of emancipation did not close the door on foreign intervention. Europe's horror at the events rapidly unfolding in America increased with the perception that the bloodiest single day's fighting in the war had ended in a stalemate, guaranteeing prolonged and bitter combat. Civilized peoples, hitherto watching the war and hoping for its quick end, now openly favored an intervention aimed at halting the conflict in the name of humanity. Also important, the certainty of a long war meant that imminent cotton shortages would cause an international economic crisis injuring England, France, and other nations conducting business with the South. Still others in both England and France had imperial interests in mind. The combination of idealistic and realistic interests constituted a powerful force for intervention in the aftermath of Antietam and the Lincoln administration's move toward emancipation.

Driven by its deep skepticism over Lincoln's purposes in the war, the Palmerston ministry reacted to emancipation in precisely the negative manner predicted by Russell in his letter to Everett in July 1861. The first British response was widespread indignation, though admittedly tempered by the grudging realization that the president had finally drawn the line between opponents and supporters of slavery. And yet some months would have to pass before the British assessed the new situation in a calm manner and fully grasped the ultimate impact of Lincoln's decision: the emancipation pronouncement unleashed an immutable force that would stop only after it culminated in the abolition of slavery throughout the United States. In the meantime, however, Russell, Gladstone, and others in England clung to intervention as the most humanitarian way to end a war that had reached a new level of intensity at Antietam. Few British observers initially recognized that the struggle had quietly taken an antislavery turn and that additional bloodletting constituted the price that both North and South must pay because of the profound social, political, and economic effects of Lincoln's move for emancipation.

Lincoln had undergone growing pressure to take a stand against slavery after his first expression of interest in emancipation during the summer of 1862. In mid-September a delegation representing the Chicago Christians of All Denominations appeared at the White House to assure him that emancipation would win the support of civilized nations. "No other step," his visitors insisted, "would be so potent to prevent foreign intervention." Northerners would gain a "glorious principle" on which to fight the war. Southerners would stand helpless while slaves walked off the plantations, gutting the Confederacy's labor force and providing the Union with a sudden infusion of black workers and soldiers. The promise of freedom, the delegation asserted to the president, would motivate the blacks to break their bonds. "What the rebels most fear," the delegates declared, "is what we should be most prompt to do; and what they most fear is evident from the hot haste with which, on the first day of the present session of the Rebel Congress, bills were introduced threatening terrible vengeance if we used the blacks in the war."[1]

Lincoln's response to the delegation's entreaties soon appeared in the *Chicago Tribune* and other papers, drawing more attention to slavery as the central issue in the war and hence a key element in foreign affairs. The president, it became clear, had pondered the matter for some time before making a public stand. "I do not want to issue a document that the whole world will see must necessarily be inoperative, like the Pope's bull against the comet! Would *my word* free the slaves, when I cannot even enforce the Constitution in the rebel States? . . . And what reason is there to think it would have any greater effect upon the slaves than the late law of Congress, which I approved, and which offers protection and freedom to the slaves of rebel masters who come within our lines?" Problems would abound from this decision, he warned. If additional slaves crossed into Union territory, *"what should we do with them?"* How would the Union meet all their needs? But this concern would not block the measure. "Nor do I urge objections of a moral nature, in view of possible consequences of insurrection and massacre of the South. I view the matter as a practical war measure, to be decided upon according to the advantages or disadvantages it may offer to the suppression of the rebellion." Slavery was "the root of the rebellion, or at least its *sine qua non*." He added, "I . . . concede that emancipation would help us in Europe, and convince them that we are incited by something more than ambition."[2]

Lincoln still regarded emancipation as primarily a military measure. The longevity of the war, he thought, had nurtured an anxious atmosphere in the Union that made it receptive to emancipation as a military weapon for winning the conflict as well as a lever for attracting greater support for the Union's cause. He also believed that the step would discourage those British observers considering intervention. How could a self-professed antislavery nation approve a policy so blatantly favorable to the slaveholding South? Lincoln's intention was not to foment slave insurrections; as he told the delegation from Chicago, any attempt to introduce moral considerations in the matter assured that terrible event. Moreover, blacks already had sufficient impetus under the Confiscation and Militia Acts to leave the South and join either the northern labor force or the Union army and fight their former masters. Emancipation, he realized, needed a wide base of support that could come only after he clarified its many attractive characteristics.

Less than a week after the Battle of Antietam, on September 22, Lincoln announced his long-anticipated preliminary proclamation of emancipation. At noon he convened his cabinet and immediately focused on the subject of the meeting. "Gentlemen," he began, "I have, as you are aware, thought a great deal about the relation of this war to Slavery." Now was the time to put these thoughts into action. The Union's forces had safeguarded the North by driving the invaders out of Maryland. At the Union's lowest point – when Lee's armies seemed poised to assault Washington, Baltimore, and Harrisburg – Lincoln had decided that if its forces held off the rebels, he would issue a proclamation of emancipation. "I said nothing to anyone; but I made the promise to myself, and (hesitating a little) – to my Maker. The rebel army is now driven out, and I am going to fulfill that promise." He emphasized that this was his decision alone and that he considered the issue closed. "I do not wish your advice about the main matter – for that I have determined for myself." He then read the document, pausing here and there to interject explanatory remarks. As of January 1, 1863, the president declared emphatically, all slaves in states still in rebellion would be "forever free."[3]

Lincoln's Emancipation Proclamation contained several notable features. In a domestic sense, it assured massive social, political, and economic changes in a projected reconstruction era – if only by implication and in the dimly defined future. Abolitionists predictably expressed displeasure with the restrictive provisions and criticized the president for refusing to declare all slaves free. But they quickly agreed with black leaders that he had moved the nation in the right direction. Legally and constitutionally, Lincoln believed that he had acted within the borders of propriety. To him, emancipation was an act of "military necessity" that fell within his constitutional powers as commander in chief to implement whatever measures he deemed necessary to win the war. He had acted legally in refusing to impose emancipation on states or areas pledging loyalty to the Union. Their property rights remained under the protection of the due-process clause of the Fifth Amendment. Lincoln had also demonstrated an acute understanding of political realities; the proclamation was so narrowly conceived that it averted confrontations with the border states, southern Unionists (especially in Tennessee), and conservative northerners, all of whom opposed a crusade for blacks. Finally, on the diplomatic front, Lincoln had effectively blunted the Confederacy's claim of resisting northern oppression by giving the war the appearance of a humanitarian crusade.[4]

Northerners at first had mixed reactions to the proclamation, many supporting its basic thrust while others expressed concern over an imminent slave rebellion that could only worsen matters. Lincoln had tried to obviate this problem by inserting two amendments into the final document at Seward's behest: that the new freedmen be urged "to abstain from all violence, unless in necessary self-defense," and that, "in all cases, when allowed, they labor faithfully for reasonable wages." As a further precaution during the hundred days before the proclamation went into effect, Lincoln later struck passages that numerous observers had criticized as inducements for rebellion – those declaring that the president would do nothing to stop blacks' efforts to win freedom and those referring to the possibilities of compensated emancipation and colonization and hence encouraging blacks to rebel.[5]

Lincoln's precautionary measures did little to ease the growing concern. McClellan was infuriated with the president for using emancipation as a military weapon. Already disinclined to support Lincoln on anything (the president had complained that his chief field officer had "the slows," and the general considered his superior an "idiot" and a "baboon"), the general spewed forth venom to his wife over the president's failure to recognize the wisdom in not chasing Lee back into the South after the Battle of Antietam. How could a civilian have a greater understanding than a professional soldier of the numbers of men needed to pursue the enemy? Was it possible to mobilize his exhausted and badly battered forces to take the offensive after such a horrific battle? These were military considerations that McClellan knew by both instinct and training. Lincoln, the general was convinced, based his thinking on an erroneous reading of the Union's failure to win the Peninsula Campaign, and now he wanted a bigger victory than that already delivered at An-

George B. McClellan. National Archives.

tietam. Further, Lincoln had injected the race issue into the war, widening the fighting between armies to include civilians. McClellan hotly refused to "fight for such an accursed doctrine as that of a servile insurrection."[6]

Even supporters of emancipation recognized that the South had brought on many of its own problems. During a celebration at Chase's home following the president's public pronouncement, the secretary of the treasury mocked the South for masterminding its own calamity: "This was a most wonderful history of an insanity of a class that the world had ever seen. If the slaveholders had staid in the Union they might have kept the life in their institution for many years to come. That what no party and no public feeling in the North could ever have hoped to touch they had madly placed in the very path of destruction." Chase soon learned from an exuberant Union official in New Orleans that the president's proclamation had resulted in "the organizing and arming of the colored population throughout the South."[7] Although this assessment exaggerated the truth, it helped to flesh out the image so deeply ingrained in many Americans' minds that emancipation promised an end to the Old South.

These suspicions of Lincoln's motives behind emancipation were not entirely ill placed. Although the president spoke only of blacks refusing to work and perhaps joining the Union army, he realized that emancipation encouraged the infectious cry for freedom among slaves and had the capacity to instigate troubles that could prove uncontrollable. The proclamation was a risky proposition; not only did it have the potential of inciting the slaves to rebellion, but it also assured stiffened southern resistance to Union subjugation. What would southerners have to lose after emancipation had upended their society and brought into being their worst nightmare? Lincoln did not prefer a racial upheaval, but he considered it a strong possibility. "From the expiration of the 'days of grace,'" he remarked to an official in the Department of the Interior, "the character of the war will be changed. It will be one of subjugation and extermination. . . . The [old] South is to be destroyed and replaced by new propositions and ideas."[8]

Stuart in Washington exemplified the fierce negative reaction of many foreign contemporaries who failed to grasp the totality of the American conflict when he accused Lincoln of underhanded action in concocting a so-called wartime measure of emancipation clearly intended to destroy the South from within. Shortly after the president's proclamation, Stuart denounced the document in a self-righteous and indignant note to Russell that resulted from a mixture of self-satisfaction over standing correct in his dire prediction and yet darkened by a foreboding sense of impending tragedy. The president's decree, Stuart declared with disgust, applied only to areas still in rebellion – where the Union had no "*de facto* jurisdiction." It demonstrated no "pretext of humanity" and was "cold, vindictive, and entirely political." The proclamation had infuriated the Confederacy, leading its Congress to shout "threats of raising the Black Flag and other measures of retaliation." The North also feared trouble. One Union governor demanded the importation of the French guillotine as a necessary deterrent to racial upheaval. If Lincoln and the Republicans won the November elections, Stuart warned, "we may see reenacted some of the worst excesses of the French Revolution." The South, Stuart later asserted without foundation in fact, had already picked up deserters from the Union and the border states. One of the president's chief objectives, he declared, was to "render intervention impossible." The other was to rip the South apart by offering "direct encouragement to servile Insurrections."[9]

The British press blasted the proclamation as a sick piece of hypocrisy. Lincoln, according to the bitterly sarcastic London *Times*, must consider himself "a sort of moral American Pope" in assuming such a righteous position on a matter he cared nothing about. His real intention was to instigate a "servile war" in those states not under Union occupation by encouraging the slaves to "murder the families of their masters" while they were at the battle front. "Where he has no power Mr. LINCOLN will set the negroes free; where he retains power he will consider them as slaves." The proclamation was "more like a Chinaman beating his two swords together to frighten his enemy than like an earnest man pressing on his cause." The London *Spectator* supported the Union but reacted with confusion to Lincoln's halfhearted stand against slavery: "The principle is not that a human being cannot justly own another, but that he cannot own him unless he is loyal to the United States." The *Bee-Hive* of London, which reversed its pro-Confederate stance after a change in editors in January 1863, denounced the proclamation for declaring slaves free in areas where Lincoln possessed no authority and leaving them in bondage where he did. The *Times* asked whether "the reign of the last PRESIDENT [was] to go out amid horrible massacres of white women and children, to be followed by the extermination of the black race in the South? Is LINCOLN yet a name not known to us as it will be known to posterity, and is it ultimately to be classed among that catalogue of monsters, the wholesale assassins and butchers of their kind?" *Blackwood's Edinburgh Magazine* called the proclamation "monstrous, reckless, devilish." To defeat the South, the Union "would league itself with Beelzebub, and seek to make a hell of half a continent."[10]

Seward had been correct in warning that unless the Union army won a clear-cut victory in the field, the British would dismiss emancipation as an act of desperation deserving only the spite of the world. Unfortunately for the Union, its victory at Antietam proved paper thin at best, while at worst it confirmed the dread of most Europeans that the war had reached a deadly stalemate that only outside intervention could break. Then, attempting to capitalize on the so-called victory, the president proclaimed emancipation in an effort to reverse the Union's fortunes and win the war. Lincoln had played "his last card," declared the *Times*. "He will appeal to the black blood of the African; he will whisper of the pleasures of spoil and of the gratification of yet fiercer instincts; and when blood begins to flow and shrieks come piercing through the darkness, Mr. LINCOLN will wait till the rising flames tell that all is consummated, and then he will rub his hands and think that revenge is sweet."[11]

British officials reacted in predictable fashion to the Emancipation Proclamation: they expressed alarm over the ever-heightening fierceness of the war and supported intervention as an act of humanity. Hammond in the Foreign Office joined Stuart in detesting the president's action and dreading its con-

PUNCH, OR THE LONDON CHARIVARI.— OCTOBER 18, 1862.

ABE LINCOLN'S LAST CARD; OR, ROUGE-ET-NOIR.

"Abe Lincoln's Last Card; or, Rouge-et-Noir." London Punch, *October 18, 1862.*

sequences. Even Richard Cobden in Parliament, who supported the Union and hated slavery, doubted the wisdom of using emancipation as a wartime expedient. Would not this measure harden southern resistance? The North, he insisted, would "half ruin itself in the process of wholly ruining the South." A quest for victory based on black collaboration would result in "one of the most bloody & horrible episodes in history."[12]

The French agreed with the British appraisal, increasing the likelihood of a foreign involvement in the war. Mercier declared that emancipation threatened to bring about the very intervention that Lincoln so feverishly resisted. He found the proclamation "so inconceivable and so serious" that it could only be a frantic effort to prevent European intervention. He nonetheless supported a joint mediation that ignored the issue of southern independence or recognition and focused on some hazy reference to union. But this omission was by design: in earlier notes to his home office, Mercier had urged political separation and economic ties with the new nation. Lincoln had played his "last card" and lost. The Peace Democrats, border states, and perhaps even war-weary soldiers in the Army of the Potomac would see the futility in trying to subjugate a rejuvenated South. Only an immediate truce in the war could prevent a rash of slave uprisings that further escalated the fighting. In Paris, Thouvenel told the Union minister, William Dayton, that even though his sympathies lay with the North, "I must say I no longer believe you can conquer the South." Indeed, no "reasonable statesman" in Europe believed it possible. The British seemed ready to recognize the Confederacy, Thouvenel asserted, carefully gauging Dayton's reaction while leaving the impression that so were the French. Indeed, Mercier had recently informed Thouvenel that the danger of a slave insurrection provided still another reason for a joint intervention aimed at ending the American war.[13]

Thouvenel's attitude surprised Dayton, even though Seward had sensed this danger and instructed his emissary to be aggressive in warning the French against intervention. Dayton expressed doubt to his host that intervention would secure cotton for either the British or the French and warned that the Union's feelings for Britain were so bad that war would result. By purposeful implication, he threatened France as well. "What [Britain] would get from interference," he insisted, "would not be equivalent to its costs." Dayton was justified in considering Britain's thoughts of intervention "the alarming feature of the conversation" and believing that France would follow because it no longer thought reunion possible. If Earl Granville from the British cabinet was accurate in his assessment, the movement toward a mediation had acquired the support of most of his colleagues in London by early October and, with French urging, could transpire within days.[14]

That same day, October 2, Thouvenel wrote Mercier what turned out to be his last dispatch before his dismissal from office resulting from disagreements with the emperor over his provocative American policy. Despite Dayton's strong statement of the Union's determination to win, "his worried look," Thouvenel declared, "betrayed his blustering language." It still seemed wise to await the outcome of the approaching congressional elections in the United States. "If the recognition which would then be irrevocable, touched off the powder keg in the North and we were forced to do our share of fighting along with England, I admit to you that I would think a long while before doing it." France already confronted problems in Mexico and Italy which, combined with the American issue, were "really too much all at once."[15]

Three days later, on the Sunday evening of October 5, the French press carried the story of the Emancipation Proclamation and, as in England, initially drew a highly negative reaction. John Bigelow reported from his consul general's post in Paris that the Union's small margin of victory at Antietam followed by the president's announcement had provided French observers with further proof of the North's inability to win. To alter French opinion, he published a recent circular from Seward declaring that the North's objectives in the war had changed from "Union and not abolition" to "Union and abolition." The president's move had not only constituted a "just and proper . . . military proceeding" for ending a terrible war, but it also demonstrated "the moderation and magnanimity [compensation to loyal Americans, or outright exemption] with which the government proceeds in a transaction of such great solemnity and importance." Bigelow soon afterward noted a change in attitude suggesting that support for emancipation would "now daily grow in grace here as it grows in age." Sanford, then in Paris from his Belgian post, praised the proclamation as attracting the support of liberals on the Continent. The most perceptive assessment of the measure came from the Orleanist *Revue des deux mondes*: "It seems that Mr. Lincoln's proclamation ought to be the decisive blow or at least the last ordeal in this unfortunate conflict. Since it was necessary to have recourse to this extreme measure, we hope that it may be indeed the beginning of the definitive abolition of slavery."[16]

Dayton, however, discerned a distinct surge of interest in intervention. "You must not be surprised if another spasmodic effort for intervention is made," he warned Seward, "based upon the assumed ground of humanity but upon the real ground that emancipation may seriously injure the cause of the South, and will interfere for years to come, at least, with the production of cotton." If Sanford was correct in noting that a great number of liberals supported emancipation, he failed to draw attention to the large numbers of French newspapers that spoke for the government in condemning the president's action. The *Constitutionnel* blasted Lincoln for permitting the slave states to stop fighting and thereby guarantee the sanctity of their peculiar institution. The *Patrie* complained that the proclamation did not promote freedom because it condoned slavery in the border states and recaptured areas now loyal to the Union. The *Presse* denounced Seward's circular. "In place of a principle," it bitterly remarked, "it is only a bomb thrown into the midst of the population of the South."[17]

As the British moved closer to intervention, a growing division in the top echelon of London's government began to harden over the question. Just when Palmerston appeared to have settled in the interventionist camp, he suddenly reverted to his former cautionary position. Despite Russell's assurances, the Union had not given up the war and its outcome remained in doubt. Consequently, on one side of the issue stood Palmerston and his secretary for war, George Cornewall Lewis, both urging continued hesitation and warning of war with the Union. On the other side were Russell and Gladstone, who called for immediate action on both humanitarian and economic grounds. As attention turned increasingly to intervention, others in the cabinet realized that they would soon have to make their positions known.

The initial result was a series of loose coalitions that shifted with the changing fortunes of the war, as well as with the continually evolving attitudes of other nations such as France and Russia. Russell and Gladstone were powerful personalities, capable of attracting a following by their sheer presence. Lewis was studious and more reserved, always respected but seldom the catalyst of an emotional following. The outcome of the imminent debate over intervention clearly hinged on Palmerston, who showed no signs of relinquishing his pragmatic principles and continued to look to the war for guidance on the interventionist question. Both British camps agreed on one essential point: the Battle of Antietam, whether a Union victory or a stalemate, had somehow convinced the Union that it could subjugate the South. The war would go on – which meant that intervention remained a constant danger to the Union and a continual ray of hope to the Confederacy.

The outcome at Antietam, the prime minister argued to Russell, meant that mediation would appeal only to the Confederacy. The South still lacked a decisive battlefield victory that would force the Union into a mediation without its having the capacity to launch a war of revenge on England. At the least, Palmerston declared, such an offer should wait until the spring thaws permitted British military and naval forces to ready themselves for action in Canada and along the Atlantic coast. Before proposing a mediation, the London ministry should offer a "friendly suggestion" to the Union that it accept southern separation as "the inevitable result of the contest, however long it may last." It would be extremely difficult to formulate meaningful armistice terms, but any number of disputes during the negotiations "would do us no harm if they did not lead to a renewal of war." The only hope for averting a war with the Union resulting from mediation was to arrange a multilateral recognition of the South. "If the acknowledgement were made at one and the same time by England, France and some other Powers, the Yankee would probably not seek a quarrel with us alone, and would not like one against a European Confederation." For the time being, however, the best policy was to wait until the war itself convinced both sides of the wisdom of a cease-fire. "The whole matter is full of difficulty, and can only be cleared up by some more decided events between the contending armies."[18]

Russell, however, had become exasperated with Palmerston's hesitation and pushed for immediate intervention. "I think unless some miracle takes place," the foreign secretary responded to Palmerston, "this will be the very time for offering mediation, or as you suggest, proposing to North and South to come to terms." The British proposal must include two points: southern separation was advisable, and England "shall take no part in the war unless attacked." British acknowledgment of southern separation did not automatically mean war with the Union, Russell insisted to Palmerston. "My only doubt [is] whether we and France should stir if Russia holds back. Her separation from our move would ensure the rejection of our proposals." But inexplicably, he seemed willing to forge ahead with France and without Russia. He could not have known that the Russian minister in Washington, Baron Edouard de Stoeckl, had already learned from his home office that it opposed any policy that jeopardized the Union's friendship. But instead of waiting for word from Russia, Russell expressed interest in Mercier's recent call for an armistice proposal that, enticingly, made no reference to separation. "If no fresh battles occur," Russell asserted, "I think the suggestion might be adopted, tho' I am far from thinking with Mercier that the North would accept it. But it would be a fair and defensible course, leaving it open to us to hasten or defer recognition if the proposal is declined."[19]

Russell had fallen victim to a defensible though emotional view of the war. No one could fault his humanitarian and economic concerns; but on the other side, no one could argue convincingly that foreign intervention – whether a mediation or an armistice – offered a harmless means for ending the war. In truth, either step extended de facto recognition to the South as a nation. Further, history demonstrates that once an intervention process begins, it takes on a life of its own. Although Russell felt confident that he could control events, the truth is that he had little sense of reality. Recognition, he had admitted more than once, would almost automatically follow a failed mediation or armistice effort. Even if recognition did not take place, the initial foreign involvement would have already done irreparable harm to the Union's prestige by implying international support for the right of secession. Russell knew that the Union had hotly warned of war on any nation that granted nationhood to the rebels. Bluster perhaps – but the chance of another Anglo-American war had sobered Palmerston and numerous other, more cautious Englishmen, who now retreated from intervention, even if prolongation of this atrocious war led to slave revolts and hurt the future flow of cotton.

And these were not the only considerations working against intervention. A failed attempt to stop the war would probably force the powers into adopting sterner measures capable of restoring their damaged prestige and, in so doing, encourage them to satisfy their own interests as payment for their efforts. Russell had admitted that the only chance for success rested on a Russian involvement that he thought unlikely at best. He was certainly aware of the risks involved in allying with the French in foreign projects. The Mexican experience alone revealed how far Napoleon would go in pursuing his New World objectives. When had the British and French ever agreed on common national interests in any international controversy? He was certainly knowledgeable enough in international law to know that any nation or nations sponsoring either a mediation or an armistice bore the responsibility of devising terms conducive to a final settlement of the dispute. What middle ground existed on the slavery question? What arguments could mollify the intense hatreds endemic to a vicious civil war that had reached shocking levels at Shiloh and Antietam? What compromise might he find between a South that demanded independence and a North that rejected anything less than full restoration of the Union?

Russell had nonetheless emerged as the chief proponent for stopping the war in the name of peace. His mediation proposal rested on an armistice that necessitated the presentation of suggested terms for a permanent settlement of the war. Rejection of mediation by either warring party, he knew, would inescapably lead to acknowledgment of southern separation soon followed by diplomatic recognition of the Confederacy. But his fears of inaction were greater than his concern over the Union's threats. From Russell's perspective, the world as he knew it stood on the verge of disaster: and thus the British government as the protector of civilization owed it to mankind to end the American war.[20]

British intervention seemed certain after Gladstone, on October 7, assured a large and boisterous public gathering in Newcastle that southern separation was irreversible. Recognition of the Confederacy suddenly appeared to be a decision already made in the private chambers of the Palmerston ministry. Thundering forth his message in the midst of wild applause, the chancellor of the exchequer proclaimed: "We may have our own opinions about slavery, we may be for or against the South; but there is no doubt that Jefferson Davis and other leaders of the South have made an army; they are making, it appears, a navy; and they have made what is more than either – they have made a nation." Lest there be doubt about his feelings, he delivered a ringing conclusion: "We may anticipate with certainty the success of the Southern States so far as regards their separation from the North."[21]

Public reaction to Gladstone's assertions was uniformly conclusive and favorable: as a cabinet official who openly advocated intervention, he appeared to express the views of the ministry, which appealed to growing numbers of British observers clamoring for mediation. Gladstone's speech, the London *Economist* declared, "echoes the general sentiment of the country, and probably the real opinion of most members of the government." If so, the Union confronted its most severe trial in the foreign relations of the war. According to a gleeful Ambrose D. Mann, the Confederacy's former commissioner and

William E. Gladstone, British chancellor of the exchequer. From H. C. G. Matthew, ed., The Gladstone Diaries, *9 vols. (Oxford: Clarendon, 1978), 6: frontispiece.*

now minister in Belgium, recognition was imminent and had caused great excitement throughout Europe. Two months afterward, Francis Lawley, a special correspondent of the London *Times* then in the Confederate capital at Richmond and openly favorable to the South, wrote Gladstone that the Confederacy expectantly awaited the establishment of "mutually beneficial relations between the two countries." Forster in England had become Adams's confidant and now urged him to inform Russell of Seward's dispatch warning of severed relations if the British government extended recognition. Adams was distraught but maintained the presence of mind to delay any response until he was certain of the British ministry's position. The chancellor, Adams wrote Seward, had always supported the South, and his speech seemed orchestrated as a prelude to recognition following the assembly of Parliament. "We are now passing through the very crisis of our fate," Adams solemnly recorded in his diary.[22]

The anxious international atmosphere made it easy to read too much into Gladstone's speech. He certainly considered southern separation a fait accompli that only the Union refused to accept; he also feared that Lincoln's emancipation policy guaranteed an outbreak of slave insurrections and widespread racial upheaval throughout the Americas. But these beliefs and fears did not mean that he favored the South or had spoken for his government in an official capacity. During a widely publicized speech at Manchester the previous April and in a personal letter just three weeks before the Newcastle uproar, Gladstone reiterated his long-held and consistent stance on the unequivocal breakup of the Union. To his correspondent, he asserted that "it has long been (I think) clear that Secession is virtually an established fact & that Jeff. Davis & his comrades have made a nation." Gladstone insisted that he remained neutral toward the war but believed that the South had earned independence and that England and other civilized nations must intervene to stop the fighting. The alternative, he had repeatedly made clear, was an imminent cotton shortage and an ever-worsening war, both outcomes made worse by presidential emancipation followed by certain slave revolts and a bitter racial conflict. The probability is that he was out of touch with the cabinet and prime minister on the status of intervention. The certainty is that he had spoken out of turn: he should have realized the gravity of a cabinet official's making a public pronouncement on the most volatile subject of the day. Whether or not he had acted officially in voicing such sentiment, he left the impression of having served as an appointed messenger heralding a new government policy.[23]

In an interesting twist of events, neither Palmerston nor Russell approved Gladstone's public indiscretion. At first not realizing its dangerous ramifications, the prime minister admitted that the chancellor was "not far wrong in pronouncing by anticipation the National Independence of the South." But Palmerston altered this lukewarm though supportive stance when the public outcry in favor of immediate intervention showed no signs of abating. Less than a week after the speech, he told Russell that Gladstone should have

"steer[ed] clear of the Future unless authorized by his colleagues to become
. . . the organ of the Govt. for announcing Decisions come to upon suitable
Deliberation." The prime minister finally reversed his position in declaring
that "Gladstone ought not to have launched into Confederate acknowledgement." Russell agreed with Gladstone's remarks but was chastened by his fear
of a public intrusion in government policy that provoked a rash decision. He
berated the chancellor for going "beyond the latitude which all speakers must
be allowed." Recognition was admittedly imminent, but Gladstone's speech
forced the issue when the time was not yet right for such action. Terms for
settlement were not yet clear. "Negotiations would seem to follow, and for
that step I think the Cabinet is not prepared."[24]

As the pressure mounted, Russell found it incumbent upon himself to re-
assure Adams that the ministry intended to abide by neutrality. The meeting
was tense because the foreign secretary found his guest highly anxious over
the prospects of war. Adams had already confided his and other legation
members' alarm to his diary: "If Gladstone be any exponent at all of the views
of the cabinet, then is my term likely to be very short." Russell attempted to
ease Adams's fears of recognition. All members of the ministry "regretted the
speech," and Gladstone himself "was not disinclined to correct, so far as he
could, the misinterpretation which had been made of it." No one in the Palmerston government had made a decision for intervention. Neutrality remained in effect and would continue its course, Russell assured Adams, as the
meeting drew to a close.[25]

Despite the appearance of deliberate falsehood, Russell had not strayed
from the truth in asserting that the government's policy would never change
from neutrality. The danger lay in his view of the ramifications of such a
seemingly detached policy. International law, Russell knew from a careful
reading of the Swiss theorist on international law Emmerich de Vattel, assigned broad parameters to neutrality that included intervention in a war that
threatened bystander nations. In a memorandum to his cabinet colleagues,
Russell urged support for an armistice as the chief means for undercutting
the "acts of plunder, of incendiarism, and of revenge" that would result from
emancipation and ultimately destroy the South. To achieve this barbarous
program, Lincoln sought to excite "the passions of the slave to aid the destructive progress of armies." The president's proclamation aimed at igniting
a massive slave revolt that would necessarily grow into a racial conflict knowing no territorial bounds. The British, he declared in what the Union would
predictably denounce as a horribly twisted piece of logic intended to justify
intervention, "must remain neutral, even were we to recognise the South &
acknowledge that Jeff. Davis has made a 'nation.'"[26]

Russell continued to demonstrate his lack of touch with reality. Admittedly, international law condoned an intervention along the lines he defined, but the probability was that his suggested interventionist action would unleash a northern fury far outmatching his greatest fears of emancipation. No sound reason exists for believing that Lincoln's proclamation assured a wave of slave revolts followed by racial war. To assume the imminence of widespread insurrection entailed the corresponding assumptions of communication among slaves, organization of effort, and accessibility to weapons. Never in America's past had such a massive rebellion occurred, despite the ambitions of black leaders such as Denmark Vesey and Nat Turner. Had not the white abolitionist John Brown during the late 1850s failed in his attempt to set up a black state because of insufficient support? And yet Russell conjured up images of horrid insurrections, no doubt resulting from recent British experiences in India and Ireland as well as earlier instances of slave rebellions among both British and French colonies in the Caribbean.[27] He continued to ignore the limited results of the Lincoln administration's already standing policies of confiscation, which had only encouraged slaves to leave the plantations and perhaps even work for the Union army.

Justified in his sense of neutrality, Russell joined Mercier in advocating an armistice as a seemingly less provocative form of intervention than either mediation or recognition. Europe's responsibility to civilization was "to ask both parties, in the most friendly and conciliatory terms, to agree to a suspension of arms for the purpose of weighing calmly the advantages of peace against the contingent gain of further bloodshed and the protraction of so calamitous a war." An Anglo-French intervention – with the lead taken by the Paris government – offered the greatest hope for success.[28]

But as the growing impact of Gladstone's speech made clear, little time remained for careful deliberation: the episode had forced the interventionist issue to the public front and, in so doing, glaringly exposed its complexities. Palmerston emphasized that no one had yet devised terms of settlement attractive to both belligerents. Would not the two sides revert again to war after a breather – particularly after reloading their arsenals and refueling their will to win? The most formidable arguments against intervention, however, came from the cabinet officer who would have to engineer a war against the United States: Secretary for War Lewis. Both in a speech in Hereford and in a memorandum to the cabinet, he insisted that the South had not yet won independence and that to intervene at this time would alienate the Union and lead to a catastrophic Anglo-American war. Compromise was impossible as long as the South demanded independence and the North countered with restoration of the Union. The war must render its own verdict.[29]

Lewis's was a sound and reasoned argument that no one of sound and reasoned mind could dispute; but Gladstone's inflammatory remarks had pushed the issue of intervention into the political arena and now threatened to force the Palmerston ministry into actions that carried greater potential for widening the war rather than bringing it to a close.

CHAPTER SIX

Autumn of Discontent:
The Crisis over Intervention

Our struggle has been, of course, contemplated by foreign nations
with reference less to its own merits, than to its supposed, and often
exaggerated effects and consequences resulting to those nations
themselves.

          President Abraham Lincoln, December 1, 1862

The autumn of 1862 emerged as the pivotal period of crisis over foreign intervention in the American war. Not only did the British focus on the issue at
the highest levels of government, but Napoleon in France produced an actual
proposal for a joint intervention that invited the Russians to join the Anglo-
French lead. Britain's motives remained a mixture of humanitarian and economic reasons, made more volatile by an inordinate fear of race war and its
ultimate international repercussions. French interest focused on the growing
need for cotton along with Napoleon's personal drive for a foothold in Mexico. Russia's feelings continued to be quixotic, pushed and pulled by ties to
the Union that repeatedly raised the question of whether an intervention
would help its friends in Washington more than its enemies in London and
Paris. In any event, foreign discontent with the unending nature of the war
had mobilized sufficient concern to put the Union in its deepest peril from
the outside. A European involvement would virtually assure southern independence, regardless of the approach.

The arguments presented by Palmerston and Lewis, combined with Gladstone's provocative speech, brought a sense of immediacy to the interventionist question and compelled the supporters of mediation to reassess their
position in light of its dangerous implications. Indeed, the imminent debate
over intervention forced them to ponder the serious consequences of alienating the Union and perhaps causing an Anglo-American war of vengeance. If
war developed, could the British trust France to stand with them? Would the

Russians seize the opportunity to restore the balance of power lost in the Crimea by aiding the Union? Most striking in this new period of assessment was the sharply diminished concern in British governing circles over the nature of the war, the imminence of slave revolts, and the loss of cotton. Of more pressing importance was the apprehension of war with the Union. Soon joining Palmerston and Lewis were an unquestioned majority that included Argyll, Granville, the Duke of Newcastle from the Colonial Office, Charles P. Villiers as president of the Poor Law Board, Sir George Grey from the Home Office, and Thomas Milner-Gibson from the Board of Trade. Only Baron Westbury, the lord chancellor, signified his support for Russell and Gladstone.[1]

The situation became more complicated when Palmerston reminded his advisers of the relevance of slavery to the interventionist question. The prime minister had taken an even firmer stand against intervention, warning of war with the Union while noting that slavery posed a "great difficulty" for England. Could the ministry, he asked Russell, "without offence to many People here[,] recommend to the North to sanction Slavery and to undertake to give back Runaways, and yet would not the South insist upon some such Conditions[,] especially after Lincoln's Emancipation Decree[?]" Thus while Russell regarded emancipation as an impetus to intervention, Palmerston considered it an obstacle. The prime minister had peered farther down the road to warn that the president's proclamation required the intervening powers to present terms of settlement that, of course, had to resolve the highly inflammatory issue of slavery. Lewis had best summarized the potential dilemma: approval of slavery would alienate the Union and the British people; its abolition would antagonize the South, with which the ministry might soon have to deal as a nation. Indeed, abolition would not meet the approval of most northerners, perhaps including the president himself. No solution existed – except for that attained by the war.[2]

Palmerston refused to budge from his realistic stand of opposing intervention until the war itself provided the occasion for a certain success. On October 22, the day before the hastily scheduled cabinet meeting, he informed Russell that he was "much inclined to agree with Lewis that at present we could take no step nor make any communication of a distinct proposition with any advantage." Neither a mediation nor an armistice would appeal to both belligerents. "All that we could possibly do without injury to our position," he continued, "would be to ask the two parties not whether they would agree to an armistice, but whether they might lean their thoughts toward an arrangement between themselves." But even this approach would prove futile. In a statement indicating Palmerston's awareness of the nonnegotiable nature of the war, he asserted that "the Northerners would say that the only condition of arrangement would be the restoration of the Union; the South would say their only condition would be an acknowledgement by the North of Southern Independence." An interventionist effort at this juncture of the war would fail. "I am, therefore, inclined to change the opinion on which I wrote you when the Confederates seemed to be carrying all before them, and I am very much come back to our original view of the matter, that we must continue merely to be lookers-on till the war shall have taken a more decided turn."[3]

Without ruling out an involvement, Palmerston called for more patience – when time might provide an opportune moment to intervene. The prime minister agreed with Russell "in fixing next Spring for the period for the acknowledgement of the Confederate States," but he still maintained that southern "independence can be converted into an Established Fact by the Course of Events alone."[4]

Palmerston's opposition to an immediate intervention forced Russell to postpone the cabinet meeting, but his resolution remained undeterred. The prime minister, after all, had not approved all aspects of Lewis's memorandum. Recognition of southern independence, Palmerston declared, did *not* have to wait "until the North had admitted it." It could come after the South had demonstrated its claim to statehood. A few cabinet members – including Lewis – gathered in London on an informal basis to discuss the possibility of an armistice offer. Despite Lewis's strongly expressed opposition to intervention, Russell maintained his position. He decided to answer Lewis's memorandum with one of his own – a call for a multiple great power mediation engineered by five European nations: England, France, Russia, Prussia, and Austria. Gladstone immediately approved the proposal and downgraded the possibility of war with the Union. The timing was propitious, he insisted in a memorandum that he too circulated among cabinet members. North and South had reached a stalemate, and the coming of winter would force a break in the fighting and make an armistice more palatable. Further, the British public clearly favored the South, and an imminent cotton famine would cause a popular eruption. The Lincoln administration could not resist an appeal based on "the common interests of humanity." Now was the time to strike.[5]

Despite the strong arguments of Russell and Gladstone, Palmerston's reluctance to move threatened to make British intervention a chimera that could fast fade into memory. Their pleas rested on well-known humanitarian and economic arguments; the position of the prime minister remained hardheaded and realistic. The chances for war with the Union, Palmerston emphasized, argued very strongly against any premature action that actually facilitated the South's move for independence. Recognition could come only after the Confederacy had already achieved its central goal.

Yet even the imminence of winter failed to quiet the issue: in late October, Napoleon revived Russell's waning hopes for intervention by proposing a joint action by France, England, and Russia that had long been under consideration. French popular views toward the Civil War continued to turn on economic interests and several other variables; Napoleon's sights remained fixed on Mexico. Before the war broke out, he and Thouvenel had supported the sanctity of the Union, even to the point of offering a mediation. Indeed, many French observers found it difficult to believe that a government built on federal principles (such as their own system in France) could condone secession as a legitimate means for promoting its own destruction. Press spokesmen for the throne, however, openly sympathized with the South and cited America's own Declaration of Independence in justifying the secessionists' insistence that "governments depend only upon the consent of the governed."[6]

It is impossible to determine whether the views expressed by the French press were its own; it repeatedly fell under the influence of government censorship and bribery. Whatever the truth, the public stance of the French government and press had undergone considerable transformation during the course of the fighting. The French government – or, rather, Napoleon – now seemed determined to act. After Thouvenel left office, the new foreign minister, Edouard Drouyn de Lhuys, learned that Napoleon planned an immediate intervention in the American war based on a joint European call for a six-month armistice, along with the Union's lifting its blockade for the period. Even though Drouyn hesitated, the emperor pushed forward, undoubtedly encouraged by the British inquiries of mid-September regarding the possibilities of an Anglo-France intervention. Under order of the emperor, Drouyn had no choice but to contact the British about the proposal.

Problems elsewhere had for a time diverted Napoleon's attention from the American situation, but they had dissipated in intensity and now permitted him to respond to widespread public pressure for intervention. Great numbers of sympathetic observers of the American scene appeared to concur with the defiant tone of Stuart's recent remark to Mercier in Washington: "If independence has ever been nobly fought for and deserved, it has been so in the case of the Confederacy." Mercier agreed that intervention "fulfilled a duty to humanity" and, in a point that fitted Russell's line of thinking, constituted "a mission assigned to neutrals by international law." Napoleon had become frustrated over British hesitation and decided to take the lead in intervention.[7]

Napoleon's overture was so striking because of its implied use of military force to compel compliance by the two American belligerents. In a private conversation on October 28 with Confederate minister John Slidell, the French emperor revealed how far he would go in an intervention that allegedly rested on both humanitarian and economic grounds. "What do you think," he asked Slidell, "of the joint mediation of France, England, and Russia? Would it, if proposed, be accepted by the two parties?" Slidell at first was dubious about either northern compliance or Anglo-Russian cooperation, even though he assured southern support. This was not a new proposal, and he did not trust England and knew that Russia was pro-Union. "France could be outvoted," Slidell countered, hoping to goad the emperor into taking the first step on his own. Perhaps accepting the challenge, Napoleon explained that his terms included a six-month armistice period during which the Union would lift its blockade. "This would put a stop to the effusion of blood, and hostilities would probably never be resumed." The Union's rejection of this offer would provide "good reason for recognition" and, in an unmistakable allusion to the use of force, "perhaps for more active intervention."[8]

The following day Napoleon pursued the topic, raising Slidell's hopes that French intervention was nigh. The emperor revealed his true propensities in the American conflict (and perhaps even prepared for the imminence of hostilities with the Union) by urging the South to contract the building of naval vessels in France. Slidell noted that British neutrality legislation had obstructed such efforts in England. "If the Emperor would give only some kind of verbal assurance that his police would not observe too closely when we wished to put on board guns and men we would gladly avail ourselves of it." Napoleon suggested a way of sidestepping objections to the construction of armed vessels. "Why could you not have them built as for the Italian Government? I do not think it would be difficult, but will consult the minister of marine about it."[9]

Southerners reacted in mixed fashion to Napoleon's invitation to a government-sanctioned subterfuge. Confederate secretary of state Judah P. Benjamin was already unhappy with Britain's refusal to declare the Union blockade ineffective and had recently blasted Russell's attitude as "discourteous and even unfriendly." President Davis even considered withdrawing Mason from his mission in England. The British ministry was "unfriendly" to the government in Richmond, Benjamin complained, leading him to express immense satisfaction with the emperor's willingness to undertake an "ulterior action which would probably follow the offer of mediation." Mason had repeatedly encountered Russell's reluctance to extend recognition and doubted the feasibility of Napoleon's offer as long as he insisted on working with England. Slidell nonetheless remained hopeful because, as he well knew, Napoleon had not mentioned to the British any possibility of further action in the event of the Union's refusal to comply with an armistice. Besides, the emperor implied, British cooperation seemed certain. King Leopold of Belgium had written a letter – while Queen Victoria was in Brussels – which

Judah P. Benjamin, Confederate secretary of state. Library of Congress.

urged the French to intervene in the American war in an effort to assure southern cotton to struggling mill workers throughout Europe. The queen's presence at the time of the letter was especially noteworthy, Slidell told Benjamin. "It is universally believed that King Leopold's counsels have more influence with Queen Victoria than those of any other living man."[10]

The greatest crisis confronting the Union in foreign affairs had materialized in the private chambers of Paris and London, and all unbeknown to American dignitaries both in London and Washington. For that matter, Confederate leaders, already rejoicing at Napoleon's apparent readiness to take the initiative, had no idea of Russell's overweening interest in intervention. Mason in England still clung to his belief that the French emperor would not act without British compliance, and Palmerston maintained his rigid opposition to an involvement until the war had established the South as victor. But Russell, on hearing of Napoleon's support for an armistice, was exuberant and prepared to move forward. Although the foreign secretary did not realize how far the French emperor was prepared to go in pursuit of his expansionist aims in the New World, he should have known from experience that Napoleon's reach knew no bounds. Had he not continued his interventionist activities in Mexico after both England and Spain had abandoned the initial project of collecting debts? The emperor was a proven adventurer without scruples. Palmerston grasped this fundamental truth about his long-time adversary. He warned Russell that the French felt free to propose any type of interventionist scheme because they were not bound by the "Shackles of Principle and of Right & Wrong." And yet Russell shoved aside this warning as well as history itself in the firm belief that Napoleon provided the chief means for arresting the war in America.[11]

A joint intervention, with or without the Russians, appeared certain. Indeed, Russell seemed to believe that the sheer momentum of an Anglo-French involvement would cause the Russians to cooperate, if only to prevent their longtime enemies from satisfying their own self-interests. Palmerston, Russell thought, would most certainly give way to such pressure.

The autumn congressional elections further muddled the already chaotic situation. Despite the confident predictions of Stuart and Mercier, the Peace Democrats did not seize control of the party and achieve a landslide victory that put them in the position of accepting either mediation or an armistice. Although the Democrats as a whole won thirty-four new congressional seats along with the governors' houses in both New York and New Jersey and a majority in the legislatures of Indiana, Illinois, and New Jersey, the Republicans surprisingly clung to seventeen of the nineteen free state governors' positions and sixteen of the legislatures. Indeed, the Republicans added five seats in the Senate and maintained a twenty-five-vote majority in the House that marked the smallest loss of congressional seats in an off-year election for twenty years. Even in six states held by the Democrats, their margin of victory was so small that if the Union soldiers – predominantly Republican enlistees – had been able to vote, they would have reversed the outcome. The Peace Democrats had failed to gain control, and yet the British chargé saw no danger in continuing to urge a mediation that he fully expected to grow into recognition. Inexplicably, he wrote London: "We might now recognize the

South without much risk to ourselves." Russell interpreted Stuart's ill-conceived optimism as the final factor in success. The new political leaders, once in office, would block resumption of the war in the spring. "I heartily wish them success."[12]

The weakened threads of Union continued to fray in early November, just as Lyons, his health restored, returned to Washington and resumed his ministerial duties. Only days after the elections, on November 5, Lincoln caused a public furor by removing McClellan from command. The Democrats, who regarded the general as their voice in the army, blasted the president's action as politically motivated and swore to bring him under control. Lyons feared that Lincoln had tightened his ties with the "Radicals" or war party and that the fighting would continue. In the midst of this angry outcry against the president, Peace Democrats called for an armistice in the war and a special convention to make changes in the Constitution aimed at persuading the South "to return to the Union." Lyons, however, believed that most Democrats thought restoration of the Union impossible and an armistice as a "preliminary to peace – and for the sake of peace would be willing to let the Cotton States at least depart." Mediation would be acceptable once they had restrained the president and if "*all* the Powers of Europe" took part – which Lyons assumed to mean "principally *Russia* in addition to England and France, and perhaps 'Prussia.'" All these conditions, Lyons inferred, made the prospect of intervention highly unlikely. Further, he thought the Democrats were actually wary of outside involvement in the war and believed that the South had not a "shadow of a desire to return to the Union." In fact, Lyons warned in a penetrating observation that contradicted Stuart's view, "Foreign intervention, short of the use of force, could only make matters worse here."[13]

Mercier became impatient with Lyons's restraint – particularly after working so closely with the more accommodating Stuart for intervention – and urged his home government to act alone and, if necessary, threaten the North into compliance. The Democrats had won the elections, the French minister maintained, and now were too "timid" to exploit their success. France should first seek a public statement of approval from England before making a unilateral offer of mediation. In this manner, he observed, the Union would be less angry with England, and France would gain the leverage of having European support. Perhaps even Russia would nod approval. Its participation, of course, would remove "the element of *intimidation*, which though kept in the background, must be felt by the United States to exist." He admitted that a mediation offer made by all the European powers "might have the effect of reconciling the pride of the United States to negotiation with the South." But he also believed that the Union would find great difficulty in rejecting an offer made by both France and England or even by France alone. Both the French and English had an "obvious and pressing interest" in ending the war and must have their naval forces prepared to satisfy that interest.[14]

For the most part, Lyons adopted a sound position in shying away from any suggestion of force and insisting to his home government that compromise between North and South was out of the question. "All hope of the reconstruction of the Union appears to be fading away, even from the minds of those who most ardently desire it." The European powers, he argued to Russell, should not consider an intervention because, contrary to Stuart's assessment, the Peace Democrats had failed to gain control of the government and the president's dismissal of McClellan had forged a fairly strong alliance between moderate Republicans and Radicals. Indeed, Lyons had learned from private conversations with a number of Democrats that they opposed mediation because it would infuriate Americans and give renewed impetus to the Radicals wanting to pursue the war. The only suitable time for mediation, Lyons argued, would be when the Democrats controlled the White House and could accept the offer without loss of honor. Above all, the British must not take the lead in what could only be a multipowered intervention. Otherwise, Lincoln and the Radicals would use mediation as a means for stirring up more domestic support for the war.[15]

Only to this point did Lyons's position make sense. But he then made a statement that reflected his own shallow understanding of international law and the intense nature of the situation: "I do not clearly understand what advantage is expected to result from a simple recognition of the Southern Government." Lyons still failed to grasp the treaty possibilities that recognition would make available to the South as a nation. Nor did he demonstrate any awareness of how the recognition issue was related to Napoleon's interests in Mexico along with his penchant for reckless behavior. Lyons blandly asserted that no European powers would "contemplate breaking up the blockade by force of arms, or engaging in hostilities with the United States in support of the independence of the South." And yet less than a week later he noted Mercier's insistence on intervention – with or without the Russians – because of the dire need for southern cotton. Surely this statement signified France's willingness to go beyond mere extension of recognition of the Confederacy and to consider some severe action aimed at satisfying French economic needs. And it followed that a reopened cotton flow would help the South and hurt the North. French intentions were clear. Whoever led the intervention, the French minister declared to Lyons, must guarantee that northern rejection of the offer "would be followed by something more in favour of the South than naked recognition." Did not this thinly veiled threat bear a remarkable resemblance to the assurance Napoleon gave to Slidell?[16]

Particularly at this point in the war – when its verdict still remained in the balance – recognition of the Confederacy would provide a tremendous boost to its morale by opening military and commercial avenues throughout Europe. Southern secession would achieve legitimacy, necessarily meaning that the Union had lost its permanency. Foreign powers now authorized to deal with the South would confront the Union blockade, thereby providing the Lincoln administration with its greatest challenge in the war. Further, Napoleon could claim a popular mandate for stern action. His French people had already warned that failure to acquire cotton could lead to domestic violence. Given Napoleon's record for unrestrained conduct, Lyons should have realized the extreme danger in extending recognition to the Confederacy, especially when the most aggressive spokesman for intervention was the French emperor.

Thus while Lincoln thought that emancipation had blocked intervention, it had instead helped to evoke the Union's greatest crisis. And what made the drama more compelling was the sheer resonance of its silence: no evidence suggests that either Adams in London or Seward in Washington was aware of the impending danger. Russell and Gladstone now prepared to present Napoleon's interventionist proposal before a November meeting of the cabinet and prime minister. Although Palmerston and the majority of his advisers still opposed interference in the American war, they were as susceptible to popular pressure as anyone in high office and could change their stand in accordance with prevailing political winds. Lyons had observed while in London that most cabinet members still opposed intervention but thought that it "might be forced upon them."[17] Indeed, the possibility remained – slim though it was – that Russia might join the venture and thereby exert additional pressure on the London ministry to participate. Had one or more European powers intervened in the war with either an offer of mediation or a call for an armistice followed by recognition of the Confederacy, the White House would have faced the unhappy choice of either capitulating to secession and outside interference in American affairs or resisting the intruders at risk of war not only with the South but with whatever nation or combination of nations had intervened. A permanent division of the United States seemed inescapable, regardless of the Lincoln administration's decision.

Lewis, however, discerned the overarching danger to world peace contained in the French proposal and, before the scheduled cabinet meeting, took the lead in opposing it as a sure step to war. Both in an extensive memorandum to cabinet members and in a series of letters that appeared in the London *Times*, the secretary for war warned that any form of intervention guaranteed a third Anglo-American war. The public letters, actually written by William Vernon Harcourt, who was Lewis's stepson-in-law and a special-

George Cornewall Lewis, British secretary for war. From Gilbert F. Lewis, ed., Letters of the Right Hon. Sir George Cornewall Lewis *(London: Longmans, Green, 1870), frontispiece.*

ist in international law, appeared under the pseudonym of "Historicus" and reiterated many of the same warnings. Intervention in another country's domestic affairs, Historicus asserted, "almost inevitably . . . results in war." Its sponsors could not assure peace "except by recourse to arms; it may be by making war upon the North, it may be by making war upon the South, or,

138

what is still more probable, it may be by making war upon both in turns." In an unmistakable allusion to the proven perils of working with Napoleon, Historicus warned that a joint mediation "would practically place our honour in the hands of our copartners in the intervention." Continued neutrality was the wisest policy. "We are asked to go we know not whither, in order to do we know not what." To believe that a mere armistice would end an "irrepressible conflict" was "childish in the extreme." An interventionist proposal without agreeable terms of settlement would demonstrate that its proponents lived in a "Paradise of fools."[18]

The South, Lewis argued, had not satisfied the requirements under international law to claim recognition as a nation. In his lengthy and sweeping memo to the cabinet, a fifteen-thousand-word treatise entitled "Recognition of the Independence of the Southern States of the North American Union" and written in part by Harcourt, the secretary for war insisted that the fighting in America had mired down the protagonists in a bloody deadlock that, primarily through the Union blockade, had inflicted "greater loss, privation, and suffering to England and France, than was ever produced to neutral nations by a war." Despite laudable calls for ending this war, the South had not established its independence. When did this moment of national awakening arrive? "It is easy to distinguish between day and night; but it is impossible to fix the precise moment when day ends and night begins." Premature intervention, he warned, would make the participants virtual allies of the South in seeking its independence. War with the Union would follow.[19]

England, Lewis insisted, must not act until the outcome of the American contest was certain. As long as a "*bona fide* struggle with the legitimate sovereign was pending," recognition of southern independence was unjustifiable. Lincoln's proclamation of emancipation proved that the war was ongoing. It was a military act, not one based on humanitarian considerations, but fully "intended to impoverish and distress the Southern planters, possibly even to provoke a slave insurrection." Recognition should not take place until evidence existed that it would produce a settlement between the belligerents. The fighting showed no signs of abating; both sides remained determined to win.[20]

Although Lewis admitted that international law justified "an avowed armed interference in a war already existing," prudence did not. He suspected that Napoleon (whom Lewis derisively dubbed the "Southern champion") preferred "armed mediation" or "dictation." But numerous logistical and practical problems prohibited serious consideration of the use of force. The Union remained a formidable power, measured in both armies and fleet – including ironclads that outmatched the Old World's wooden vessels. Any European effort to dispatch a fighting contingent across three thousand miles of ocean would encounter major problems. If the intervening nations should succeed in ending the American war, they would then confront the enigma of having to draft peace terms. Not only would they have trouble satisfying North and South, but they also could disagree among themselves. If the concert collapsed, "England might stand alone."[21]

In the midst of great public and ministerial excitement over the question of intervention, Lewis had injected the voice of reason. He accepted Russell's legal and even humanitarian justifications for involvement in the American war but ultimately rejected any form of intervention on the realistic ground of British self-interest. First and foremost was the possibility of war with the Union. But also important, and not unrelated to his primary concern, was the danger inherent in any cooperative scheme involving Napoleon. Even a mediation raised more problems than it resolved: the related necessity of devising peace terms posed an insurmountable obstacle to settling differences between two peoples who had already chosen war as the final solution. And, as always, there was the ever-present reality that any form of intervention automatically would help a slaveholding people achieve their goal.

Neutrality remained the only proper course – as long as that policy did not take on the expanded meaning advocated by Russell. The war had admittedly caused economic hardships for other nations as well, but the time had not yet come for those nations to intervene. The South had not proved itself on the battlefield, and the British must not become involved at a crucial juncture in the war in which such action could determine the outcome of that war – particularly if that outcome safeguarded slavery.

Russell convened the cabinet on November 11, and even though the ensuing discussions became heated and extended over two days, Lewis's memorandum had predetermined the final decision against intervention. No argument could surmount the obstacles set forth by Lewis. Indeed, Russell did not even make the attempt. He first informed his colleagues that the French ambassador in London had presented a proposal to invite England to join France and Russia in asking the two belligerents in America to accept a six-month armistice, combined with a suspension of the blockade for the same period. Russell explained that word had just arrived of Russia's refusal to participate in the plan, but, happily, it had declared a willingness informally to support any Anglo-French project that the Union found acceptable. Hoping to exploit the obvious loophole injected by the Russians, Russell tried to win cabinet support by arguing that the interventionist scheme would encourage the peace advocates in America. He also warned that British refusal to participate in the armistice project might encourage Russia to join the French and thereby leave England standing alone. He then opened the French proposal for discussion, and the cabinet, in Lewis's words, "proceeded to pick [it] to pieces." The primary concern was the likelihood of a war with the Union resulting from a stipulated six-month suspension of the blockade that was "so grossly unequal, so decidedly in favour of the South." The cabinet overwhelmingly voted against intervention.[22]

Although soundly defeated by his colleagues, Russell still did not give up hope of an involvement aimed at stopping the American war. His ensuing note to France declining the offer held out the prospect of a future intervention because of the horrendous amount of bloodshed and increased likelihood of a slave uprising. Four times in the course of the note – approved by the cabinet – the foreign secretary implied the possibility of a joint move "upon grounds and in terms," Gladstone wrote his wife, "which leave the matter very open for the future." Indeed, the British position remained unchanged: continued neutrality unless the South won a decisive battle and proved its viability as a nation. Russell lamented that there was "no ground at the present moment to hope that the Federal Government would accept the proposal suggested, and a refusal from Washington at present would prevent any speedy renewal of the offer." A change in American public opinion might someday warrant a tripartite "friendly counsel."[23]

Although the French had felt no moral compulsion to intervene in the American war over slavery, they nevertheless feared that, in addition to the war's negative effect on the cotton flow, an outbreak of slave revolts would further exacerbate this already terrible situation. Napoleon had had his eye on the Emancipation Proclamation soon to go into effect when he approved Drouyn's dispatch to England and Russia expressing concern over the "added fears of a servile war which would put the finishing touch on so many irreparable misfortunes." A trilateral intervention "would have fulfilled a duty to humanity more especially called for in a war where passions make so difficult any effort at direct negotiations between the two enemies." Such a peace overture was "a mission assigned to neutrals by international law" because the war had been "causing so much suffering and compromising such important interests throughout the whole world."[24]

Despite Napoleon's strong statements to Slidell just before Drouyn's note, French policy toward the American war remained uncertain, primarily because the emperor's views differed from those of his foreign minister. Even though the Palmerston ministry turned down the French proposal, Russell had encouraged the French to try again when he signified that present conditions could change. Additional encouragement came from the French press, which overwhelmingly praised Napoleon's unsuccessful attempt to mediate the American war in an effort to acquire cotton. Whereas both the emperor and his chief adviser on foreign affairs believed southern separatism irreversible and a prolonged war injurious to French economic interests, they could not agree on how to end the war. As demonstrated in his October 28 conversation with Slidell, Napoleon stood ready to use force in imposing an armistice that more than likely would have resulted in recognition of the South; Drouyn was more cautious, preferring an overture less challenging than even a mediation in an attempt to avert an uproar in the Union over recognition.[25]

But the Union's minister in Paris, William Dayton, realized that any outside intervention posed a threat to the Union and ingeniously put Drouyn in the uncomfortable position of appearing to oppose Lincoln's move against slavery. The mere offer of a peace proposal, Dayton told Drouyn on November 12, implied French reservations about the Union's war effort. And if the Lincoln administration rejected the offer, it would take on the image of a warmonger and facilitate the South's bid for recognition by peace-loving states. Most of all, the sheer vagueness of Drouyn's proposal promised trouble. No truce terms could satisfy both sides, Dayton declared; the North sought a restored Union and the South demanded independence. He then turned the conversation to slavery. The North had long been in a quandary about how to destroy slavery without violating the law. "Now, in the exercise of the war powers, the favorable opportunity has occurred." Then, in a clear jab at France and other nations considering an intervention that could help only the South, the Union minister cagily remarked, "I wonder if it would be worthy of the great nations of the world, in this nineteenth century, to step in and prevent it." To this scarcely veiled reproach, Drouyn testily shot back: "I am no friend of slavery!" While Drouyn fumed, Dayton unfolded a huge map on the desk between them and listed the slaveholding states along with the numbers of blacks still in bonds. Louisiana, Florida, and Texas, he asserted, had come to the United States after wars and large monetary expenditures. It would not "yield them up without a death struggle; France, I am sure, would not!"[26]

The heated meeting came to a close, but not without Drouyn's chastening experience at the hands of Dayton and his becoming even more determined to restrain Napoleon's actions regarding American affairs. Within the week, Drouyn sent Mercier a strikingly mild note instructing him only to stand ready for any opportunity to offer France's good offices in settling the conflict.[27]

In the meantime, the Lincoln administration became irate on learning of this series of events soon after the French note to Russell appeared in the London *Times* on November 13.[28] In an effort to demonstrate his fidelity to the French working classes, Napoleon had declared in the press on November 10 that he proposed joint intervention to England and Russia. Three days later, knowing unofficially that his plan had drawn no support in either London or St. Petersburg, he released to the press the full texts of the diplomatic notes concerning the attempt, hoping to throw all blame for failure onto England and Russia. Russell fell back on Palmerston's argument that intervention threatened to cause war with the Union. The public exposure of Napoleon's interventionist proposal should have proved comforting to the Lincoln administration: the move signified British opposition to intervention, now capitalized by a breakdown of the Anglo-French concert regarding American affairs.

But the entire business infuriated Seward, who severely chastised both Lyons and Mercier for their home governments' having the audacity to discuss America's domestic problems as a concern of their own. Seward's ire particularly focused on the French. Napoleon's "aggressive designs" were not surprising; French military forces remained in Mexico in clear contravention of the Union's wishes. "This Government will in all cases," Seward hotly wrote his minister in Paris, "seasonably warn foreign Powers of the injurious effect of any apprehended interference on their part." After the war, "the whole American people will for ever afterwards be asking who among the foreign nations were the most just and the most forbearing in their country in its hour of trial." Certainly England and France would not be on that list.[29]

More than a few contemporaries regarded this latest attempt at intervention as a mere setback and now insisted that Napoleon would take the lead, with or without British involvement. Even after news of the British cabinet's rebuff of the French plan had reached Paris, Slidell assured Mason that public opinion in England would force the Palmerston ministry into joining France in intervention. Should England still resist, Slidell continued, "my opinion is that France will act alone." Lindsay laid the blame on Russell. In a cunning display of mendacity, the southern sympathizer wrote Mason from Paris, Russell had led Napoleon to believe that his proposal would find acceptance in England, only to reject it in an attempt to drive a wedge between France and the Union. "I cannot believe," Lindsay wrote, "after what the Emperor said to me more than once and after what took place in regard to his despatch of March last that he would make any official proposal to England on the subject of American affairs unless he had a tacit understanding beforehand that it would be accepted." To recover prestige, Lindsay concluded, Napoleon would act alone. The Union's consul general in Paris, John Bigelow, agreed with this assessment. The emperor, Bigelow wrote Seward, "will compel us to make peace or fight him . . . before he takes any steps backward." Slidell sent the same message to Benjamin at the Confederate capital. Even if Napoleon did not expect approval of his proposal, Slidell wrote, Napoleon's "character and antecedents" would not allow him "to leave his work unfinished." He "will act alone."[30]

Although this crucial period in the ongoing interventionist crisis had passed, both the British leaders in this enterprise – Russell and Gladstone – and those in the White House remained alert to new possibilities. The British foreign secretary and the chancellor of the exchequer continued to watch for the opportune moment to put a halt to the steadily mounting carnage in America, whereas the president attempted to dismiss the external danger as a "mistaken desire to counsel in a case where all foreign counsel excites distrust." Indeed, Lincoln assured Congress in early December that even though "the condition of our relations with other nations is less gratifying than it has usually been at former periods, it is certainly more satisfactory than a nation so unhappily distracted as we are, might reasonably have apprehended." But Lincoln also knew that the outside danger remained constant because the European nations acted primarily out of self-interest. The American struggle, he explained, had come under close foreign scrutiny "less to its own merits, than to its supposed, and often exaggerated effects and consequences resulting to those nations themselves."[31]

Lincoln and Seward recognized that they had only narrowly escaped a perilous situation and that the mere announcement of emancipation had not killed the interest in intervention. The British cabinet had declined the French invitation this time.

What assurance existed that the matter might not surface again and arouse a different reaction?

The imminent effective date of the Emancipation Proclamation – January 1, 1863 – returned the president's attention to the relevance of slavery to the Union. Lincoln disappointed many contemporaries when, in his congressional message of December 1862, he again raised the possibility of compensated emancipation followed by colonization. Had not the Emancipation Proclamation taken care of slavery? And yet Lincoln's reluctance to drop the gradualist approach revealed his deep concern over the workability of even his restrained form of emancipation. Privately, he predicted that the proclamation "would not make a single negro free beyond our military reach." To clergymen visiting the White House, he related a case in which an attorney tried to convince a western court that a calf had five legs by referring to its tail as a leg. "But," Lincoln observed, "the decision of the judge was that *calling* the tail a leg, did not make it a leg, and the calf had but four legs after all." The lesson was clear, said the president: "Proclaiming slaves free did not make them free." The proclamation applied only to slaves in areas still in rebellion and therefore had no impact on either the border states or the Upper South. Further, it had legal standing only as a wartime measure. The sole remedy, he concluded, was a series of constitutional amendments that authorized federal compensation to any state abolishing slavery by January 1, 1900; assured freedom to all slaves who "enjoyed actual freedom by the chances of the war" but compensated those masters who had not participated in the rebellion; and approved federal funds for "colonizing free colored persons, with their own consent, at any place or places without the United States."[32]

But Lincoln realized that his call for compensated emancipation and colonization had aroused little support and that emancipation by itself, though burdened with hardships, afforded the only feasible route to resolving the problem. Once the proclamation went into effect, he feared, the blacks' transition from slavery to freedom would become infinitely more difficult because of a widespread racism that crossed sectional lines. White slave owners in the border states would doubtless question their loyalty to the administration, and any hope of attracting white support in the Deep South would sharply diminish. Moreover, the Republican party threatened to lean toward the Radicals, who called for an immediate end to slavery. Although the proclamation pointed the way to eventual abolition, it also raised intense racial animosities and assured a prolonged war.[33]

Lincoln thought that the republic had reached a milestone in history and told Congress that the question was not, "can *any* of us *imagine* better?" but "can we *all* do better?" History had challenged the present generation to save the Union. "The dogmas of the quiet past, are inadequate to the stormy present. . . . As our case is new, so we must think anew, and act anew." Thus did Lincoln encapsulate his central view toward contemporary events and history in general. He still called for gradual compensated emancipation and colonization, but he also recognized that the times had changed – so profoundly that the Union as it had existed at the outset of the war had become a relic that no longer bore relevance to the present and future. The time had come to move beyond present social, political, and economic strictures to institute a new way of life that more nearly matched the idealistic vision of the Declaration of Independence. "In *giving* freedom to the slave, we *assure* freedom to the *free*." The destruction of slavery, he had come to realize, constituted a vital step in saving the Union.[34]

CHAPTER SEVEN

The Emancipation Proclamation: An Act of Justice, Warranted by . . . Military Necessity

On the first day of January, in the year of our Lord one thousand eight hundred and sixty-three, all persons held as slaves within any State or designated part of a State, the people whereof shall then be in rebellion against the United States, shall be then, thenceforward, and forever free.
President Abraham Lincoln, January 1, 1863

The Emancipation Proclamation marked the defining moment in the Civil War because it promoted the president's central goal of preserving the Union and, after some more cause for alarm, further closed the door on foreign intervention. Critics who have attempted to denigrate the impact of that document by showing that it legally freed no slaves have failed to grasp the president's larger purpose. Those who blasted his words as hypocritical and amoral have missed their results. The proclamation became the heart and soul of a revolutionary action that soon established emancipation as an integral part of the administration's steady movement toward an even better Union.[1]

Only a constitutional amendment could end slavery legally and permanently, but Lincoln's pronounced assault on the institution set the revolution in motion that eventually assured the final demise of human bondage in the United States. "Great is the virtue of this Proclamation," the philosopher-poet Ralph Waldo Emerson keenly noted. "It works when men are sleeping, when the army goes into winter quarters, when generals are treacherous or imbecile." Once the Emancipation Proclamation went into effect on January 1, 1863, the momentum began to build for supporting black freedom as an essential part of the struggle for a more perfect Union, making it extremely difficult for either England or France to consider any form of intervention that might prolong the life of slavery. Emancipation would at long last take its place with liberty and, with the Union, become one and inseparable.[2]

Especially critical to the ultimate warm reception accorded the Emancipation Proclamation was the absence of slave insurrections. Both Seward in

Washington and Russell in London had feared such an outbreak, the former because of British meddling in American domestic affairs and the latter because of his belief that Lincoln had purposely instigated a black upheaval in an effort to destroy the South from within. Indeed, Seward's use of the threat of slave uprisings as a lever for keeping the British out of the war had actually increased the chances of their involvement. Despite these racial fears on both sides of the Atlantic, nothing of the sort transpired.[3]

By early 1863 the British government finally realized that the Lincoln administration had taken a move against slavery, and it dropped all official talk of intervention. Southern supporters outside governing circles, however, remained active well into 1864, establishing organizations such as the Manchester Southern Independence Association, the London Southern Independence Association, and the London Society to Promote the Cessation of Hostilities in America. But these efforts marked the last cries of a dying cause. Even Russell had grown weary of the struggle and conceded the lead to Mercier. To Lyons, the foreign secretary declared in mid-February 1863 that "till both parties are heartily tired and sick of the business, I see no use in talking of good offices." Southern supporters outside England's inner circle of government, however, bided their time, waiting for a change in the American war that might revive the chances of intervention. Even William Gregory, the first vocal supporter of intervention in 1861, gloomily told Mason that the House of Commons opposed any such action as "useless to the South" and a possible cause of war with the Union. "If I saw the slightest chance of a motion being received with any favour I would not let it go into other hands, but I find the most influential men of all Parties opposed to it."[4]

But, ironically, the Union remained in peril from the outside because, with the slavery issue seemingly settled by the Emancipation Proclamation, the French interventionists could now push their doctrine for economic and imperial reasons without alienating anyone over the moral issue of human bondage. It should come as no surprise that the strongest proponents of intervention following the crisis of fall 1862 remained the French – or, more specifically, Napoleon. For the first time in the American war, he could support the Confederacy without fear of political or moral repercussions at home over slavery. Slidell, Lindsay, Mason, and other Confederate supporters were perhaps correct in their exultation: the French emperor could act alone.

At this moment, another strong impetus to intervention developed when two staunch southern sympathizers in Parliament, William Lindsay and John Roebuck, took it upon themselves to promote an Anglo-French recognition of the Confederacy. Roebuck planned to introduce such a motion in Parliament, but before doing so he and Lindsay crossed the Channel to discuss the prospect with Napoleon. They found him intrigued by its possibilities. The threat of foreign intervention remained, fueled in Paris by self-interest and by apparent British official approval.

The danger of French intervention rose and fell throughout much of 1863 in proportion to the designs of Napoleon and the capacity of his advisers to control his provocative conduct. The emperor confronted major economic problems at home and still entertained high hopes in Mexico, both issues he hoped to resolve by extending recognition to the Confederacy. Not by coincidence did the *Documents diplomatiques* in Paris publish an anonymous pamphlet entitled *La France, le Mexique et les Etats-Confédérés*, which strongly criticized the American Union and called for southern independence as a major step in the regeneration of Spanish America. The pamphlet, many believed, had been Napoleon's inspiration. Sanford in Belgium had warned for some time of the emperor's imperial ambitions in the Western Hemisphere and declared that he had heard boastful talk almost *"ad nauseum* in Parisian Salons" about advancing the "Latin Race."[5]

Not all Confederate spokesmen lost sight of the fact that Napoleon, like the British, acted primarily out of self-interest and would support the South only if conditions proved conducive to his objectives. Ambrose Mann in Belgium warned Benjamin of Napoleon's reputation for perfidy. "I shall be agreeably disappointed if we do not, in after years, find France a more disagreeable neighbor on our Southern frontier than the United States." Napoleon's intentions in America, Mann declared, should cause "general uneasiness in the minds of our citizens." Benjamin had earlier become concerned about France's openly expressed interest in Texas and must have been receptive to Mann's warning that Napoleon "will remain anxious for us to believe that he is silently our friend. Mexico first, and then Mexico as she was previous to her dismemberment is the resolutely and faithfully cherished end at which he aims."[6] Thus Mann appeared to believe that as long as France needed cotton and the American war seemed to turn in the Confederacy's favor, Napoleon considered it necessary to recognize the South – even if such action came at the risk of conflict with the Union. But if either or both of these variables changed, the value of the South to Napoleon's machinations would drastically diminish.

As most contemporaries expected, the hundred days of grace between the announcement and the enactment of emancipation passed without the Confederacy revealing any disposition to end the fighting. Two major battles in December 1862 and early 1863 had failed to break the Confederate will – Fredericksburg in Virginia, which resulted in a devastating Union defeat, and Murfreesboro in Tennessee, which ended in a bloody stalemate. Lincoln's September warning had not persuaded southerners to give up their dream of an independent republic based on slavery. On schedule, the president signed the Emancipation Proclamation into effect on January 1, 1863.

From the announcement of the proclamation in September 1862 to its implementation a bare three months later, the call for emancipation drew a mixed reaction that highlighted the widespread failure to grasp the long-range meaning of the document. Some observers expressed disappointment with the lack of eloquence in the president's words and the absence of a moral denunciation of slavery. Count Adam Gurowski, the whimsical translator for the State Department, remarked that the proclamation was "written in the meanest and the most dry routine style; not a word to evoke a generous thrill, not a word reflecting the warm and lofty . . . feelings of . . . the people." Karl Marx, coauthor with Friedrich Engels of the *Communist Manifesto* in 1848 and now correspondent for a London newspaper, likewise lamented the terse tone of the emancipation document. And yet in making this criticism, he joined other detractors in curiously ignoring the universal power that pulsated in its closing words: "Upon this act, sincerely believed to be an act of justice, warranted by the Constitution, upon military necessity, I invoke the considerate judgment of mankind, and the gracious favor of Almighty God."[7]

In a strange twist of events, Marx's chastisement of Lincoln for presenting such a sterile and amoral document actually brought attention to its greatest strengths. He conceded that the "most formidable decrees which [the president] hurls at the enemy and which will never lose their historic significance, resemble – as their author intends them to – ordinary summons, sent by one lawyer to another." Skeptics erroneously denounced Lincoln for freeing the slaves only in areas where he had no jurisdiction; the truth is that he acted correctly in freeing them in regions that fell into his domain as commander in chief exercising his war powers. His action was legal and constitutional, as befitted his careful wording in this legal document. In a move that clearly exempted the border states, he declared in the preliminary announcement that his only purpose was to restore "the constitutional relation between the United States, and each of the states, and the people thereof."[8] Thus the primary motive behind the proclamation was to preserve the Union. The freedom sought by Lincoln rested on a solid legal base because he wove it into the protective cloth of the Constitution.

The basic thrust of the Emancipation Proclamation signified Lincoln's commitment to a new and improved Union that was revolutionary in spirit and impact. Slavery had been an integral part of a stained and troubled republic before the war; it must cease to exist afterward. Wartime exigencies had forced him from the more moderate stance of antislavery into the direction of abolition. How could slavery exist anywhere in the United States once a plea for universal freedom had undergirded an "act of justice"? And yet he had to tread softly in light of the deep strains of racism that ran throughout the nation. Slavery had sullied the vision that the Founding Fathers had crafted for the new American republic. Was the Constitution capable of resolving certain racial problems between white and black in the aftermath of slavery?

For the moment, however, the president had to meet the immediate needs of the war by increasing the size of the Union army and bolstering the morale of his people. The Union's defeat at Fredericksburg had combined with the mutual slaughter at Murfreesboro to force the administration to institute a military draft aimed at filling a rapidly depleting manpower supply. As national conscription went into effect on March 3, 1863, Lincoln fervently defended the war effort as a necessary prelude of suffering to a rebirth of hope. At the end of the month, on March 30, he issued a presidential proclamation that established a national day of fasting and afforded him an opportunity to appeal to higher principles in explaining the burden of such a horrible war. "Insomuch as we know that, by His divine law, nations like individuals are subjected to punishments and chastisements in this world, may we not justly fear that the awful calamity of civil war, which now desolates the land, may be but a punishment, inflicted upon us, for our presumptuous sins, to the needful end of our national reformation as a whole People?"[9] Lincoln realized that the American people must first feel the deepest despair before they could accept revolutionary change.

The hundred days between the preliminary Emancipation Proclamation and its formal enactment was a critical period for several reasons. Not only did the European powers gain the time to reflect on the measure's ramifications for slavery, but the South had the opportunity to ponder the consequences of emancipation and perhaps reconsider the wisdom of secession. In the interim, Lincoln still shied away from abolition in declaring himself receptive to any resolution of the slavery issue that fitted the principles of the Republican party; but he knew that this outcome was highly unlikely because southerners had already chosen war over any arrangement aimed at stopping the expansion of slavery. How could they now accept an emancipation program that pointed ultimately to abolition? Recent Confederate successes in the field meant that resistance would not abate, sending a message that no southern state would resume its place in the Union on Lincoln's terms. Nor did he expect – and perhaps even want – them to do so before emancipation took effect. No longer could he seek a mere restoration of the prewar Union. Numerous constitutional and legal issues remained unsettled that, when resolved, would necessarily change the nature of that Union. "The central idea of secession," Lincoln had declared in his Inaugural Address, "is the essence of anarchy." The order and stability so vital to liberty, he unmistakably implied, derived only from a strong Union. And the danger was more than domestic in consequence: the internal chaos spawned by secession encouraged predator nations to intervene.[10]

Secession had emerged as even more explosive when it became entangled with slavery and the problems of race. Only a thorough defeat of the South could squelch that doctrine and take slavery with it. Emancipation provided a vital element to achieving victory, for it would doubtless build an irrepressible force that culminated in the destruction of slavery everywhere – including in the border states. Lincoln continued to deny that he acted on moral grounds, thereby maintaining his distance from the abolitionists. The only justification for the proclamation, he insisted to Chase, was as a military measure; it had to have a constitutional or legal base. "If I take the step must I not do so, without the argument of military necessity, and so, without any argument, except the one that I think the measure politically expedient, and morally right? Would I not thus give up all footing upon constitution or law?" In truth, however, Lincoln's emphasis on military necessity had become inseparable from emancipation, tying antislavery to the war effort and eventually convincing the British and the French that the proclamation had declared an all-out war on the South that could end only with its unconditional surrender and the death of slavery.[11]

The most immediate and revolutionary aspect of the president's new emancipation policy was the impetus it gave to black enlistments into the Union army. The specter of ex-slaves killing their former white masters embodied the South's worst fear and further shook its edifice from within. Lincoln had at first expressed little interest in putting uniforms on runaway slaves, but he soon gave the measure his strong endorsement. In March 1863 he wrote Andrew Johnson, military governor of Union-occupied Tennessee: "The bare sight of fifty thousand armed, and drilled black soldiers on the banks of the Mississippi, would end the rebellion at once. And who doubts that we can present that sight, if we but take hold in earnest?" By the autumn of that same year, 50,000 blacks were in uniform, stirring Lincoln to declare publicly that "the emancipation policy, and the use of colored troops, constitute the heaviest blow yet dealt to the rebellion." Before the war ended, some 180,000 black soldiers had worn Union blue (along with 29,000 more in its navy, or a fourth of its rolls), which had a doubly devastating impact on the South by their making up nearly 12 percent of the North's fighting force in 1865 while depleting much of the Confederacy's labor supply.[12] The presence of black Union soldiers contributed to the difficulty that any so-called progressive European nation might have in extending recognition to the slaveholding South.

But an effective foreign policy can be only as strong as its domestic base, and emancipation at first showed little signs of arousing widespread popular favor even among Union loyalists. And yet if the Emancipation Proclamation initially drew little support from the Union army, that support slowly grew as increasing numbers of soldiers realized how the measure benefited the Union for both realistic and idealistic reasons. Those soldiers who opposed slavery at the outset of the war rejoiced at the president's move. A Pennsylvania private asserted that after the proclamation "foreign nations will now have to come out flat-footed and take sides; they dare not go with the South, for slavery, and consequently they will all be ranged on our side." An Iowa volunteer called slavery a "blighting curse" that had brought on "this wicked rebellion," which, according to two Union officers from Ohio and Massachusetts, only the war and emancipation could destroy. The battle was not simply "between North & South," a captain from Pennsylvania proudly asserted, "but a contest between human rights and human liberty on one side and eternal bondage on the other." A New York private echoed that sentiment: "Thank God . . . the contest is now between Slavery & freedom, & every honest man knows what he is fighting for." "The God of battle will be with us," an Iowa sergeant declared, "now that we are fighting for *Liberty* and Union and not Union and Slavery." An escaped slave from North Carolina serving in the Union navy wrote in his diary that we fought "for the holiest of all causes, Liberty and Union."[13]

Other Union soldiers, however, did not assess the proclamation on idealistic grounds. Many did not grasp the crucial relationship between Union and emancipation and felt betrayed by Lincoln for seemingly changing the war's objective from Union to abolition. Under no circumstances would they fight for black freedom. And yet most officers and soldiers supported emancipation, if not for moral reasons, then in the belief that the measure encouraged blacks to fight for the North and thereby dealt a mortal blow to the South. A private from Ohio bitterly denounced the proclamation until he came to believe that slavery had caused the war and that only emancipation would end it. An Illinois soldier asserted that God was on the Union's side now that Lincoln had taken a stand against slavery.[14] If the military establishment mirrors the feelings of society as a whole, the evolutionary change in attitude among the soldiers toward emancipation suggested that Lincoln was in a safe political position in adopting an antislavery policy that profoundly affected both domestic and foreign affairs.

The greatest immediate impact of the Emancipation Proclamation lay in the inescapable moral tone it imposed on the war and the resultant uplifting influence this sense of crusade had on the soldiers' thinking. Union troops gradually identified with an objective that rested on the personal liberties guaranteed by the Constitution. Both before and after the Emancipation Proclamation, numerous letters and diaries attested to widespread concern over the future of the republic and how it would advance the universal principles of right over wrong. "I believe that slavery (the worst of all curses) was the sole cause of this Rebellion," an Iowa private declared in January 1862, "and untill this cause is removed and slavery abolished, the rebellion will continue to exist." A Minnesota private agreed. "The war will never end," he declared in December 1861, "until we end slavery." "Every soldier [knows] he [is] fighting not only for his own liberty," recorded a captain from New York in 1864, "but [even] more for the liberty of the human race for all time to come." Later that same year, a wounded Union private expressed the popular belief "that the present struggle will do more to establish and maintain a republican form of government than the Revolutionary war." A typhoid-ridden private in his hospital bed wrote his missionary parents in Hawaii that he wanted to rejoin his fighting comrades to help "the holy cause for which I am fighting. . . . I say, better let us all *die* fighting for *union* and *liberty*, than to yield one inch to these 'rebel slave mongers,' as Charles Sumner justly calls them." As the war ground on, increasing numbers of soldiers in blue considered emancipation critical to preserving the Union.[15]

Confederate soldiers, however, insisted that they fought for liberty and against slavery – the latter defined as northern enslavement in much the same way that the colonists resisted the mother country in the Revolution. "Sooner than submit to Northern Slavery, I prefer death," asserted an officer to his wife in a statement strikingly similar to numerous other letters of the period. "I am engaged in the glorious cause of liberty and justice," an Alabama corporal declared in his diary – "fighting for the rights of man – fighting for all that we of the South hold dear." The inability of either side to compromise becomes clear: as liberty and Union were one and inseparable to Lincoln, so were liberty and slavery one and inseparable to the South.[16]

Thus in an ironic twist of logic, southerners saw no discrepancy between fighting both for liberty and for slavery. Southerners believed in their right as human beings to own slaves. "Our cause," declared one volunteer in a statement affirmed by many others, "is the sacred one of Liberty, and God is on our side." A South Carolinian asserted that "a stand must be made for African slavery or it is forever lost." Slavery, another soldier declared, created "a bond of union" in the Confederacy that was "stronger than any which holds the north together." With slavery condoned, southerners claimed primary responsibility for upholding the experiment in republicanism set out in 1776, which now faced its greatest threat from tyrants in the North. The purpose of emancipation, or so southern spokesmen professed to believe, was not to stamp out an institution that Lincoln and his supporters hypocritically denounced as immoral; rather, the proclamation provided further proof of an effort by power-seeking northerners to control the southern states. "Sooner than submit to Northern slavery, I prefer death," asserted a slaveholding officer from South Carolina. The entering wedge was emancipation, which initially aimed at removing a chief cornerstone of southern civilization and ultimately sought the demise of self-rule.[17]

Only in this double-edged manner can one understand the spirited reaction to emancipation by both North and South, along with each antagonist's intense feelings toward foreign intervention. Each side thought itself the chief protector of American republicanism against its transgressors. Both proclaimed support for self-government and liberty in combating tyranny – whether it emanated from a government (the South's view) or from a white slaveholding class (the North's view). Above and below the Mason-Dixon Line, the most fervent supporters of the war thought the republic in its deepest peril and sought to preserve that sacred heritage by claiming to be the true progenitors of the American Revolution. From the Union's perspective, emancipation defined northerners as patriots, while identifying southerners as traitors. The southern vantage point was profoundly different: emancipation constituted the first step in a long-range program aimed at squelching states' rights, thereby defining northerners as traitors and southerners as patriots.

Emancipation had more than a domestic impact; its enactment led to a change in British attitude toward the proclamation which suggested that the Lincoln administration had finally achieved its central objective in foreign affairs of keeping England out of the war. During the hundred-day period following the president's preliminary announcement of emancipation, British indignation steadily gave way to the realization that the Confederacy's defeat necessarily meant the ultimate death of slavery. Argyll had joined Cobden and John Bright in Parliament in making this argument on the eve of emancipation but had failed to convert many of their colleagues. In early October 1862, however, the *Morning Star* of London provided evidence of a slight swing away from Lincoln's critics. The Emancipation Proclamation, according to the paper, marked "a gigantic stride in the paths of Christian and civilized progress . . . the great fact of the war – the turning point in the history of the American Commonwealth – an act only second in courage and probable results to the Declaration of Independence."[18]

Workers north of London, too, had identified early with the president's bold move, encouraged by the presence of nearly forty African Americans who actively promoted the Union cause by lecturing and holding meetings

The great Union and emancipation meeting held at Exeter Hall, London. One of many demonstrations in England for the American Union and emancipation. Harper's Weekly, *March 14, 1863.*

that highlighted the movement against slavery. In huge and highly charged rallies beginning in December 1862, British labor groups cheered Lincoln for promoting the rights of people everywhere with his proclamation. "The great body of the aristocracy and the commercial classes," Adams observed, "are anxious to see the United States go to pieces," whereas "the middle and lower class sympathise with us." They "see in the convulsion in America an era in the history of the world, out of which must come in the end a general recognition of the right of mankind to the produce of the labor and the pursuit of happiness." Adams received countless letters, petitions, and resolutions from working groups (and emancipation societies) in support of the president, all suggesting that his strategy had succeeded. From January through March 1863, the public outcry in favor of Lincoln's emancipation policy had virtually muted the southern sympathizers in England.[19]

The president had played no small role in molding British workers' opinion toward the war. American funds, kept hidden from public knowledge, helped to finance the huge meetings in England that praised the Union and exalted emancipation. Charles Sumner had a large coterie of friends overseas and worked closely with the president in drafting missives to British workers that expressed concern over unemployment and attributed the cotton shortage to "the actions of our disloyal citizens" rather than to the Union blockade. Self-interest, Lincoln wrote the workers in Manchester, could easily have directed them into supporting the Confederacy; instead, they had made their decision on high principles and cast their lot with the Union. British workers had gone through a "severe trial" in resisting Confederate efforts to attract their support for an unjust cause. Their stand provided "an instance of sublime Christian heroism which has not been surpassed in any age or in any country." To workers in London, Lincoln called the war a test of "whether a government, established on the principles of human freedom, can be maintained against an effort to build one upon the exclusive foundation of human bondage."[20]

To seal the matter, Lincoln prepared a resolution in April to share with British supporters of the Union, which demonstrated again his awareness of the intricate relationship between domestic and foreign affairs. The basic objective of the rebels, the president asserted, was "to maintain, enlarge, and perpetuate human slavery." The Union therefore resolved that "no such embryo State [the Confederacy] should ever be recognized by, or admitted into, the family of christian and civilized nations."[21]

Although in the short run Antietam and emancipation had given added momentum to the interventionist crisis, in the long run these two epoch-making events forced British leaders to shy away from such a dangerous move. Lincoln, it was clear, sensed the British mood and drew more public attention to emancipation than to the Union by focusing on the need to preserve freedom. His shift in emphasis, however, did not signal a change in his wartime objective. Lincoln's central goal remained the preservation of the Union, though now it was to undergo major improvement by emancipation. That this fundamental truth still eluded the British was of no consequence. Most important was their fear of war with the Union, made even more unpalatable by the thought of becoming the virtual ally of a slaveholding people. The noninterventionists in England had taken an almost insurmountable lead in their battle against involvement in the American war and now banded together with the workers in hailing the Emancipation Proclamation as the death knell of slavery.

This is not to say that Lincoln's September 1862 pronouncement against slavery had erected an insurmountable moral obstacle to British intervention. Such idealistic sentiment did not determine the November decision of the cabinet. The key consideration was British concern over antagonizing the Union. Indeed, neither side on the intervention issue in England highlighted opposition to slavery as its chief motive. But even though slavery did not emerge as a moral consideration in the heated British deliberations over intervention, it nonetheless remained a dominant force in the background by threatening to stir up a major political fallout from any ministerial decision supporting the slaveholding South and by encouraging the ever-present fear of slave uprisings caused by emancipation. Still, the British decision against intervention turned more on the chances of war with the Union than on any issue, moral or otherwise, relating to slavery. Both camps on the interventionist issue united in a sincere quest for peace that rested on a shifting mixture of idealistic and realistic factors; they differed over how to achieve this goal.

Ironically, slavery played a more important role in British views toward American events *after* the interventionist struggle had come to a close. Just as the Emancipation Proclamation had initially spurred an already strong British interest in intervention, so did it become a palliative in the period after the cabinet's negative decision by making it easier for the defeated interventionists to save face following their overwhelming defeat. Who could argue against a program destined to bring slavery to an end, even if its primary purpose was military rather than moral? In the meantime, fears of slave revolts and race war sharply dissipated when no violence erupted during the hundred days preceding actual emancipation.[22]

Unlike the British, however, the French maintained a strong interest in intervention, but not because of their views toward slavery. The South's proslavery stand had acted as a major restraint on Napoleon, repeatedly reminding him of his people's opposition to the peculiar institution and causing him to wait for the British lead. But by the end of 1862 domestic economic problems had threatened to erupt in violence and thereby provided a major motivation for the Paris government's decision to take the initiative in an intervention aimed at ending the American war and acquiring southern cotton.[23]

Throughout 1863 the French government, along with several individuals on both sides of the ocean, tried to interest the Lincoln administration in a peace proposal. The South's mid-December 1862 victory at Fredericksburg had bolstered its confidence and encouraged its interest in an armistice. Russell had led Drouyn to believe that, even though declining Napoleon's November proposal, the Palmerston ministry had left the way open for a change in policy if the Union became amenable to intervention. The French became convinced that they had to act in view of their steadily deteriorating economy. Chances for peace had seemingly increased because of the growing dissatisfaction in the Union over its army's failures.[24]

Consequently, in January 1863 and only coincidentally with the implementation of the Emancipation Proclamation, Drouyn and other cabinet members formulated what they thought was a harmless approach aimed at ending the war. Approved by the emperor a month earlier, the proposal went to Washington on January 9. At first glance, it seemed innocuous in simply asking representatives of North and South to meet on neutral ground to discuss a resolution of their differences. Slidell immediately opposed the suggestion, failing to realize that such a meeting would enhance the South's status and fearing instead that the move might result in some solution other than recognition of the Confederacy. Despite his opposition to the idea, his superiors in Richmond agreed to meet with northern representatives *if* the Lincoln administration first announced its willingness to attend. To ease the Union's apprehensions over intervention, Drouyn wrote the Lincoln administration that "if it believes it must reject all foreign intervention, could it not honorably accept the thought of direct conversations with the authority which represents the Southern States?" Such talks, he emphatically added, did not signify a cease-fire.[25]

Dayton was perplexed about France's motives and arranged to see Drouyn. "This is not an effort to mediate," the foreign minister declared. "It proposes no interference of any kind by a foreign power in the American affairs, and it does not even suggest a cessation of hostilities pending the negotiation." Dayton remained unconvinced. "Such a suggestion from abroad, however well-intentioned, is unnecessary." When the time was right for peace talks, he told Drouyn, delegates would be appointed by the two belligerents and not at the behest of an outside power. Americans distrusted Napoleon in light of his recent armistice proposal and his ongoing war in Mexico. "They do not like to see His Majesty's hand always in their business." Drouyn denied any permanent intentions in Mexico and, in fact, called that war "a great annoyance to us." The French "want to leave Mexico as soon as we have obtained satisfaction there." Such a statement may have seemed a promise of restraint to Drouyn, but it could not have eased Dayton's fears of Napoleon's well-known absence of self-control. Dayton remained doubtful of the emperor's capacity to discipline his own imperial instincts. Drouyn sensed this skepticism and, as the meeting drew to a close, made a vain attempt to allay Dayton's concerns: "As to the implication that we have any purpose or design on the United States in connection with our proceedings in Mexico, it is madness to think of it."[26]

If Drouyn was telling the truth, and no reason exists to think otherwise, the situation once again highlights the danger of Napoleon's diplomacy. He had not given up on his desire to satisfy French interests in the New World, and this latest interventionist proposal seems to have fitted nicely with an attempt to assure his people in economic distress that he was doing everything in his power to stop the war. Dayton thought so. After reading a series of newspaper articles that often served as the voice of the government, he concluded that French leaders wanted to convince their constituency "that they are making every possible effort to relieve" the nation's economic hardships.

Napoleon had chosen this time to make a proposal that, even if it failed to arouse Union interest, would prove to his unemployed people at home that he was still trying to stop the war.[27] The problem, however, lay in his well-deserved reputation for imprudent actions designed to promote his own acquisitive interests. His involvement in Mexico provided ample evidence of his lack of restraint when the moment proved opportune. Whether Napoleon *intended* to intervene in American affairs was not the issue; to leave the *impression* of an imminent intervention constituted an ill-advised piece of risky diplomacy – particularly when the Union had clearly warned of war against meddlesome nations.

In Napoleon's annual address to the legislature in mid-January 1863, he asserted that "the Empire would be flourishing if the war in America had not exhausted one of the most fruitful of our industries." He had earlier acted out of "sincere sympathy" in inviting other powers to help him end the war, but they had not "thought themselves yet able to join me" and "I have been obliged to postpone to a more propitious season the mediation which had for its object the checking of bloodshed and the prevention of the devastation of a country whose future should not be indifferent to us." The legislature accepted Napoleon's moving argument. It expressed regret that mediation had failed to resolve the problems that southern secession had caused for French trade with America and for the workers in French industrial areas.[28]

While Drouyn's proposal was under consideration, the Peace Democrats (derisively called "Copperheads") actually *invited* outside involvement in the war by proposing a French mediation. Taking advantage of their favorable showing in the fall 1862 congressional elections, they launched a bitter assault on the president that focused on his alleged dictatorial policies, the public's war weariness, and, in particular, the West's resentment for the Emancipation Proclamation that, they feared, would lead to a labor glut resulting from a massive migration of black freedmen from the South. Ohio representative Clement L. Vallandigham in mid-January 1863 denounced Lincoln's war effort as an "utter, disastrous, and most bloody failure," called his government "one of the worst despotisms on earth," and invited the intervention of a friendly outside nation to secure "an informal, practical recognition" of the South. The question of reunion was irrelevant, he insisted. "The will is yet wanting in both sections. . . . Stop fighting. Make an armistice – no formal treaty."[29]

Even Horace Greeley, editor of the *New York Tribune* and arch-supporter of the Union and emancipation, so desperately wanted the war to end that he now seemed willing to sacrifice the administration's advances against slavery by promoting a mediation plan that likewise rested on the French taking the lead. By early 1863 he considered the war hopeless and publicly exhorted fellow northerners to restore "the Union as it was." In making this plea through an editorial, he ignored the implementation of the Emancipation Proclamation (which he had staunchly supported) and called for a mediation "in a conciliatory spirit" by either England, France, or Switzerland. Greeley advocated the argument of an adventurous mining entrepreneur, William Cornell Jewett, who had recently returned from Paris with a mediation proposal from the ever-persistent emperor. According to its terms, the French government would host a meeting of the two American antagonists at some neutral location, where they would discuss the alternatives of either reunion or a division of the United States into two nations. Excited about the prospects for peace, Greeley had rushed to Washington to seek the assistance of the pro-separatist French minister, Henri Mercier, and to discuss the idea with the president, Sumner, and other leading Republicans. Mercier soon talked with Sumner and several western Republican congressmen, while Jewett unveiled the plan to the new Democratic governor of New York, Horatio Seymour, and the influential editor of the *New York Herald*, James G. Bennett.[30]

Greeley's most ambitious and unrealistic step in this venture was his attempt to reconfigure Napoleon III into a peace-loving humanitarian by writing laudatory articles in the *New York Tribune* that actually contradicted the editor's own earlier writings. Whereas the emperor formerly was the Union's "one substantial enemy in Europe" and the "destroyer of the French republic," he suddenly emerged as the most ardent republican in all Europe and "more popular with his people than any other European monarch." Conveniently forgetting his previous staunch opposition to mediation, Greeley now blasted the *Herald* for criticizing Napoleon, praised the emperor's armistice proposal as "an excellent act," and asserted that anyone opposed to foreign mediation was providing "aid and comfort to the Rebels."[31]

Not surprisingly, Greeley's mediation proposal aroused no interest in Washington. No one could believe in the miraculous metamorphosis of the treacherous French emperor into a selfless proponent of peace. The president predictably refused to make a commitment to what still was, despite the careful language, a foreign intervention. How could he approve an outside involvement that threatened to reverse all the progress he had made in thwarting a move so injurious to American integrity? How could anyone expect him to revert to a prewar Union that condoned slavery and therefore undermined his long fight for the Emancipation Proclamation? Sumner urged Greeley to be patient – that the Union armies would ultimately prevail. But Greeley refused to change course. He informed Henry J. Raymond, editor of the *New York Times*, of the mediation plan. Asked the president's response to the proposal, Greeley confidently replied to Raymond: "You'll see . . . that I'll drive Lincoln into it."[32]

By now, the Lincoln administration saw the danger developing and decided to put a halt to the Greeley proposal. Seward likewise appealed to Raymond (his longtime friend), who published an article accusing Greeley of breaking the law by engaging in "personal negotiations" with Mercier aimed at foreign mediation. If so, the *Times* declared, Napoleon must immediately recall Mercier. Indeed, Greeley had violated the long-standing Logan Act, which forbade private U.S. citizens from negotiating with foreign governments. At one point Lincoln tried to shuck off the intervention proposal with his characteristic humor. Greeley's peace effort, the president jested, had probably done more "to aid in the successful prosecution of the war than he could have done in any other way." His plea had, "on the principles of antagonism, made the opposition urge on the war." But just as he joked about Greeley's plan, so did he regard it as a serious challenge to the Union.[33]

Lincoln refused to condone any arrangement that awarded governmental status to the Confederacy. Under no conditions would he accept a breakup of the Union; too much blood had been shed to change direction and concede that the supreme sacrifice was all in vain. He approved Seward's recommendation to reject the proposal. Nearly all American newspapers supported the White House decision, including the usually critical *New York Herald*, which, in a remarkable change of form, praised Seward's "masterly diplomacy" and Lincoln's "sagacity, consistency and steadiness of purpose" in keeping him in the administration when so many Americans demanded his ouster.[34]

The most bitter irony was that the prolongation of the American war, seemingly encouraged by the Emancipation Proclamation, had fostered a climate in Paris actually conducive to intervention for reasons peculiar to that nation's own interests. As in England, slavery did not emerge as a moral determinant in French deliberations, although both governments recognized the domestic political danger in adopting any policy advantageous to the slaveholding South. They also knew that in light of the latest French mediation attempt, the Lincoln administration still maintained a stronger position than did the Copperheads and rigidly maintained its opposition to intervention as a severe strike against the Union's integrity.[35] Intervention could take place only when economic problems stemming from the continued fighting threatened the internal stability of either England or France (or both). Palmerston did not believe that time imminent; Napoleon did.

Especially noteworthy about the continued French interest in intervention following the Emancipation Proclamation was the absence of concern about slavery. Lincoln had eliminated slavery from the interventionist controversy, but in doing so, he had encouraged the French to consider the wisdom of intervention on other grounds. Economic and political objectives guided Napoleon's policy, making it more amenable to southern interests and hence extremely dangerous to the Union. No longer was the question of slavery woven into French thoughts to complicate the other issues. Lincoln had removed this emotional issue from the highly charged question of outside involvement in American domestic affairs, but he had been incorrect in believing that emancipation would kill any further thoughts of foreign intervention. In the immediate sense, the Emancipation Proclamation actually encouraged the interventionists in both England and France to continue their efforts; in the long run, the document convinced the British to drop the cause of intervention, whereas it invited the French (i.e., Napoleon) to use intervention as a lever for satisfying economic and imperial interests in Mexico that, in turn, posed still another crisis for the Union.

CHAPTER EIGHT

The Final Impact of Slavery on Intervention: Napoleon's Grand Design for the Americas

The abolishment of slavery [marked a] great moral victory . . . [for] the country and the whole world.

President Abraham Lincoln, February 1, 1865

The Emancipation Proclamation had had the unforeseen effect of encouraging France to explore other interventionist schemes. With slavery no longer an international concern, Napoleon felt free from any moral or political restraints to pursue his imperialist aims in the Western Hemisphere. His interest in the Mexican venture and in alleviating economic problems at home remained constant into the summer of 1863 as he became involved in a highly unconventional attempt by two members of the British House of Commons to extend recognition to the Confederacy. William Lindsay and John Roebuck, strong supporters of the Confederacy, arrived in Paris to discuss the matter unofficially with the emperor during the late spring of that year and returned home fully confident that he was prepared to intervene in the war.

Further, the chances for British compliance with such an intervention seemed to experience a revival in light of recent public criticism of the ministry for appearing to capitulate to the Union on two important maritime cases. A Union cruiser in February 1863 had captured the British steamship *Peterhoff* near the Danish West Indies for carrying contraband to the Confederacy via Matamoros, Mexico. That same year, coming in the midst of a long and heated controversy over the building in Liverpool of a commerce raider christened the *Alabama*, British authorities relented to Union pressure and seized the warship *Alexandra*, then also under construction for the Confederacy. Battlefield events then combined with British frustration over the war to renew talk of intervention. Lee's army had just routed the Union forces at Chancellorsville, perhaps finally convincing the Lincoln administration that it could not win.

Thus the ironies continued to appear in Civil War diplomacy. The imminent demise of slavery in the United States had provided the final consideration in moving the Palmerston ministry farther from intervention because such an action would place England in the camp of the slaveholding Confederacy. But even while the Emancipation Proclamation was finally contributing to the Union's central objective of keeping the British out of the war, it had unleashed the adventurous Napoleon III to launch one of the greatest potential threats not only to the United States but to the entire Western Hemisphere: the establishment of a monarchy in Mexico as the first step toward ending republicanism throughout the Americas.

Napoleon considered the year 1863 a particularly auspicious time for intervention in the American war. He was about to solidify his position in Mexico by placing a new ruler on the throne, and the French National Assembly had eased the threat of domestic disturbances by appropriating relief funds for distressed workers. He also thought that good relations with the Confederacy would provide a further guarantee to French interests in Mexico along with access to southern cotton. Indeed, he even had a solution to the slavery issue that, he thought, added respectability to his scheme. Consequently, he made clear his heightened interest in intervention.

The Confederacy likewise felt intervention so vital that it supported Napoleon's ventures in Mexico, even though his imperialist actions in the past offered a clear indication of his long-range motives and thereby posed a threat to southern interests in the region, both during the war and afterward. The Central American isthmus linked the commerce of the Atlantic with that of the Pacific and was therefore integral to the cotton traffic. It provided places of refuge for blockade runners and offered the possibility of seizing Union gold that passed from California to Asia via either the Panama Railroad or the water passages through Nicaragua. How could the Confederacy be sure that a French presence in Mexico would not block southern expansion both west and south while also posing a threat to Texas and Louisiana? Was a French alliance worth such a risk?[1]

Napoleon also revealed a sense of desperation by regarding the unauthorized arrival of Lindsay and Roebuck as a sign of growing support in England for an intervention that might pressure the Palmerston ministry into action. The political reputations of these two maverick politicians, especially that of Roebuck, should have provided ample warning against the chances of their plan receiving a favorable reception in England. Not only were they operating outside regular diplomatic channels, but Roebuck, in particular, had established a record of cavalierly ignoring the political process at home. Hotze thought that Roebuck held "a singularly isolated position" in the

Commons, always opposing the government, no matter who sat in power. A leading social critic and writer, Thomas Carlyle, put it succinctly when he described Roebuck as "an acrid, barren, sandy character, dissonant speaking dogmatist, with a singular exasperation: restlessness as of diseased vanity written over his face when you came near it." Henry Adams, son of the Union minister in England, declared Roebuck "rather more than three-quarters mad." But Napoleon's pervasive interest in intervention put him out of touch with reality, leading him to believe that this extraordinary visit by two parliamentary members signified widespread popular dissatisfaction with Palmerston's refusal to act. Perhaps, at last, the moment had arrived for a joint Anglo-French action aimed at ending the American war.[2]

The ongoing uprising in Poland against harsh Russian policies, combined with the expanding French military involvement in Mexico, provided the international setting for this new interventionist attempt. France and England differed in policy toward this European crisis that had erupted in February 1863. On several occasions, Russell urged Drouyn to take forceful action on behalf of the suffering Polish people; but then England itself refused to furnish support. The French populace sympathized with the rebels and urged Napoleon to help them. But such a move would have placed him in direct conflict with Russia and Prussia, the former still searching for revenge after the Crimean War, the latter wanting him toppled so badly that it would go to war with France in 1870 and emerge triumphant. Russia and Prussia, simply put, wanted to destroy Poland. When Napoleon followed his familiar American policy of deferring to England's lead, his government came under heavy criticism both at home and abroad. Pressured into action, Drouyn pushed for a diplomatic settlement built on Russia's easing its treatment of the Poles, but one also aimed at preserving the balance of power on the Continent by restricting the Russians' growing influence in eastern and central Europe. As Henry Sanford in Belgium cynically assured the White House, at the bottom of nearly all international turmoil was that "perpetual nightmare, the Emperor."[3]

Napoleon, in fact, sought to exploit the Polish problem by tying it to his goals in Mexico. In exchange for European concessions from Austria that bolstered the French defense and promoted their acquisition of parts of Denmark, Italy, and Poland, Napoleon made an astounding move: he privately agreed to sponsor Habsburg Archduke Ferdinand Maximilian of Austria as emperor of Mexico.[4]

In the spring of 1863, the Union became increasingly suspicious over the French military presence in Mexico. Most ominous, Drouyn no longer offered assurances against interference with the government. Now, in a subtle rewording of the pledge, he declared that France had no interest in controlling the Mexican government and wanted only to leave that country after resolving the debt problem. When Dayton expressed concern that the French might "leave a puppet behind," Drouyn coyly replied, "No, the strings would be too long to work." Dayton warned the White House against trusting the French. "Truthfulness is not, as you know, an element in French diplomacy or manners. No man but a Frenchman," he told Seward, "would ever have thought of Talleyrand's famous *bon mot* that the object of language is to conceal thought."[5]

Napoleon's interventionist efforts regarding the American war were inseparable from his interventionist designs in Mexico. French forces occupied Mexico City in June, encouraging him to implement a secret plan developed earlier during the January mediation project. Both the Union and the Confederacy were correct in their fears. Napoleon sought to block both northern and southern expansion southward by devising a North American balance of power based on a "hyphenated confederation" patterned after that of Germany. The confederation would consist of the North, the South, the West, and Mexico, each holding the same degree of power. Dismemberment of the United States would result, leaving a French-dominated Mexico to expand northward to incorporate Texas and perhaps even the former colony of Louisiana.[6]

Ambitious plans no doubt, but Napoleon suffered from many maladies, not the least of them unbounded ambition. Benjamin in Richmond suspected the French emperor of wanting Texas in an effort to thwart southern expansion, and seasoned diplomat and scholar Edward Everett, now an adviser in the State Department, warned the Lincoln administration that Napoleon sought to resurrect a scheme first tried in 1844: the creation of a hemispheric state consisting of Texas and all Mexican territories west of Texas to the ocean, including California and perhaps even Louisiana. Even though Drouyn's chief concern was the Polish situation, Napoleon's remained the expedition in Mexico, which, in turn, underlay his interests in the American war.[7]

Napoleon meanwhile received several reports from America that, even though contradictory, further encouraged him to believe that the time had arrived to mediate an end to the war. The French consul Shouchard in Boston asserted that New Englanders had become increasingly disenchanted with Washington's leaders and doubted the Union's capacity to defeat the South. Any kind of peace seemed preferable to continued war. Indeed, according to Shouchard in March, some Americans in the North spoke of secession. The next month, however, he totally confused the situation by reporting the opposite. War sentiment, he insisted, had revived as a result of the Peace Democrats' failure to draw a favorable response to their calls for talks. From the South came equally conflicting accounts of the blockade's effectiveness. At one point Benjamin proclaimed that the Union had lifted its blockade of Charleston, Galveston, and Sabine Pass; but less than a month afterward, the French consul in Richmond, Alfred Paul, assured Paris that the Confederacy was undergoing an "economic and commercial crisis" of "alarming proportions." Regardless of the truth on either matter, the chief consideration remained the unending war. With its verdict still in doubt, the chances of a foreign involvement had increased.[8]

In early April Napoleon expressed his mounting frustrations over England's American policy to Lord Cowley, its ambassador in Paris. "If Great Britain would recognize the Confederacy," the emperor asserted, "cotton would become available." France remained in economic trouble and, by implication, would likewise extend recognition. Lindsay chose this propitious moment to take the lead. He had approached Napoleon a year earlier about extending recognition and, failing in that effort, continued to work with Mason in trying to persuade the British to take the first step. In May, Lindsay invited Mason to his country residence near London to meet with him and Roebuck to discuss the possibility of securing a parliamentary resolution intended to force the Palmerston ministry into recognizing the South. Soon afterward Roebuck informed the House of Commons that he would submit a motion calling for recognition.[9]

Meanwhile, in Paris, Slidell sought another meeting with Napoleon to argue again for recognition. England, the Confederate commissioner thought as he prepared for that meeting, would never grant recognition because it preferred a long American war as a means of weakening a major commercial competitor; France, he realized, found it in its best interests to have two American republics capable of challenging England's maritime position. Indeed, Slidell concluded that French intervention was more important than the danger it posed in threatening Confederate expansion south and perhaps even costing it control over Texas and Louisiana. His most immediate objective was French assistance against the Union. Without foreign intervention, the war would grind on endlessly, wrecking the South (as well as the North) while helping only the British. Concerns over French territorial interests were secondary to the overarching need for their intervention in the war. Once established as a nation, the South could deal with Napoleon's expansionist schemes. Slidell's priority was clear: France must recognize the Confederacy.[10]

At this point Roebuck's strategy began to mesh with Slidell's persistence. In early June the Palmerston ministry made known its opposition to Roebuck's motion and, in a well-managed distortion of the truth, sought to undermine the interventionists by claiming that Napoleon, too, had recently decided against recognition. Roebuck suspected chicanery and invited Lindsay to accompany him on a special visit to the emperor. Mason meanwhile informed Slidell of the Roebuck-Lindsay mission.[11]

On June 18 Slidell met with Napoleon, only to learn that even though the emperor still favored recognition, he once again had reverted to his original position of preferring to act only after the British took the initial step. Intervention, Napoleon explained, probably meant war with the Union, and he could not take that chance without the support of the British fleet. Apparently others in the Paris government had convinced him of the danger of war induced by a foreign intervention. Whatever the reason for Napoleon's consistently changing position, Slidell was both stunned and exasperated. Recovering only slightly from this surprising setback, Slidell assured Napoleon that all powers on the Continent would join him in recognizing the South and argued out of desperation that the Spanish fleet was sufficient alone to yield success. Napoleon, Slidell somehow thought, would act with Spain if that government proved willing. France's refusal to lead undermined the commissioner's hope for some broader form of concerted European action.[12]

But the Spanish fleet was not the Royal Navy, and Slidell had no choice but to appeal once more for a joint Anglo-French intervention, this time bolstering his plea with a reference to the motion planned by Roebuck. Was Palmerston correct, Slidell asked Napoleon, in asserting that he no longer supported recognition? His interest in recognition remained as strong as ever, was Napoleon's quick response, and Slidell could speak with imperial authorization in assuring Roebuck of this fact. Informed of the Roebuck-Lindsay mission, Napoleon declared that he "would be pleased to converse with them on the subject of Mr. Roebuck's motion." In fact, he cagily observed, "I think that I can do something better – make a direct proposition to England for joint recognition. This will effectually prevent Lord Palmerston from misrepresenting my position and wishes on the American Question." Slidell was elated over Napoleon's continued determination to recognize the South and assured Mason that the emperor's decision to approach England with a joint proposal was "by far the most significant thing that the Emperor has said, either to me or to the others." It now made little difference what England did.[13]

Slidell's relief over Napoleon's apparent willingness to assume the lead lasted for only the brief time it took to realize that the emperor had inserted a qualification that again constituted a retreat onto safe diplomatic and political ground. "I shall bring the question before the cabinet meeting today," Napoleon asserted; "and if it should be decided not to make the proposition now, I shall let you know in a day or two . . . what to say to Mr. Roebuck."[14]

Not surprisingly, the cabinet reacted negatively to Napoleon's proposed joint Anglo-French recognition, but it nonetheless left the door open for an intervention by declaring the timing "inopportune." In addition, the French ministers "did agree to deny, as far as the British cabinet is concerned, the reports which falsely attribute to us sentiments and a policy less favorable for the South." Several times, they wished to convey to London, their government had proposed an intervention that the Palmerston ministry declined. The French position had not changed – "quite the contrary." Napoleon could inform the British that the French "shall be charmed to follow them up, and if they have any overtures to make to us in a like spirit to that which has inspired ours, we shall receive them with quite as much eagerness as pleasure." Within a week – on June 23 – Drouyn notified London of the French ministry's sustained interest in intervention.[15]

In the meantime Slidell approached Drouyn about the possibility of recognition and came away from a meeting on June 21 convinced that the French had refused to act because they distrusted the British. If the French took the initiative, Drouyn explained, the British would doubtless refuse and reveal the proposal to the Lincoln administration. Even if hostilities did not follow, the Union would be infuriated with the French and demand their departure from Mexico. The resulting confrontation might "compel the Emperor to declare war, a contingency which he desires to avoid and which England would aid in creating."[16]

Such an explanation, of course, was too simple, but Slidell sought a simple solution and took Drouyn's words at face value. French cabinet advisers certainly distrusted the British, but they also had other considerations. The French position in Mexico was tenuous at best and recognition might drive the Union into helping that beleaguered country and tip the delicate balance in its favor. Napoleon had taken advantage of the American war to intervene in Mexico. He had calculated that Confederate success would weaken the United States and do more to solidify the French stay than would a Union triumph and the predictable postwar realignment of North and South against the intruder in the hemisphere. Only out of self-interest did the French government exhibit any concern for southern recognition. But now that the French faced the likelihood of conflict with the Union – and without British naval support – they found themselves in the position of having to avert any action favorable to the South at least in part because of the Mexican intervention. Ironically, the French had encouraged the South by becoming involved in Mexico, only now to refuse to help the South because of their involvement in Mexico.[17] Slidell failed to grasp the many nuances of French recognition of the Confederacy and mistakenly believed that only Anglo-French rivalry stood in the way.

The following day, June 22, Napoleon met with Roebuck and Lindsay at Fontainebleau to discuss the possibility of a joint intervention. Although the accounts of this meeting are contradictory, evidence suggests that, again ironically, all renditions are accurate insofar as each recorder interpreted the conversation. Lindsay claimed that Napoleon refused to send another formal request to London (as he had done the previous fall of 1862) because, he declared, "that application was immediately transmitted to the United States Government, and I cannot help feeling the object of that proceeding was to create bad blood between me and the United States." Instead, he had instructed his ambassador in London, Baron Gros, to inquire whether the British shared his views on recognition and, in Napoleon's words, to "suggest any mode for proceeding for the recognition of the Southern States which I so desire." At the end of the meeting, according to Lindsay, the emperor authorized his British visitors to inform Parliament of his continued interest in recognition.[18]

Napoleon's account differs markedly from Lindsay's. The emperor denied having said anything that Roebuck could construe as even a conditional assurance of recognition and insisted that he had not authorized Roebuck to make such an announcement in the House of Commons. Indeed, he expressed astonishment that Roebuck could have discerned a promise to cooperate with the British in recognizing the Confederacy. In view of England's rejection of his November 1862 call for recognition, Napoleon had decided against submitting another proposal without a prior assurance of acceptance. He nonetheless instructed the French ambassador in London to inform the Palmerston ministry that if it recommended recognition as a means for stopping the war, the French government would be party to the proposal. To Drouyn, Napoleon reluctantly admitted that he should not have been so straightforward with Roebuck and Lindsay. Since the conversation took place in English, the emperor noted, his visitors probably misunderstood the exchange. "It was enough," Napoleon explained, "to make [Roebuck] understand that I could not address to the English Government an official proposition to recognize the South without first knowing its intentions, because the official act of the month of last October was not accepted, and it came back to me (which however I doubted) that the English Government boasted in Washington for having refused our offer of mediation."[19]

Dayton had already become suspicious of French involvement with Roebuck, but an article in the pro-government *La France* solidified his worst fears by suggesting new clandestine activities by Napoleon that aimed at recognizing the Confederacy. According to the writer, a pattern of conspiracy had developed: the emperor had talked privately with Slidell; the Confederacy praised the recent French military victories in Mexico; Roebuck and Lindsay had had a secret conference with Napoleon; and Spain, the writer erroneously declared, had entered negotiations with the Confederacy over the possibility of granting recognition in exchange for assurances regarding Cuba. "The cause of the Confederates," the writer continued, "gains new sympathies every day and their heroic resistance on the one side, on the other the impotence of the armies of the North prove that there is in them a people strongly organized, worthy in fact to be admitted among the independent states." Dayton detected a dangerous shift in the French position and rushed to Drouyn's office to ask "if any change in the policy of this government towards us is contemplated? Whether anything is in agitation?"[20]

Drouyn at first tried to allay Dayton's concern by alleging that he knew of no change in policy, but this staid response failed to calm the agitated Union minister. Drouyn asserted that "I have not seen the emperor for some days and I cannot therefore answer for what he has said and done. I am satisfied that he has seen Mr. Slidell here in Paris, and I believe that he has seen Misters Roebuck and Lindsay in Fontainebleau, but of this I cannot speak with certainty." Dayton remained unconvinced and conveyed his anxiety to Seward. Slidell, Dayton feared, had tried to win Napoleon's favor by approving his actions in Mexico. The emperor's history of intrigue especially disturbed Dayton. Indeed, Drouyn's assurances seemed unreliable because of the "self-judging, governing and reticent power behind him." The danger of recognition remained real, Dayton warned Washington, because "these foreign governments do not believe it would be a just cause for war, nor that it would lead to it."[21]

Dayton had accurately gauged the French threat, regardless of whether Drouyn was in complicity with the emperor. Indeed, if Drouyn's reaction was sincere, the situation emerged as even more dangerous to the Union because Napoleon would be moving solely on his own. His interest in the New World was no secret, and it required no great leap in logic to see a connection between the emperor's support for recognition of the South and his ongoing enterprise in Mexico. French recognition of the Confederacy combined with Confederate support for the French expedition in Mexico seemed a feasible arrangement for the South's assuring its independence. Dayton had brought focus to another great challenge to the Union – indeed, to the entire United States.

There the issue rested until, on June 30, Roebuck stood before Parliament to introduce his motion for recognition of the Confederacy and where he quickly demonstrated that only his hatred for the Union outdid his zeal for the South. Confidently, even arrogantly, Roebuck lashed out at his peers and the ministry itself for withholding a right to nationhood that the Confederacy had earned by its very existence over the past two years. Indeed, the

Union capital in Washington stood in danger of invasion. England, he insisted, could only profit from the demise of the United States. Recognition would bring cotton to Lancashire and permanently divide and weaken a major maritime competitor and Britain's most hated enemy. In leering fashion, Roebuck reminisced that, until the present war in America, that proud nation

> bestrode the narrow world
> Like a colossus; and we petty men
> Walked under her huge legs and peeped about
> To find ourselves dishonoured graves.[22]

As expected, Roebuck called for joint Anglo-French recognition of the South; but he then shocked his peers by revealing the contents of his private and unofficial conversation with Napoleon regarding the issue. "France is the only power we have to consider," Roebuck asserted, "and France and England acknowledging the South, there would be an end of the war." He then detailed every item of his and Lindsay's conversation with Napoleon, including the emperor's charge that the Palmerston ministry had betrayed him by revealing his interventionist proposals to the Union.[23]

Despite Roebuck's bluster over his alleged assurances from Napoleon, he had no chance for success. His revelations were so clearly unauthorized that even fellow southern sympathizers were embarrassed and quickly distanced themselves from him. Russell had already denied receiving any French overture, making it difficult for Roebuck to convince his colleagues that Napoleon stood poised to act once the British had taken the lead. Roebuck insisted that the emperor had held back only because he feared that the Palmerston ministry would again break a confidence by sharing any private proposal with the Lincoln administration. But he remained willing to follow the British lead. According to Roebuck, the emperor had instructed his ambassador in London to assure the British cabinet of his willingness to act.[24]

Members of Parliament reacted with angry disbelief that Roebuck had risked endangering relations with both the Union and France over such an explosive issue. Why would Napoleon ignore normal diplomatic channels and entrust such an important matter to an unofficial representative of the British government? If England went to war with the Union, Bright and Forster warned, it would lose wheat as well as cotton. Even Gladstone, one of the most persistent advocates of intervention, finally admitted that the war must exact its own verdict. Neither England nor France, he declared, could claim impartial neutrality because both nations had great economic and political interests at stake. They stood powerless while the embittered relations between blacks and whites in the South, along with the suspension of constitutional liberties in the North, threatened to discredit republicanism itself. The Union, Gladstone insisted, would resent any outside interference. England could not, indeed should not, take any action regarding the American war.[25]

The outcome was predictable: Russell and his supporters in the Commons roundly defeated the motion. According to Hotze, the entire country laughed at Napoleon's antics as "a sort of farce in which Mr. Roebuck acted a broadly comic part." Mason was inconsolable. Having been with Slidell when Napoleon affirmed his interest in recognition, the Confederate minister believed Roebuck's account and called the whole episode a "mess" that resulted largely from Napoleon's duplicity. Roebuck tried again in early July to amass support for his motion, but in less than two weeks, on July 13, he formally announced its withdrawal.[26]

Dayton was so alarmed by the events in Parliament that he again sought out Drouyn for an explanation. Roebuck should not have divulged the contents of "an unofficial and private conversation," the foreign minister lamented. Surely the emperor had not authorized such a disclosure. Moreover, Drouyn emphatically assured Dayton, "in point of fact *no official communication of any kind* has recently passed on this subject between France and England." Doubtless the emperor informed Roebuck that his stand on recognition remained constant and that he would act only with England. But these statements were unofficial and did not suggest a formal proposal.[27]

Drouyn had spoken truthfully, but he did not assuage Dayton's anxieties. Too many actions by the emperor seemed uncontrolled and potentially dangerous. Both Drouyn and Russell had carefully denied any *official* overtures, strongly suggesting that Roebuck had told the truth and that a proposal outside regular channels had passed hands. Dayton insisted that even if the French government sent no official note to London, the possibility that Napoleon had authorized Roebuck to reveal the contents of a private discussion took on a "'quasi-official character and is therefore the fair subject of inquiry and explanation." Drouyn admitted that if Roebuck had had authorization, his revelation would have been tantamount to an official communication. But again, Drouyn denied that the emperor had granted Roebuck this authority. As the tense meeting came to a close, Drouyn declared his willingness to consider any British recommendation that sought to end the American war. "It certainly will not be brought to a close by a recognition of the South," Dayton tersely replied. Then, after a pause, he added an ominous warning: "Such an act might extend and enlarge the war by drawing other nations into it." At this particular juncture in the war, Dayton knew that Lee's forces had already engaged the Union armies at Gettysburg but had not learned the results. "If Lee should take Pennsylvania and drive the government out of Washington," Dayton darkly warned Seward after the meeting, "the effect would be immediate recognition from all of the European States."[28]

The Lincoln administration remained concerned about the possibility of recognition, and even though it expected the recent good news from the Gettysburg battle front to ease Dayton's apprehensions, that news had not yet arrived in Europe. The Union's forces had pushed Lee back into Virginia after his defeat at Gettysburg and, in the meantime, had captured the Mississippi River fortress at Vicksburg. But just as Dayton was not yet aware of these positive developments at home, Seward feared that this same lack of knowledge in Paris and London might further encourage an intervention designed to terminate a war that still appeared to be endless. Roebuck's speech, combined with French calls for mediation in late 1862 and early 1863, suggested the imminence of some interventionist effort before news of the Union's victories at Gettysburg and Vicksburg reached Europe.

So serious did Seward regard this time interlude that he sent two letters of instructions to Dayton by special messenger. "Any new demonstration of activity by [Napoleon] prejudicial to the unity of the American people," Seward declared, would be "necessarily regarded as unfriendly." If the emperor took any "official act" that threatened the Union's sovereignty, Seward wrote Dayton: "*your functions will be suspended.*" If he went any farther than to propose either unilateral or joint intervention, the Lincoln administration would not "be induced to depart from the course [it had] so distinctly indicated in regard to foreign intervention." At no other time during the Civil War did the Union come so close to severing diplomatic relations with France.[29]

Seward meanwhile sought clarification on French policy toward the war. He had learned from a reputable source that the French ambassador in London had informed the Palmerston ministry of Napoleon's growing interest in recognizing the Confederacy. Indeed, the emperor intended again to ask England to extend recognition, and if refused, he planned to take the step alone. In Washington, however, Mercier knew that Confederate forces had lost at Gettysburg and Vicksburg and, in a striking change of form, wanted his home government to inform the South's leaders that recognition was no longer possible. Buoyed by the exhilarating impact of the battles at home and wishing to buy some time for the news to have a sobering effect on the interventionists in Paris, Seward instructed Dayton to secure from Drouyn "an explanation of the policy of the Emperor in regard to the Civil War existing in the United States." When Napoleon's proposed Anglo-French recognition of the Confederacy appeared in the *Moniteur*, Seward wrote a blunt note to Dayton that he read to Drouyn: "The President," Seward declared, "has read this announcement with surprise and regret." In a studied reference to the danger of war, Seward asserted that "the Emperor has not been left by this government in doubt upon the point that a recognition of the insurgents would be regarded by it as an unfriendly proceeding."[30]

Before Dayton received his new instructions, however, the immediate crisis with France had passed. News had arrived in Europe of the Union's victories at Gettysburg and Vicksburg, and Spain had maintained its refusal to extend recognition without England and France taking the initiative. But Drouyn, too, reflected the new attitude born of the Union's good fortunes and now assured Dayton that no communication whatsoever had gone to London. "Baron Gros never made such remarks; he never said anything of the kind either officially or unofficially, public or private." Regarding the emperor's policy toward the American war, Drouyn declared that "he has none; he awaits events." Dayton felt confident that Drouyn had grasped the significance of the Union's recent battlefield successes and planned no intervention. Indeed, the French consul in the Confederate capital at Richmond wrote home that even though the South cheered French progress in Mexico, "these are the dreams of an unhappy people" whose illusions had been shattered.[31]

Napoleon had characteristically distorted the truth in this long controversy over intervention. In the fall of 1862 he led Slidell to believe that French armed force would accompany an intervention. The very wording in the emperor's armistice proposal to England suggested the same resort to force – or so the Palmerston ministry interpreted the note in rejecting a measure that virtually assured conflict with the Union. When the French proposal became public, Napoleon predictably retreated into the safe position of agreeing to recognize the South only if the British took the first step. Then, to Slidell again, Napoleon maintained that he could not make another proposal of recognition because, he claimed, the British had maliciously divulged this information to the Union in an effort to hurt its relations with France. This charge, one must note, carried no weight since the French press (speaking for the government) carried the details of the proposal *before* it appeared in British newspapers.[32] Now, in writing to Drouyn, Napoleon expressed doubt that the British had tried to damage French relations with the Union. Finally, he denied any ill feelings against the United States, and yet he was willing to intervene in a manner that could help only the South while hurting only the North. He realized that any form of intervention would alienate the Union. "I did not want to put myself in the wrong," he remarked to Drouyn, "without being sure of the help of England." Napoleon admitted to his own indiscretion: "I spoke to the misters Lindsay and Roebuck openly; I should have been more diplomatic."[33]

More controversy exists over the alleged instruction to the French ambassador in London. On June 22, just after Napoleon's meeting with Roebuck and Lindsay, he wrote Drouyn: "I wonder whether Baron Gros may not be instructed to state unofficially to Lord Palmerston that I am resolved on recognizing the independence of the Southern Provinces. We could not be compromised by such a declaration," the emperor insisted, "and it might determine the British Government to take a step." The following day, Drouyn telegraphed Gros: "See Lord Palmerston and in the course of conversation give him to understand that the Emperor has no objection to recogniz[ing] the independence of the South." The problem is clear: Napoleon's directive was strikingly different from Drouyn's telegram. Whereas Napoleon declared that he was "resolved on recognizing" the South's independence, Drouyn wrote that the emperor had "no objection to recogniz[ing]" its independence. The difference is monumental and could have been no accident. Gros later admitted to Drouyn that in talking with Russell in London, "it is very likely that I incidentally said to him that having no official communication to make to him on the recognition of the Southern States, I was personally persuaded that the emperor was disposed to recognize them."[34]

Drouyn had toned down Napoleon's instruction because it guaranteed additional trouble with the Union. The foreign minister had been alarmed by Napoleon's unorthodox diplomacy regarding Roebuck and Lindsay as well as by his general willingness to venture into another country's affairs without considering the consequences. The emperor's interventionist proposal of the previous fall had been a call for an armistice that he outwardly professed to be innocent because it carried no promise of recognition. But as Slidell knew at the time and others correctly suspected, Napoleon stood prepared to use force if the British joined the project.

The emperor's proposal had predictably caused a furor in Washington because, no matter how well meaning the stated motive, any form of intervention constituted an involvement in American affairs that gave credence to secession and benefited only the Confederacy. Drouyn saw the danger. He knew that any interventionist proposal, regardless of its source or terms, assured another fiery reaction by the Lincoln administration that, combined with the earlier outburst, could prove far more dangerous. Consequently, Drouyn acted on his own (but in harmony with the cabinet's wish to act only after the British took the lead) in toning down the emperor's original instruction without violating his directive. Further, Gros may have been hazy in recalling the substance of his meeting with Russell, but the thrust of his message clearly leaned heavily toward that contained in Drouyn's instruction. Napoleon upheld his promises to Slidell, Roebuck, and Lindsay, and Drouyn acted in accordance with his colleagues in avoiding a provocative policy conducive to war.[35] Everyone had behaved honorably – at least according to each individual's personal code of honor.

Despite all the careful political maneuvering, the Roebuck-Lindsay affair further disrupted international relations. As Drouyn had feared, Napoleon's unofficial flirtation in diplomacy left him vulnerable to varying interpretations that suited each party's objectives. The emperor's vague and noncommittal language, related in what he admitted was his own inferior English, offered great potential for misunderstanding. Yet he felt comfortable enough in his position to make no effort to keep his statements private. When asked by Roebuck and Lindsay if they could repeat his words in London on possible French recognition of the Confederacy, he immediately approved: "They are no secret."[36] Best intentions notwithstanding, the Anglo-French concert suffered a severe blow from Napoleon's armistice proposal that clouded all issues afterward: he had entrusted a proposal for intervention with Russell, who had seemingly turned against the French by revealing its contents to Adams in London. Not only did the resulting ill feelings between France and England continually plague any possible joint involvement in American affairs, but they interfered with Anglo-French cooperation regarding the Polish crisis. In the meantime, Napoleon's continued interest in intervention, combined with his ongoing involvement in Mexico, encouraged the Confederacy and infuriated the Union, pointing the way to raw Franco-American relations in the period following the American war.

Shortly after the Roebuck debacle, the Confederate government in Richmond ordered Mason to leave England. Several considerations had forced this decision, but the primary causes were the Palmerston ministry's refusal either to extend recognition or to challenge the Union blockade as illegal. Consequently, in early August 1863 President Davis finally came to the realization that the British government had no intention of recognizing the Confederacy and instructed Mason to leave London. When Mason informed Russell of his imminent departure, the foreign secretary crisply replied that his reasons for refusing to accept the emissary on an official basis were "still in force" and that it was "not necessary to repeat them." Mason soon received a new appointment as commissioner in Europe after joining Slidell in Paris.[37]

Particularly galling to the South in this already embittered atmosphere was the continued presence of foreign consuls in Richmond whose exequaturs, or permits to carry out their duties, came from the government in Washington. Their presence had been tolerable until early in 1862, when Britain (and France and Spain) had not granted recognition of the Confederacy in what the *Charleston Courier* called "a reasonable time." More than a year later, in March 1863, the *Montgomery Advertiser* denounced the consuls' behavior as "offensive" to the Confederacy and called for their dismissal. "If we wish to gain the countenance of the world," claimed the *Advertiser*, "we must act as becomes an independent nation, and self-respect and independence alike cry out against the further toleration of officers, whose only titles to official recognition are derived from the Government at Washington." Confederate legislators in Richmond joined the growing popular demand that the consuls either depart the South or signify their recognition of the Confederacy by requesting exequaturs from its government.[38]

The continued presence of the foreign consuls provided an added irritant to the growing southern animosity toward England. The failed joint mediation attempt of November 1862, combined with Russell's cold treatment of Mason, had convinced southerners that, in a view ironically similar to that of the Union, Britain's central objective was to wreck the United States before seeking a peace. The *Richmond Whig* complained that British leaders "'secretly rejoice in the fact that the late United States are arrayed against each other in bitter strife, literally threatening the complete annihilation of each other, thus relieving her of a powerful rival, of whom she lived in continual dread." This "cold-blooded selfishness of the British ministry towards the Confederate States [is] fast engendering toward that country a bitterness of feeling in this country that cannot fail to tell upon future relations." The *Richmond Enquirer* bitterly remarked that, despite victory after victory, "neither England nor France pretends to have any knowledge of our existence." When, in April 1863, the full text of Russell's rejection of Mason's pleas relating to recognition and the blockade appeared in the press, the public reacted with anger. The *Enquirer* called Britain "(next to the Yankees) our worse and deadliest enemy." Exasperated by the turn of events, Benjamin forbade the British consuls to remain inside the Confederacy.[39]

Even as the Confederacy broke with England, it carefully reiterated its welcome to French representatives. King Cotton diplomacy had collapsed, leaving the Confederacy's languishing hopes to lie only with the French. Richmond's leaders knew that Napoleon still had his hands in Mexico and that, sooner or later, he had to work with them in solidifying his control over the country. Perhaps the quid pro quo for southern assistance could be French recognition of the Confederacy – or so its spokesmen claimed as they continued to operate under the illusion of expecting to achieve independence simply by surviving the war rather than winning it.

Napoleon's efforts in Mexico, however, had woven a tangled web that threatened to undo everything he had already accomplished. Even though he knew that the success of his Mexican venture depended primarily on southern independence, he also realized that he could not take any interventionist action without risking war with the Union. Seward's repeated warnings against any permanent French aggrandizement in Mexico weighed heavily on Napoleon's mind as he pondered the South's renewed quest for recognition in exchange for its supporting his ambitions in Mexico.[40]

When in the fall of 1863 it became clear that the rumors were true – that Napoleon intended to install Austrian Archduke Maximilian as emperor of Mexico – the Confederacy decided to use the new monarch as a means for securing either an alliance with France or an intervention on behalf of the South. For either of these guarantees, the South would assure no interference in Napoleon's plans in Mexico.[41]

Not surprisingly, the fall of 1863 marked the beginning of a serious deterioration in relations between the Union and Mexico. Concern over Maximilian's possible ascension to the throne had reached the Union, leading Dayton in late August to make inquiries of Drouyn. France did not seek either Mexican territory or governmental interference, the foreign minister replied. Napoleon intended to withdraw his forces from Mexico as soon as the two countries had resolved the debt problem and stability returned to the torn nation. The Lincoln administration remained dubious about these assurances and dispatched troops to Texas under the command of Gen. Nathaniel Banks. Perhaps their presence would dissuade Napoleon from expanding his Mexican interests northward.[42]

Drouyn was either telling less than the truth or he was incredibly naive about the emperor's intentions in Mexico. The previous November (1862) *Le Moniteur* published an article providing the nation with Napoleon's justification for the involvement in Mexico. In January 1863 the *Documents diplomatiques* elaborated on the emperor's objectives. A short time afterward, an anonymous pamphlet, entitled *La France, le Mexique et les Etats-Confédérés*, appeared in Paris and strongly advocated southern independence while explaining how to regenerate Spanish America. In late September Americans learned the details when the *New York Times* published a translation of that pamphlet. Within two weeks, another translation appeared as a separate tract in New York City. William Henry Hurlbert, internationally known journalist and editorial writer for the *New York Times* before becoming editor of the *New York World*, prefaced his translation with the claim that the pamphlet deserved "world-wide notoriety as embodying the first coherent view which has been made public of the designs of Napoleon III in the New World." Doubtless inspired by Napoleon, the pamphlet was seemingly the work of his longtime adviser Michel Chevalier.[43]

An entrepreneur of some note, Chevalier had long expressed the ideas found in this pamphlet and had a great influence on Napoleon's policies. In the 1830s Chevalier had visited the United States to study the nation's transportation system in canals and railroads. He also traveled throughout the country and into Mexico and Cuba. His succeeding publications, both in book and pamphlet form, highlighted the vast economic potential of the New World. He rose to power in late 1851, when he cast his lot with Louis Napoleon in his successful coup d'état and became a high-ranking official of the Second Empire and a fervent socialist. Particularly important in establishing the ties between Chevalier and Napoleon was their interest in constructing a canal between the Atlantic and Pacific Oceans. In addition, Chevalier published two articles in the *Revue des deux mondes* in 1862 that detailed the poor conditions in Mexico. Then, in 1863, he published a two-volume work on the French expedition in Mexico, *Le Mexique, ancien et moderne*, which focused on the need to curb U.S. expansion, stabilize Spanish America by installing monarchical rule, and encourage the immigration of talented Europeans to assure reform in Mexico. The Old World would gain raw materials and new markets, establishing Napoleon as the chief guarantor of the Latin peoples in both Europe and the New World. Thus armed with material goods and a heightened international stature, he would block "the absorption of Southern America by Northern America" and thereby prevent "the degradation of the Latin race on the other side of the ocean." French recognition of the Confederacy would assure its independence along with a grand future for Mexico and neighboring states. The anonymous pamphlet that appeared in 1863 contained the same ideas.[44]

The two reproductions of the pamphlet provided Americans with Napoleon's so-called Grand Design for the Americas. To protect the Latin peoples in the New World, according to the writer, France intended to work closely with the Confederate States. Recognition of the South would be "the consequence of our intervention." In an idea aimed at appealing to aristocrats and military spokesmen at home, Napoleon declared his intention to "regenerate" French commerce in the Atlantic as a spur to the nation's industry. The grain and gold of Mexico would provide the substance of major growth, but only after a new government had rid the country of its anarchy born of chronically poor leadership. The French Empire had refined socialism and eradicated anarchy at home. "This it is that the empire is to do in Mexico, and this it cannot do securely and properly until the Confederate States have been recognized."[45]

The most striking feature of Napoleon's Grand Design was his dismissal of slavery as a consideration in extending recognition to the Confederacy. America's ill treatment of the Indians, according to the pamphlet in a derisive tone, provided an indication of how little significance it attached to human rights and hence to the abolition of slavery. Were the Union to win the war, "the poor negroes would find their way to liberty a path of thorns." The first European nation to recognize the Confederacy would gain "a right to obtain much more for the negro than the Federals could secure for him through their 'Union by victory.'" Only during peacetime could abolition come; "an alliance with the South will effect that great social renovation." Thus the pamphlet concluded, "Slavery cannot possibly be made a serious argument against the recognition of the South." French influence would achieve "the gradual emancipation of the slaves without making slavery a ground for refusing recognition." Once the French had removed the "phantom of slavery" from the issue of intervention, other powers – including the British, Spanish (with interests in Havana), and Austrians (with Maximilian on the Mexican throne) – would likewise recognize the Confederacy. The Union, facing the French navy, would have no choice but to give up the war.[46]

Confederate independence was essential to Napoleon's vision of establishing a commercial and strategic stronghold in the Western Hemisphere. The new southern nation would ally with the French in safeguarding Mexico from the Union. Mexico would become a progressive, industrialized nation that provided raw materials for factories along with the rich land and bountiful silver mines of the north. During the fall of 1863, Napoleon directed his commander in chief of the French military expedition in Mexico to "get confidential information about the mines of Sonora and advise me if it would be possible to occupy that state." The area sought by the emperor included nearly the entire northern half of Mexico, a vast land stretching from the Rio Grande River at the Gulf of Mexico to the bottom of Baja California at the Pacific Ocean two thousand miles away. To erect this great buffer state against the North, France intended to encourage the entry of immigrants from the United States and Europe by granting generous tax reductions on mining. Under the facade of safeguarding the new miners, France would guarantee Mexico's security against the United States and thereby avoid the charge of imperialism.[47]

Maximilian, too, became a captive of his own illusions. He came from a long line of Austrian emperors and, not surprisingly, supported Napoleon's call for monarchy as a remedy for the debasing influence of republicanism. From the American legation in Austria came a virtual lamentation over a certain tragedy. The historian John Lothrop Motley asserted in dazed wonderment that the archduke "firmly believes . . . he is going forth . . . to establish an American empire, and that it is his divine mission to destroy the dragon of democracy."[48]

The Lincoln administration did not know all the details of Napoleon's plan for the Americas, but it had heard enough to expect trouble. The president and his secretary of state had no choice during the Civil War but to clarify their opposition to France's presence in Mexico and wait until the end of the fighting to act. The Union's recent victories at Gettysburg and Vicksburg had emboldened Seward to sharpen the tone of his words to France. The Union, he declared, had relied on French assurances against imperial designs in Mexico and had therefore maintained neutrality during the Franco-Mexican conflict. But the Union's position had become increasingly difficult to maintain in view of Maximilian's imminent arrival. The French must settle their affairs in that country "upon the basis of the unity and independence of Mexico" and then leave. The American people sought to avoid "any cause of alienation" with France, but they would not shrink from the challenge once their war with the Confederacy had ended in victory. "The sensibility I have described," wrote Seward to Dayton in a follow-up dispatch, "increases with every day's increasing of the decline of the insurrection in the United States."[49]

The fall of 1863 offered the only propitious time for Napoleon either to recognize the Confederacy and arrange an alliance or to abandon these thoughts and pull out of Mexico. Without southern independence, he had no hope for success in Mexico. Maximilian had won the throne after a so-called plebiscite, but he must have been somewhat sobered when almost everyone agreed that the election did not reflect popular sentiment in Mexico. So uncertain was Maximilian of his new position that he initiated overtures to the Confederate government before it had had a chance to announce an official reaction. In a November conversation with a friend of President Davis's who had received an invitation to the palace of Miramar outside Trieste, Maximilian expressed great support for the South's independence and sought to build some sort of familial tie by declaring its precarious position analogous to that of Mexico. England and France, Maximilian thought, should recognize the Confederacy before he took the Mexican throne. Indeed, Maximilian asserted to another of the South's contacts in Europe, Confederate victory in the war was "identical with that of the new Mexican empire." Elated by the prospects of French recognition, Slidell sought a meeting with Maximilian while he was in Paris discussing the Mexican venture with Napoleon. But the archduke, in an abrupt change of form, did not respond to Slidell's request. According to Ambrose Mann in Belgium, who was angry over the rebuff, Napoleon had "enjoined upon Maximilian to hold no official relations with" Confederate officials, either in France or Mexico.[50]

Once again, the Confederacy had failed in its attempts to secure recognition from France. Slidell warned Maximilian's aide-de-camp of the severe consequences of refusing to recognize the Confederacy. "Without the active friendship of the South," the minister emphatically declared, Maximilian "will be entirely powerless to resist Northern aggression." Benjamin could not understand why neither Napoleon nor Maximilian realized that "the safety of the new empire is dependent solely upon our success in interposing a barrier between northern aggression and the Mexican territory." Slidell assured the Mexican ministers in Paris and London along with Drouyn himself that the American war would soon end with southern independence and that the two new governments would enter an "offensive and defensive alliance, for the establishment of an American policy on our continent, which will result in the suppression of monarchical institutions in Mexico."[51]

But no tactic moved the French from their position, whether a Confederate offer to drop the Monroe Doctrine and ally with France or a threat to join the North in defending the Americas against violations of the Monroe Doctrine. Slidell remained so convinced of imminent victory in the war that he dismissed Napoleon's fears of war with the Union over intervention as unduly alarmist. Even if war was a possibility, Slidell seemed to think, Napoleon would gain far more in running that risk because cooperation with the South would assure his success in Mexico and gain him great bonanzas in silver and cotton to secure his rule at home.

The threat of war with the Union, however, acted as a decisive restraint on Napoleon. Paradoxical as it seems, he could take no interventionist action on behalf of the South because, even though slavery was no longer a barrier and he believed that southern independence would virtually guarantee his success in Mexico, he also feared that recognition of the Confederacy meant a war with the Union in which he would have no allies. In late November 1863 he had told a British diplomat that such a war "would spell disaster to the interests of France and would have no possible object." Consequently, France and the Union maintained their fiction of an amicable arrangement whereby Napoleon professed to have no permanent designs in Mexico and the Lincoln administration professed to believe him.[52]

And yet Seward repeatedly made clear that the only legitimate reason for the French intrusion in Mexico was to resolve the debt issue. Maximilian's arrival in Mexico assured trouble with the Union because the move violated Napoleon's pledge to seek only a claims settlement. Regardless of the French emperor's assurances that Maximilian's rise to power had come from a popular election, Seward refused to recognize the new monarch as legitimate ruler and, as long as the war with the Confederacy continued, maintained a stern, foreboding silence on the matter. Napoleon could only hope that continued patience would pay off in the form of an ultimate southern victory in the war that would, in turn, secure his control in Mexico.[53]

Napoleon tried to curb the Union's interference with his plans in Mexico by alleging that Lincoln had agreed to recognize Maximilian's government in exchange for a French promise not to negotiate with the Confederacy. The assertion had no basis in fact, but Mercier arrived in Paris in early March 1864 to inform Slidell of such an arrangement. In addition, the London

Globe reported the same story. The basis for Napoleon's claim doubtless came from Dayton's recent remark to Drouyn that the Union held no grudge against the coming monarchy in Mexico and would "enter into relations with it" once in place. Napoleon only momentarily seemed chastened when at this very time the House of Representatives in Washington passed resolutions against recognition of the new government in Mexico and the Senate seemed ready to follow suit. Both the French press and Mercier insisted that the resolutions would not dissuade Napoleon from his course. The *Moniteur* and the *Constitutionnel* saw no danger of the Union's interfering in Mexican affairs. Slidell was infuriated with Mercier, complaining that the minister had been allegedly a friend of the Confederacy while really trying to be "every thing to every body."[54]

The real culprit in this controversy was Napoleon, who was willing to sell out the Confederacy to assure the Union's reception of Maximilian. Benjamin, however, attributed the French emperor's refusal to grant recognition to Seward's phony warnings of war. The secretary of state's strategy was "so transparent," Benjamin hotly asserted, that he found it difficult to believe that Napoleon could give in so easily to such a deception. Confederate leaders had underestimated the impact of Seward's angry threats of war and continued to delude themselves into believing that their longevity had legitimized their existence and that recognition was only moments away. A large part of their failure in foreign relations lay in their naïve belief that one way to achieve intervention was to convince Europe of the righteousness of their cause. In truth, self-interest guided both British and French policies throughout the American war. King Cotton diplomacy had failed to deliver recognition from the British, and the Mexican enticement had likewise failed to deliver recognition from the French.[55] Most likely the South had only the remotest chance for a joint Anglo-French intervention, given those two nations' long history of mutual distrust and conflicting interests. If so, Napoleon's irresponsible, inept, and provocative diplomacy provided a false hope to the Confederacy that (along with British flirtations with intervention) perhaps prolonged the war, while leaving a legacy of Union animosity for both European governments that only the passage of time could ease.

In early 1867 Napoleon abandoned his Mexican project and ordered his troops home. The Union's string of military victories in late 1864 and early 1865 had dictated this ignominious retreat. With the war finally approaching an end, it became clear that the French would soon confront an angry United States. Indeed, even before the fighting came to a close, the elderly Jacksonian Democrat Francis P. Blair had recommended a peace proposal to the president that included a call for the North and South to unite against the French menace as a means toward setting aside their differences. Although

Lincoln showed no interest in the Mexican part of the proposal (which sounded too much like his secretary of state's April 1861 plan to avert a civil war by starting a conflict with either Spain or France), he and Seward met with Vice-President Stephens and other Confederate officials at Hampton Roads, Virginia, in February 1865, only to see this peace effort collapse in the face of the president's demand for unconditional surrender.[56] In the meantime, Gen. William T. Sherman's army left a broad path of destruction as it made its way through Georgia and to the sea, and Gen. Ulysses S. Grant's forces hammered away at Lee's fading army until he surrendered at Appomattox Courthouse in Virginia in April 1865. Just days afterward Lincoln died from an assassin's bullet, bringing into the presidency the outspoken Andrew Johnson of Tennessee, who had recently promised military retribution against the French for invading Mexico. Napoleon's forces were already en route out of the country as the American guns became silent in 1865.

Maximilian, however, made the ill-fated decision to remain. In an ending that fitted the audacity of this fiasco's beginning, President Benito Juárez and his guerrilla forces captured the emperor in mid-May 1867 and, after a court-martial found him guilty of subverting the republic, executed him by a firing squad a month later.[57]

Thus by the opening of 1864, the possibility of foreign intervention in the war had ceased to exist, thereby costing the Confederacy its last slender hope for independence. The French had finally joined the British in realizing that their best interests lay in staying out of the war and averting a conflict with the Union. Each side on the slavery question – North and South – had taken a stand conducive to a foreign intervention that might have assured a breakup of the United States into two republics, one slave and the other free, while leaving the northern half of the hemisphere vulnerable to British expansion and the southern half to the French. Lincoln was correct on February 1, 1865, the day after Congress passed the Thirteenth Amendment abolishing slavery, when he pronounced that decision a "great moral victory . . . [for] the country and the whole world."[58]

Ironically, Lincoln's move for emancipation ultimately restrained Britain while it released France to pursue Napoleon's Grand Design for the Americas that, because of his unstable nature, posed an even greater threat to the United States and the hemisphere than did England. A French bastion of monarchical power in the New World would have confronted the Union in the postwar era as it sought to regain the momentum for republicanism while searching for a common ground with Britain's expanding commercial interests in the hemisphere. Such a volatile situation had the potential of causing another heated international rivalry reminiscent of the Anglo-French conflicts during the era preceding the American Revolution.

Lincoln's efforts to prevent foreign intervention proved successful, even if he did not understand why and how every international scheme failed. One suspects, however, that he fully grasped the profound effect that intervention would have had on both American and international history.

Epilogue: To Create a More Perfect Union

The moment came when I felt that slavery must die that the nation
might live!
President Abraham Lincoln, 1864

At the beginning of the war, President Lincoln did not envision either the
death of slavery or the profound social, political, and economic revolution
that would result from its passing. But he eventually came to regard the war
as a crucible for forging an improved Union whose most salient feature was
the absence of slavery. Human bondage, he declared in his Second Inaugural
Address, was "one of those offences which, in the providence of God, must
needs come, but which, having continued through His appointed time, He
now wills to remove [through] this terrible war, as the woe due to those by
whom the offence came." Lincoln started as a reluctant revolutionary, but
once the revolution had begun he became determined to finish the task by
abolishing slavery. In November 1863 he tried to justify the bloodshed by de-
livering an address on the Gettysburg battlefield that over time has taken on a
mystical aura as one of the most profound expressions of republican theory
ever penned. Not until the postwar period, however, did Americans begin to
grasp the universal importance of the Gettysburg Address, which highlighted the chief legacy of the Civil War as a Union more perfect because it
offered a new birth of freedom based on the death of slavery.[1]

Even the Confederacy recognized the power afforded the Union by its move
to abolition. Late in 1864, desperation hit the South, causing it to resort to a
surprising and self-destructive measure: an offer to free its slaves in exchange
for diplomatic recognition from England and France. Such a step demonstrated its awareness of the impact of slavery, but it also reiterated the South's
continued capacity to delude itself into believing that recognition was still
possible. Neither Anglo-French interest in cotton nor Napoleon's involvement in Mexico had yielded the desired result. And, to be sure, the abolition

of slavery would have undermined the South from within and thereby promoted the Lincoln administration's central objective of preserving the Union. But little evidence suggests that Confederate leaders even considered these dire probabilities. They believed their cause righteous and simply assumed that independence would come as a matter of course. The harsh realities of diplomacy – that wise decisions rested on self-interest rather than sentiment – continued to elude them.[2]

The Confederacy's resort to emancipation was a foolhardy attempt to salvage victory out of a lost cause. Britain had already decided against intervention for reasons unrelated to slavery; France had kept intervention alive for considerations that also bore no relation to slavery. The Emancipation Proclamation had eliminated slavery as a major factor in international affairs, allowing both Britain and France to make decisions regarding intervention on grounds of self-interest. Lincoln's antislavery initiative, regardless of its motives, had placed the Union in the front of the battle against the peculiar institution. Now, in the aftermath of the Union's emancipation policy, southern emancipation would not only leave the appearance of a cheap stunt born of desperation but would undermine the Confederacy's way of life and signal an inglorious capitulation to the abolitionists – and, even worse, to Lincoln. Finally, the big slaveholders could never have countenanced an idea that removed a great share of their wealth, virtually gutted the cotton economy, and guaranteed a challenge to white supremacy. Abolition would have destroyed the South's social, political, and economic base. In short, it would have dismantled the Old South.

Lincoln's success in removing slavery from international matters had a double impact, one an encouragement to better foreign relations, the other an impediment. Questions of morality had raised universal issues of right and wrong that made the slavery issue much more divisive and difficult to resolve. When Lincoln finally succeeded in drawing the line between the slave South and the free North, he removed the major obstacle to a realistic foreign policy on both sides of the Atlantic and thereby brought a rational approach to intervention that rested on self-interest. The threat of British involvement in the war ultimately receded because, as Palmerston feared, the outcome would be a war with the Union that served only the slaveholding South. Paradoxically, however, the removal of the slavery issue from the war encouraged the French to seek Mexico and southern cotton – even at the risk of war with the Union.

Fortunately for the Union, its twin victories at Gettysburg and Vicksburg in July 1863, followed by Lincoln's inspiring words on the Gettysburg battlefield in the autumn of that year, sealed the Union's direction in the war.

Confederate forces had sustained their most severe blows to independence: convincing defeats on the battlefield, followed by Lincoln's Gettysburg Address, so critical to defining the war's higher purpose. Lincoln found it necessary to deify death as essential to life. The butchery of the battle at Gettysburg became the greatest test of the republic – a crucible of fire from which the experiment in liberty emerged in the form of a much improved Union.[3]

In the first part of the war, Lincoln's use of the Union and slavery in diplomatic affairs more than once tipped the delicate balance against intervention in both England and France by reminding each nation's leaders that involvement automatically placed them on the side of the slaveholding South. At pivotal times in this early stage of the war – most notably in the autumn of 1862 – both European nations seemed poised to intervene by either a mediation or an armistice offer. Although both proposals appeared innocent of selfish motive, these were appearances only. Both nations had much to gain in North America from a breakup of the Union, whether or not this was their primary motive in considering intervention. The Union regarded any form of intervention as an insult to its national integrity and an implicit approval of secession – particularly when both England and France premised their ideas on southern separation and therefore seemed to be taking the initial step to recognition of the Confederacy. The chief restraint on their actions was the certainty of war with the Union; but also causing them to exercise great care at this early point in the war was the uncomfortable reality of siding with the slaveholding South.

Frederick Douglass, a former slave who became a major spokesman for black people, was like most others of his time in failing to grasp the intricate relationship between Union and slavery. He did not agree with those who referred to Lincoln as the "Great Emancipator" because he remained "preeminently the white man's President" in seeking the Union above the end of slavery. Still, Douglass knew that Lincoln could not rid America of the "great crime of slavery" if he acted outside the dictates of present-day racial restraints. "Had he put the abolition of slavery before the salvation of the Union," Douglass publicly declared, "he would have inevitably driven from him a powerful class of the American people and rendered resistance to rebellion impossible." Abolitionists regarded Lincoln as "tardy, cold, dull, and indifferent," but in relation to the prevailing sentiment of his people, "he was swift, zealous, radical, and determined." The president, as Douglass finally acknowledged, sought only what public feeling and the law allowed in the 1860s.[4]

The Civil War, Lincoln realized, served as an important transition between the destruction of slavery and the continuing progress toward universal freedom. The Declaration of Independence, he had argued in the 1850s, "contemplated the progressive improvement in the condition of all men everywhere." The Founding Fathers "did not mean to declare all men equal *in all respects*." Their ideal was a "free society . . . constantly looked to, constantly labored for, and even though never perfectly attained, constantly approximated and thereby constantly spreading and deepening its influence, and augmenting the happiness and value of life to all people of all colors everywhere." We cannot halt the movement toward an improved Union, to which events were "tending."[5]

"Liberty *and* Union, now and forever, one and inseparable!" These words, first uttered by Webster in the Senate in 1830, expressed Lincoln's central understanding of the Civil War. Liberty could not exist without the Union, Lincoln insisted, for the Union was the chief guarantor of republicanism. Sanctifying the Constitution, he asserted to a friend, carried with it the "duty of preserving, by every indispensable means, that government – that nation – of which that constitution was the organic law. Was it possible to lose the nation, and yet preserve the constitution?" Preservation of the Union provided the chief prerequisite to the destruction of slavery. "I could not feel that, to the best of my ability, I have even tried to preserve the constitution, if, to save slavery, or any minor matter, I should permit the wreck of government, country, and Constitution all together." The "general law" called for the protection of "life *and* limb." So "often a limb must be amputated to save a life; but a life is never wisely given to save a limb."[6] The meshing of liberty and Union provided Lincoln's paramount aim in the war and afterward.

Liberty, Lincoln believed, was "the heritage of all men." To place a single man in bondage heightened the chances of the same plight for others. "He who would *be* no slave, must consent to *have* no slave. Those who deny freedom to others, deserve it not for themselves." The enslavement of any human being was the chief sign of tyranny and a serious threat to liberty. Consequently, he asserted, "The moment came when I felt that slavery must die that the nation might live!" The United States, he declared in another attempt to identify the Union with freedom, offered the "last best, hope of earth."[7]

Lincoln regarded the movement against slavery as universal in meaning. In late December 1861, he told Congress that the struggle was "not altogether for today. It is for a vast future," for it "presents to the whole family of man, the question, whether a constitutional republic, or a democracy – a government of the people, by the same people – can, or cannot, maintain its territorial integrity, against its own domestic foes." In the Gettysburg Address, he applied these principles to all human beings when he declared that Americans were engaged in a struggle to determine whether a nation "con-

ceived in Liberty, and dedicated to the proposition that all men are created
equal . . . can long endure."[8]

A mystical and permanent Union based on the inherent rights of mankind
and the sanctity of republicanism: in the intricately related world of domestic and foreign affairs, Lincoln as president never strayed from these great
principles.

Notes

PROLOGUE

1. Allan Nevins, *War Becomes Revolution*, Vol. 2 of *The War for the Union* (New York: Charles Scribner's Sons, 1959–71), 242. For the discussion of a five-power intervention and the warnings against such a move, see George Cornewall Lewis (secretary for war), *Recognition of the Independence of the Southern States of the North American Union*, Nov. 7, 1862, a pamphlet printed for cabinet use and found in the William E. Gladstone (chancellor of exchequer) Papers, British Library, Additional Manuscripts, 44,595, DX, London; Gladstone, "Memorandum on Border for North and South States of America," July 31, 1862, *Gladstone and Palmerston: Being the Correspondence of Lord Palmerston with Mr. Gladstone, 1851–1865*, ed. Philip Guedalla (Covent Garden, Eng.: Victor Gollancz, 1928), 230–31; numerous dispatches from Lyons to Lord John Russell (foreign secretary), Russell Papers, Public Record Office (PRO), Kew, England, all cited throughout this work.

2. See Gary W. Gallagher, "'Upon Their Success Hang Momentous Interests': Generals," in *Why the Confederacy Lost*, ed. Gabor S. Boritt (New York: Oxford University Press, 1992), 99–103; Lincoln to Gasparin, Aug. 4, 1862, *The Collected Works of Abraham Lincoln*, 9 vols., ed. Roy P. Basler et al. (New Brunswick: Rutgers University Press, 1953–55): 5:355–56. Hereafter cited as *CWL*.

3. David H. Donald, *Lincoln* (New York: Simon and Schuster, 1995), 15, 114, 337, 514–15; Benjamin P. Thomas, *Abraham Lincoln: A Biography* (New York: Knopf, 1952), 108–9.

4. Speech at Peoria IL, Oct. 16, 1854, *CWL*, 2:276.

5. Lincoln, Emancipation Proclamation, Jan. 1, 1863, *CWL*, 6:30.

6. Hammond quoted in Frank L. Owsley, *King Cotton Diplomacy: Foreign Relations of the Confederate States of America*, revised by Harriet C. Owsley (Chicago: University of Chicago Press, 1959), 16; *Mercury* quoted in Owsley, *King Cotton Diplomacy*, 25; Varina Davis, *Jefferson Davis, Ex-President of the Confederate States of America: A Memoir by His Wife*, 2 vols. (New York: Belford, 1890), 2:160.

7. Adams quoted in Owsley, *King Cotton Diplomacy*, 20; Russell quoted in Owsley, *King Cotton Diplomacy*, 21.

8. Owsley, *King Cotton Diplomacy*, 138, 140.

9. Owsley, *King Cotton Diplomacy*, 30–31, 37, 39, 46, 49; James M. McPherson, *Battle Cry of Freedom: The Civil War Era* (New York: Oxford University Press, 1988), 383–84.

10. *Times* (London), Nov. 21, 1860, Jan. 4, 1861, *Economist*, Jan. 12, 1861, *Edinburgh Review*, Apr. 1861, *Saturday Review*, Mar. 2, 1861; *Chronicle* (London), Mar. 14, 1861, *Dublin News*, Jan. 26, 1861, and *Review* (London) (n.d.), all cited or quoted in Owsley, *King Cotton Diplomacy*, 180–81; *Moniteur* (n.d.), *Patrie* (n.d.), *Pays*, Nov. 22, 1860, *Constitutionnel*, Jan. 20, May 16, 1861, *Journal des d'débats*, Dec. 4, 30, 1860, Jan. 10, Feb. 20, May 17, Oct. 19, Dec. 10, 14, 1861, *Revue des deux mondes*, Nov. 1, 1861, all cited or quoted in Owsley, *King Cotton Diplomacy*, 197–201.

11. Alfred J. Hanna and Kathryn A. Hanna, *Napoleon III and Mexico: American Triumph over Monarchy* (Chapel Hill: University of North Carolina Press, 1971), xv, chap. 1.

12. James M. McPherson, *Abraham Lincoln and the Second American Revolution* (New York: Oxford University Press, 1991), viii, 31–32; Brooks D. Simpson, *America's Civil War* (Wheeling IL: Harlan Davidson, 1996), 89; Merrill D. Peterson, *Lincoln in American Memory* (New York: Oxford University Press, 1994), 383; William C. Harris, *With Charity for All: Lincoln and the Restoration of the Union* (Lexington: University Press of Kentucky, 1997), 1, 77, 97.

13. Allan Nevins, *The Statesmanship of the Civil War* (1953; rpr. New York: Collier Books, 1962), 99, 104, 117, 119–20; James G. Randall, *Lincoln the Liberal Statesman* (New York: Dodd, Mead, 1947), ix, 194; Mark E. Neely Jr., *The Fate of Liberty: Abraham Lincoln and Civil Liberties* (New York: Oxford University Press, 1991), 214–17.

14. Nevins, *Statesmanship of the Civil War*, 111, 113; Lincoln's speech at Peoria IL, Oct. 16, 1854, *CWL*, 2:249.

15. Robert W. Johannsen, *Lincoln, the South, and Slavery: The Political Dimension* (Baton Rouge: Louisiana State University Press, 1991); LaWanda Cox, *Lincoln and Black Freedom: A Study in Presidential Leadership* (Columbia: University of South Carolina Press, 1981).

16. Proclamation Appointing a National Fast Day, Mar. 30, 1863, *CWL* 6:156; James M. McPherson, *Drawn with the Sword: Reflections on the American Civil War* (New York: Oxford University Press, 1996), 183–84.

17. Cecil Woodham-Smith, *The Great Hunger: Ireland, 1845–1849* (New York: Harper & Row, 1962), 406–9; Goldwin Smith, *England: A Short History* (New York: Charles Scribner's Sons, 1971), 333–34; G. Kitson Clark, *The Making of Victorian England* (Cambridge MA: Harvard University Press, 1962), 76;

Lawrence J. McCaffrey, *The Irish Question, 1800–1922* (Lexington: University of Kentucky Press, 1968), 64–66.

18. Howard Jones, *Union in Peril: The Crisis over British Intervention in the Civil War* (Chapel Hill: University of North Carolina Press, 1992).

19. Garry Wills, *Lincoln at Gettysburg: The Words That Remade America* (New York: Simon and Schuster, 1992), 90.

I. LINCOLN ON SLAVERY

1. Randall, *Lincoln the Liberal Statesman*, 133; Harold M. Hyman, *A More Perfect Union: The Impact of the Civil War and Reconstruction on the Constitution* (New York: Knopf, 1973); Cox, *Lincoln and Black Freedom*, 6.

2. Lincoln's speech at Bloomington IL, Sept. 12, 1854, *CWL*, 2:230.

3. Lincoln's speech at Peoria IL, Oct. 16, 1854, *CWL*, 2:282; Don E. Fehrenbacher, *Prelude to Greatness: Lincoln in the* 1850's (Stanford: Stanford University Press, 1962), 81–82, 85.

4. Lincoln's speech at Peoria IL, Oct. 16, 1854, *CWL*, 2:282; Lincoln's speech at Alton IL, Oct. 15, 1858, *CWL*, 3:315; Fehrenbacher, *Prelude to Greatness*, 76–77, 107; Pauline Maier, *American Scripture: Making the Declaration of Independence* (New York: Knopf, 1997), 201–15.

5. Richard N. Current, *The Lincoln Nobody Knows* (New York: Hill and Wang, 1958), 221–22.

6. Lincoln to Mary Speed, Sept. 27, 1841, *CWL*, 1:260; Cox, *Lincoln and Black Freedom*, 20; Current, *Lincoln Nobody Knows*; Don E. Fehrenbacher, "Only His Stepchildren: Lincoln and the Negro," *Civil War History* 20 (Dec. 1974): 293–310; Lincoln's notes for speeches, ca. Sept. 1859, *CWL*, 3:399; George M. Fredrickson, "A Man but Not a Brother: Abraham Lincoln and Racial Equality," *Journal of Southern History* 41 (Feb. 1975): 39–58; Stephen B. Oates, "'The Man of Our Redemption': Abraham Lincoln and the Emancipation of the Slaves," *Presidential Studies Quarterly* 9 (Winter 1979): 15–25.

7. Lincoln to Joshua F. Speed, Aug. 24, 1855, *CWL*, 2:320; Donald, *Lincoln*, 165–66.

8. Protest in Illinois Legislature on slavery, Mar. 3, 1837, *CWL*, 1:75.

9. Lincoln's remarks in Illinois Legislature concerning resolutions in relation to fugitive slaves, Jan. 5, 1839, *CWL*, 1:126, 126 n. 1; Johannsen, *Lincoln, the South, and Slavery*.

10. Lincoln to Williamson Durley, Oct. 3, 1845, *CWL*, 1:347–48; fragment: What General Taylor Ought to Say, (Mar. ?) 1848, *CWL*, 1:454; Lincoln's speech in U.S. House of Representatives, July 27, 1848, *CWL*, 1:505; Lincoln's speech at Worcester MA, Sept. 12, 1948, *CWL*, 2:3; Lincoln's speech at Boston, Sept. 15, 1848, *CWL*, 2:5; Lincoln's speech at Lacon IL, Nov. 1, 1848, *CWL*, 2:14.

11. Eulogy on Henry Clay, July 6, 1852, *CWL*, 2:130; Lincoln to James N.

Brown, Oct. 18, 1858, *CWL*, 3:327; Lincoln's first debate with Douglas at Ottawa IL, Aug. 21, 1858, *CWL*, 3:16.

12. Fehrenbacher, *Prelude to Greatness*, 111–12; Lincoln's speech at Quincy IL, Oct. 13, 1858, *CWL*, 3:249.

13. Lincoln's speech at Peoria IL, Oct. 16, 1854, *CWL*, 2:274; Lincoln's speech at Hartford CT, Mar. 5, 1860, *CWL*, 4:11; Lincoln's speech at New Haven CT, Mar. 6, 1860, *CWL*, 4:22; Lincoln's speech at Springfield IL, June 26, 1857, *CWL*, 2:404.

14. Winthrop D. Jordan, *White over Black: American Attitudes Toward the Negro, 1550–1812* (Chapel Hill: University of North Carolina Press, 1968), 44–98; Juliet E. K. Walker, "Whither Liberty, Equality or Legality? Slavery, Race, Property and the 1787 American Constitution," *New York Law School Journal of Human Rights* 6 (spring 1989): 310, 315–16; David B. Davis, *The Problem of Slavery in Western Culture* (Ithaca NY: Cornell University Press, 1966), 57; Paul Finkelman, *Slavery and the Founders: Race and Liberty in the Age of Jefferson* (Armonk NY: M. E. Sharpe, 1996), 3–7.

15. Walker, "Whither Liberty," 300–302; David B. Davis, *The Problem of Slavery in the Age of Revolution, 1770–1823* (Ithaca NY: Cornell University Press, 1975), 331–35, 340; Davis, *Problem of Slavery in Western Culture*, 3–4.

16. William W. Freehling, "The Founding Fathers and Slavery," *American Historical Review* 77 (Oct. 1972): 81–83; William W. Freehling, *The Road to Disunion: Secessionists at Bay, 1776–1854* (New York: Oxford University Press, 1990), 121–31; Walker, "Whither Liberty," 303, 333; Taney quoted in Walker, "Whither Liberty," 334; Jordan, *White over Black*, 350–51.

17. James Madison, "Federalist No. 54" (Feb. 12, 1788), *The Federalist: A Collection of Essays Written in Favor of the New Constitution*, ed. George W. Carey and James McClellan (Dubuque IA: Kendall/Hunt, 1990), 283; Edmund S. Morgan, *American Slavery American Freedom: The Ordeal of Colonial Virginia* (New York: Norton, 1975), 4–5, 316–37; Walker, "Whither Liberty," 307–9, 349; Davis, *Problem of Slavery in the Age of Revolution*, 258–62.

18. Eulogy on Clay, July 6, 1852, *CWL*, 2:130; Lincoln's debate with Douglas at Ottawa IL, Aug. 21, 1858, *CWL*, 3:29.

19. Johannsen, *Lincoln, the South, and Slavery*, 5. Lincoln's speech at Edwardsville IL, Sept. 11, 1858, *CWL*, 3:92; fragment on slavery, July 1, 1854 (?), *CWL*, 2:222; Lincoln's speech at Peoria IL, Oct. 16, 1854, *CWL*, 2:249; Lincoln's speech at Chicago, July 10, 1858, *CWL*, 2:492; Lincoln's last public address, Apr. 11, 1865, *CWL*, 8:405; Fehrenbacher, *Prelude to Greatness*, 95; McPherson, *Lincoln and the Second American Revolution*, 125–26; Cox, *Lincoln and Black Freedom*, 5; Finkelman, *Slavery and the Founders*, 35–37.

20. Lincoln's speech at Winchester IL, Aug. 26, 1854, *CWL*, 2:227; Lincoln's

speech at Carrollton IL, Aug. 28, 1854, *CWL*, 2:227; Lincoln to John M. Palmer, Sept. 7, 1854, *CWL*, 2:228; Lincoln's speech at Bloomington IL, Sept. 12, 1854, *CWL*, 2:230–31; Eric Foner, *Free Soil, Free Labor, Free Men: The Ideology of the Republican Party before the Civil War* (New York: Oxford University Press, 1970), 28–30.

21. Lincoln's speech at Bloomington IL, Sept. 26, 1854, *CWL*, 2:239; Lincoln's speech at Peoria IL, Oct. 16, 1854, *CWL*, 2:266.

22. Lincoln's speech at Springfield IL, Oct. 4, 1854, *CWL*, 2:245; Lincoln's speech at Peoria IL, Oct. 16, 1854, *CWL*, 2:250, 255, 274–76, 281–82.

23. Lincoln's speech at Peoria IL, Oct. 16, 1854, *CWL*, 2:255–56, 274–76, 281–82.

24. McPherson, *Lincoln and the Second American Revolution*, 126; Lincoln's speech at Peoria IL, Oct. 16, 1854, *CWL*, 2:255, 274–76, 281–82.

25. Lincoln's speech at Peoria IL, Oct. 16, 1854, *CWL*, 2:255–56.

26. Lincoln's speech at Peoria IL, Oct. 16, 1854, *CWL*, 2:270, 282; Lincoln's speech at Bloomington IL, May 29, 1856, *CWL*, 2:341; "A House Divided," Lincoln's speech at Springfield IL, June 16, 1858, *CWL*, 2:461.

27. Lincoln's speech at Chicago, July 10, 1858, *CWL*, 2:501; Lincoln's speeches at Springfield IL, June 26, 1857, July 17, 1858, *CWL*, 2:406, 520–21.

28. Johannsen, *Lincoln, the South, and Slavery*, 51; McPherson, *Drawn with the Sword*, 200.

29. McPherson, *Battle Cry of Freedom*, 253.

30. Lincoln to Congressman William Kellogg of Illinois, Dec. 11, 1860, *CWL*, 4:150; Lincoln to Elihu B. Washburne, Dec. 13, 1860, *CWL*, 4:151; Lincoln to Thurlow Weed, Dec. 17, 1860, *CWL*, 4:154; Lincoln to John D. Defrees, Dec. 18, 1860, *CWL*, 4:155; Lincoln to Seward, Feb. 1, 1861, *CWL*, 4:183; Lincoln to James T. Hale, Jan. 11, 1861, *CWL*, 4:172; Thomas, *Lincoln*; Glyndon G. Van Deusen, *William Henry Seward* (New York: Oxford University Press, 1967), 243; Robert E. May, *The Southern Dream of a Caribbean Empire, 1854–1861* (Baton Rouge: Louisiana State University Press, 1973), 22–76, 163–89.

31. Lincoln's speech in Independence Hall, Philadelphia, Feb. 22, 1861, *CWL*, 4:240; McPherson, *Lincoln and the Second American Revolution*, 126, 164 n.30.

32. First Inaugural Address, Mar. 4, 1861, *CWL*, 4:268; Message to Congress in Special Session, July 4, 1861, *CWL*, 4:426.

33. McPherson, *Lincoln and the Second American Revolution*, 135–38.

2. LINCOLN, SLAVERY, AND PERPETUAL UNION

1. Lincoln to Stephens, Dec. 22, 1860, *CWL*, 4:160; Gary W. Gallagher, *The Confederate War* (Cambridge MA: Harvard University Press, 1997); Maury Klein, *Days of Defiance: Sumter, Secession, and the Coming of the Civil War* (New

York: Knopf, 1997); Michael A. Morrison, *Slavery and the American West: The Eclipse of Manifest Destiny and the Coming of the Civil War* (Chapel Hill: University of North Carolina Press, 1997).

2. Davis cited in Dunbar Rowland, ed., *Jefferson Davis, Constitutionalist: His Letters, Papers, and Speeches*, 10 vols. (Jackson: Mississippi State University Press, 1923), 4:357; Stephens quoted *in Augusta (Ga.) Daily Constitutionalist*, Mar. 30, 1861, cited in James M. McPherson, *What They Fought For, 1861–1865* (Baton Rouge: Louisiana State University Press, 1994), 80 n. 2.

3. Kinley J. Brauer, "The Slavery Problem in the Diplomacy of the American Civil War," *Pacific Historical Review* 46 (Aug. 1977): 441, 443–45.

4. McPherson, *Battle Cry of Freedom*, 284, 311–12; J. G. Randall and David H. Donald, *The Civil War and Reconstruction*, 2d ed. (Lexington MA: D. C. Heath, 1969), 370–71; J. G. Randall, *Lincoln the President*, 2 vols. (New York: Dodd, Mead, 1945), 2:126–27; Jones, *Union in Peril*, 16.

5. *Times* (London), May 11, 1861, *Pays*, Nov. 22, 1860, all other British news citations, and French citations in Owsley, *King Cotton Diplomacy*, 189, 191, 197; Charles Francis Adams to Charles Francis Adams Jr. (hereafter CFA and CFA Jr.) June 21, 1861, Worthington C. Ford, ed., *A Cycle of Adams Letters, 1861–1865*, 2 vols. (Boston: Houghton Mifflin, 1920), 1:14–15.

6. Sadie D. St. Clair, "Slavery as a Diplomatic Factor in Anglo-American Relations during the Civil War," *Journal of Negro History* 30 (July 1945): 262; Charles Greville (the Englishman) to Earl of Clarendon (former foreign secretary), Jan. 26, 1861, Herbert Maxwell, *The Life and Letters of George William Frederick, Fourth Earl of Clarendon*, 2 vols. (London: Edward Arnold, 1913), 2:237; Lynn M. Case and Warren F. Spencer, *The United States and France: Civil War Diplomacy* (Philadelphia: University of Pennsylvania Press, 1970), 316–17; Ephraim D. Adams, *Great Britain and the American Civil War*, 2 vols. (New York: Longmans, Green, 1925), 1:35.

7. Lincoln to Seward, Apr. 1, 1861, CWL, 4:316–17; Seward's memo, "Some thoughts for the President's Consideration," Apr. 1, 1861, CWL, 4:317–18; Kinley J. Brauer, "Seward's 'Foreign War Panacea': An Interpretation," *New York History* 55 (Apr. 1974): 136–37, 153–57; Case and Spencer, *U.S. and France*, 32–34; Bremen envoy quoted by Case and Spencer, *U.S. and France*, 33; Jones, *Union in Peril*, 14–15.

8. Palmerston to Russell, Dec. 30, 1860, Apr. 14, 1861, Russell Papers, PRO 30/22/21; Herbert C. F. Bell, *Lord Palmerston*, 2 vols. (London: Longmans, Green, 1936), 2:276–77, 291.

9. Russell's dispatch regarding the Italian crisis, Oct. 27, 1860, quoted in A. Wyatt Tilby, *Lord John Russell: A Study in Civil and Religious Liberty* (London: Cassell, 1930), 185; see also, 189, 193, 197, 211–13; Russell to Lyons, Apr. 12, 1861, no. 89, Gladstone Papers, British Library, Add. Mss., 44,593, vol. 508;

Russell to Lyons, Jan. 10, 1861, Russell Papers, PRO 30/22/98. Vattel was the author of the highly influential work *The Law of Nations, or, Principles of the Law of Nature Applied to the Conduct and Affairs of Nations and Sovereigns* (Philadelphia: Abraham Small, 1817).

10. Palmerston to Queen Victoria, Jan. 1, 1861, cited in Jasper Ridley, *Lord Palmerston* (New York: E. P. Dutton, 1971), 548.

11. *Economist* (London), May 15, 25, June 29, 1861, all quoted in Owsley, *King Cotton Diplomacy*, 194, 195; see also 196.

12. Brauer, "Slavery Problem," 450; Russell to Lyons, Dec. 29, 1860, Russell Papers, PRO 30/22/96; Eugene H. Berwanger, ed., *William Howard Russell, My Diary North and South* (Philadelphia: Temple University Press, 1988), 51 (Mar. 28, 1861).

13. Yancey quoted in Adams, *G.B. and Civil War*, 2:5 n.3; Henry Blumenthal, "Confederate Diplomacy: Popular Notions and International Realities," *Journal of Southern History* 32 (May 1966): 151–52, 155, 162–64, 169; Russell to Lyons, May 11, 1861, Great Britain, Foreign Office, *British and Foreign State Papers.* 116 vols. (London: William Ridgway, 1812–1925), *1860–1861*, 51:186–87 (hereafter cited as *BFSP*; Owsley, *King Cotton Diplomacy*, 57.

14. Berwanger, ed., *Russell, Diary*, 126 (May 7, 1861); Yancey and Mann to Robert Toombs, May 21, 1861, James D. Richardson, ed., *A Compilation of the Messages and Papers of the Confederacy, Including the Diplomatic Correspondence, 1861–1865*, 2 vols. (Nashville: U.S. Publishing Co., 1905), 2:37; Confederate commissioners to Richmond, May 21, 1861, U.S. Naval War Records Office, *Official Records of the Union and Confederate Navies in the War of the Rebellion*, 2d ser., 3 vols. (Washington DC: U.S. Government Printing Office, 1894–1927), 3:214–16 (hereafter cited as *ORN*; W. Stanley Hoole, ed., "Notes and Documents: William L. Yancey's European Diary, March-June, 1861," *Alabama Review* 25 (Apr. 1972): 134–42.

15. Seward quoted in David H. Donald, *Charles Sumner and the Rights of Man* (New York: Knopf, 1970), 21; Phillip S. Paludan, *The Presidency of Abraham Lincoln* (Lawrence: University Press of Kansas, 1994), 90.

16. Lincoln's First Inaugural Address, Mar. 4, 1861, *CWL*, 4:264–65.

17. Others who feared race war were Attorney General Edward Bates and Lincoln's secretary, John Hay. See Howard K. Beale, ed., *The Diary of Edward Bates, 1859–1866* (Washington DC: U.S. Government Printing Office, 1933), 179 (Mar. 31, 1861); Tyler Dennett, ed., *Lincoln and the Civil War in the Diaries and Letters of John Hay* (New York: Dodd, Mead, 1939), 22 (May 10, 1861).

18. "British Proclamation for the Observance of Neutrality in the Contest Between the United States and the Confederate States of America, May 13, 1861," *BFSP, 1860–1861*, 51:165–69. Spain joined France in June 1861 in declaring neutrality. See Henry Wheaton, *The Elements of International Law* (1836), 8th ed.,

ed. Richard Henry Dana Jr. (Boston: Little, Brown, 1866), Dana's notes, 167 n.84; Sumner quoted and Seward cited in Norman A. Graebner, "Northern Diplomacy and European Neutrality," in *Why the North Won the Civil War*, ed. David Donald (1960; rpr. New York: Collier, 1962), 60–61; Seward to CFA, May 21, 1861, quoted in Brian Jenkins, *Britain and the War for the Union*, 2 vols. (Montreal: McGill-Queen's University Press, 1974, 1980), 1:106; Charles Francis Adams Jr., "The British Proclamation of May, 1861," *Massachusetts Historical Society Proceedings* 48 (1915): 190–241.

19. Lyons to Seward, Apr. 29, 1861, U.S. Department of State, Notes from the British Legation in the United States to the Department of State, 1791–1906, National Archives, Washington DC [hereafter cited as NFBL (NA); Lyons to Russell, May 2, 1861, Great Britain, *British Parliamentary Papers, 1801–1899*, 1,000 vols. (Shannon: Irish University Press, date varies by volume), *Civil War*, 16:22 (hereafter cited as BPP); Vattel, *Law of Nations*, bk. 3, chap. 7, secs. 103–4, chap. 18, secs. 293–94; Wheaton, *Elements of International Law* (1836 ed.), pt. 1, secs. 23, 26; Kenneth Bourne, *The Foreign Policy of Victorian England, 1830–1902* (Oxford: Clarendon, 1970), 92; Robert E. Johnson, "Investment by Sea: The Civil War Blockade," *American Neptune* 32 (Jan. 1972): 45–46.

20. Wheaton, *Elements of International Law* (1836 ed.), pt. 1, secs. 21, 23; Dana's notes, Wheaton, *Elements of International Law* (1866 ed.), 31 n.15.

21. Argyll to Russell, Sept. 11, 1861, Russell Papers, PRO 30/22/25; Forster to Austen Henry Layard (under secretary), Sept. 11, 1861, Layard Papers, Brit. Lib., Add. Mss., 39,101, vol. 171; T. Wemyss Reid, *Life of the Right Honourable William Edward Forster*, 2 vols. (London: Chapman and Hall, 1888), 1:289–92, 337–39; Norman B. Ferris, *Desperate Diplomacy: William H. Seward's Foreign Policy, 1861* (Knoxville: University of Tennessee Press, 1976), 41.

22. Adams, *G.B. and Civil War*, 2:79–82, 97–98.

23. Martin P. Claussen, "Peace Factors in Anglo-American Relations, 1860–1865," *Mississippi Valley Historical Review* 26 (Mar. 1940): 512; Frank J. Merli, *Great Britain and the Confederate Navy, 1861–1865* (Bloomington: Indiana University Press, 1970), 58–59; Warren F. Spencer, *The Confederate Navy in Europe* (University: University of Alabama Press, 1983), 9–10; Martin Duberman, *Charles Francis Adams, 1807–1886* (Boston: Houghton Mifflin, 1961), 259–60; Charles Francis Adams Jr., *Before and After the Treaty of Washington: The American Civil War and the War in the Transvaal* (New York: New York Historical Society, 1902), 15–18.

24. "British Proclamation of Neutrality," *BFSP, 1860–1861*, 51:165–69.

25. CFA to Seward, May 21, 1861, no. 2, U.S. Department of State, *Papers Relating to Foreign Affairs, Accompanying the Annual Message of the President to the Second Session of the Thirty-Seventh Congress, 1861* (Washington DC: U.S. Govern-

ment Printing Office, 1861), 91–92 (hereafter cited as *FRUS 1861*); CFA to Seward, May 21, 1861, CFA letterbook, Adams Family Papers, Massachusetts Historical Society, Boston; Russell to Lyons, May 21, 1861, no. 140, Gladstone Papers, Brit. Lib., Add. Mss., 44,593, vol. 508; *Economist* (London), May 18, 1861, quoted in Adams, *G.B. and Civil War*, 1:174; CFA diary, May 26, 1861, Adams Family Papers.

26. Russell to Lyons, Dec. 19, 1860, Russell Papers, PRO 30/22/96; Lyons to Russell, May 6, 1861, Russell Papers, PRO 30/22/35; Clarendon to Secretary for War George Cornewall Lewis, Jan. 24, 1861, Clarendon Papers, Bodleian Library; Lyons to Russell, May 12, 1861, BPP: *Civil War*, 16:79.

27. *Parliamentary Debates*, 168:134 (Commons, May 27, 1861); CFA to Seward, May 31, 1861, no. 4, *FRUS 1861*, 96; Russell quoted in Tilby, *Russell*, 196–97.

28. CFA to Richard Henry Dana Jr., June 14, 1861, and CFA to Everett, July 26, 1861, CFA letterbook; CFA diary, July 25, 1861; CFA to Seward, June 21, 1861, no. 9, *FRUS 1861*, 109–10; CFA to Seward, June 28, 1861, no. 10, *FRUS 1861*, 110–11.

29. *Times* (London), Aug. 27, Sept. 4, 1861, quoted in Owsley, *King Cotton Diplomacy*, 196; Yancey, Rost, and Mann to Russell, Aug. 14, 1861, *BFSP, 1860–1861*, 51:219–28.

30. Russell to Yancey, Rost, and Mann, Aug. 24, 1861, *ORN*, 2d ser., 3:248.

31. Jones, *Union in Peril*, chaps. 2 and 3.

32. Reference to Russell's letter to Everett of July 12, 1861, found in Everett's reply to Russell, Aug. 19, 1861, Russell Papers, PRO 30/22/39; miscellaneous draft in unidentified hand and undated, Russell Papers, PRO 30/22/118A; Tilby, *Russell*, 50.

33. Everett's reply to Russell, Aug. 19, 1861, Russell Papers, PRO 30/22/39; Tilby, *Russell*, 197; Russell to Cowley, British ambassador in Paris, Apr. 15, 1865, Russell Papers, PRO 30/22/106.

34. Everett to Russell, Aug. 19, 1861, Russell Papers, PRO 30/22/39.

35. Russell to Lyons, Nov. 2, 1861, Russell Papers, PRO 30/22/96; *Bee-Hive* (London), Nov. 23, Dec. 7, 1861, cited in Philip S. Foner, *British Labor and the American Civil War* (New York: Holmes and Meier, 1981), 29; Donald Bellows, "A Study of British Conservative Reaction to the American Civil War," *Journal of Southern History* 51 (Nov. 1985): 512–13, 522; Douglas A. Lorimer, "The Role of Anti-Slavery Sentiment in English Reactions to the American Civil War," *Historical Journal* 19 (June 1976): 407, 409, 420.

36. *Economist* (London), Sept. 28, 1861, quoted in Owsley, *King Cotton Diplomacy*, 185.

37. Russell to Palmerston, Oct. 7, 1861, Spencer Walpole, *The Life of Lord John Russell*, 2 vols. (London: Longmans, Green, 1889), 2:344; Russell and Pal-

merston quoted in Adams, *G.B. and Civil War*, 1:199–200; Palmerston to Russell, Oct. 18, 1861, *Economist* (London), Oct. 12, 1861, both cited in Owsley, *King Cotton Diplomacy*, 73 and 85.

38. Yancey to Hunter, Dec. 31, 1861, *ORN*, 2d ser., 3:312–13.

3. SOUTHERN SLAVERY, NORTHERN FREEDOM

1. Jones, *Union in Peril*, chap. 4; Gordon H. Warren, *Fountain of Discontent: The Trent Affair and Freedom of the Seas* (Boston: Northeastern University Press, 1981); Norman B. Ferris, *The Trent Affair: A Diplomatic Crisis* (Knoxville: University of Tennessee Press, 1977); D. P. Crook, *The North, the South, and the Powers, 1861–1865* (New York: Wiley, 1974), 99–170.

2. Lyons to Russell, Nov. 24, 1861, Russell Papers, PRO 30/22/36; Lyons to Russell, Nov. 29, 1861, Russell Papers, PRO 30/22/14C; Lyons quoted in Lord Newton, *Lord Lyons: A Record of British Diplomacy*, 2 vols. (London: Edward Arnold, 1913), 1:59; Argyll to Gladstone, Dec. 30, 1861, Jan. 1, 1862, Gladstone Papers, Brit. Lib., Add. Mss., 44,099, vol. 14.

3. Dayton to Seward, Nov. 6, Dec. 6, 24, 1861, all cited in Owsley, *King Cotton Diplomacy*, 71–72; Hanna and Hanna, *Napoleon III and Mexico*, 38–39. The three powers signed the London Treaty on October 31, 1861; see Carl H. Bock, *Prelude to Tragedy: The Negotiation and Breakdown of the Tripartite Convention of London, October 31, 1861* (Philadelphia: University of Pennsylvania Press, 1966).

4. Theodore C. Pease and James G. Randall, eds., *The Diary of Orville Hickman Browning*, 2 vols. (Springfield: Illinois State Historical Library, 1925), 1:526 (Jan. 18, 1862); Lyons to Russell, Jan. 20, 1862, quoted in Adams, *G.B. and Civil War*, 2:80; see also 1:271–72, 272 n.1; Russell to Gladstone, Jan. 26, 1862, Gladstone Papers, Brit. Lib., Add. Mss., 44,292, vol. 207.

5. Seward to CFA, Feb. 4, 1862, no. 178, U.S. Department of State, *Papers Relating to Foreign Affairs Communicated to Congress, December 1, 1862* (Washington DC: U.S. Government Printing Office, 1863), 21 (hereafter cited as *FRUS 1862*); Zebina Eastman (consul) to Lincoln, Dec. 10, 1861, quoted in Hans L. Trefousse, *Lincoln's Decision for Emancipation* (Philadelphia: J. B. Lippincott, 1975), 29; Benjamin Moran Diary, Feb. 7, 8, 10, 20, Mar. 6, May 8, 9, 1862, Library of Congress. Russell's warnings of a race war doubtless struck a responsive chord in the Lords because of the rebellion in Haiti during the 1790s, the results of emancipation in the West Indies, the Sepoy rebellion in India of 1857, and England's continuing problems in Ireland. See Crook, *The North, the South, and the Powers*, 237–38; McPherson, *Battle Cry of Freedom*, 558.

6. *Times* (London), Mar. 6, 10, 1862, quoted in Owsley, *King Cotton Diplomacy*, 196.

7. References to Schurz and to Lincoln quote in Adams, *G.B. and Civil War*, 2:91–92; Prince de Joinville to Lincoln, Feb. 8, 1862, Prince Jerome to Everett,

Feb. 18, 1862, both quoted in Trefousse, *Lincoln's Decision for Emancipation*, 29; Moran Diary, Apr. 16, 1862.

8. CFA to Seward, Feb. 21, 1862, no. 119, CFA letterbook; Seward to CFA, Mar. 10, 1862, no. 203, *FRUS 1862*, 46; Seward to CFA, Apr. 1, 1862, no. 218, *FRUS 1862*, 60; D. P. Crook, "Portents of War: English Opinion on Secession," *Journal of American Studies* 4 (1970): 175.

9. Jones, *Union in Peril*, 117; McPherson, *Battle Cry of Freedom*, 353; Case and Spencer, *U.S. and France*, 317–18; CFA diary, Mar. 19, 1862; Russell to Lyons, Mar. 22, 1862, Russell Papers, PRO 30/22/96; Adams, *G.B. and Civil War*, 2:82–83.

10. Lincoln's Message to Congress, Mar. 6, 1862, CWL, 5:144–46; Paludan, *Presidency of Lincoln*, 127–28; Donald, *Lincoln*, 362.

11. Phillips quoted in Paludan, *Presidency of Lincoln*, 130.

12. Lyons to Russell, Mar. 31, Apr. 8, 1862, Russell Papers, PRO 30/22/36; Seward to CFA, Apr. 8, 1862, no. 226, *FRUS 1862*, 65; text of treaty in BPP: *Papers Relating to Slave Trade, 1861–74*, 91:161–70.

13. Adams, *G.B. and Civil War*, 1:275, 2:10, 90; A. Taylor Milne, "The Lyons-Seward Treaty of 1862," *American Historical Review* 38 (Apr. 1933): 511; Conway W. Henderson, "The Anglo-American Treaty of 1862 in Civil War Diplomacy," *Civil War History* 15 (Dec. 1969): 314.

14. Adams, *G.B. and Civil War*, 2:83–84; Benjamin P. Thomas and Harold M. Hyman, *Stanton: The Life and Times of Lincoln's Secretary of War* (New York: Knopf, 1962), 232–33; Lincoln to Congress, Apr. 16, 1862, CWL, 5:192; see also 370–71 n.1.

15. Seward to CFA, May 28, 1862, no. 260, U.S. Department of State, Dispatches from United States Ministers to Great Britain, 1792–1870, National Archives, Washington DC [hereafter cited as Disp., GB (NA)]; CFA Diary, June 20, 1862.

16. Dayton to Seward, Apr. 11, 1862, cited in Owsley, *King Cotton Diplomacy*, 270; Slidell to Benjamin, Apr. 14, 1862, ORN, 2d ser., 3:392–95.

17. *Economist* (London), May 17, 1862, *Times* (London), May 21, 1862, the first cited and the second quoted in Owsley, *King Cotton Diplomacy*, 196; Graebner, "Northern Diplomacy and European Neutrality," 66–67.

18. Palmerston to Russell, June 13, 1862, Russell Papers, PRO 30/22/22.

19. Donald, *Lincoln*, 362; President's message to Congress, Mar. 6, 1862, CWL, 5:144–46; Lincoln's proclamation revoking Gen. David Hunter's May 9, 1862, order of military emancipation, May 19, 1862, CWL, 5:223; Lincoln's appeal to border-state representatives to favor compensated emancipation, July 12, 1862, CWL, 5:318, CWL, 5:319 n.1; McPherson, *Lincoln and the Second American Revolution*, 34; Current, *Lincoln Nobody Knows*, 221–23.

20. Donald, *Lincoln*, 362; Howard K. Beale, ed., *Diary of Gideon Welles: Secre-*

tary of the Navy Under Lincoln and Johnson, 3 vols. (New York: Norton, 1960), 1:70–71 (July 13, 1862); Gideon Welles, "The History of Emancipation," *Galaxy* 14 (Dec. 1872): 842–43; Stephen B. Oates, "Lincoln's Journey to Emancipation," in Stephen B. Oates, *Our Fiery Trial* (Amherst: University of Massachusetts Press, 1979), 76–77; McPherson, *Battle Cry of Freedom*, 503–4; Thomas and Hyman, *Stanton*, 238.

21. Cobden to Bright, July 12, 1862, Cobden Papers, Brit. Lib., Add. Mss., 43,652, vol. 6; Palmerston to Queen Victoria, July 14, 1862, quoted in Bell, *Palmerston*, 2:327; Mason to State Department in Richmond, July 15, 1862, and Slidell to Mason, July 16, 1862, Mason Papers, Library of Congress; Stuart to Russell, July 15, 1862, Russell Papers, PRO 30/22,36; Louis M. Sears, "A Confederate Diplomat at the Court of Napoleon III," *American Historical Review* 26 (Jan. 1921): 262–63; CFA to Seward, July 17, 1862, no. 186, *FRUS 1862*, 136–37; CFA diary, July 15, 1862; Jenkins, *Britain and the War for the Union*, 2:94.

22. Dayton to Seward, Sept. 27, 1861, quoted in Owsley, *King Cotton Diplomacy*, 509.

23. Hanna and Hanna, *Napoleon III and Mexico*, 98–100, 183, Maximilian's quote on 100.

24. Castilla and Spanish minister quoted in Hanna and Hanna, *Napoleon III and Mexico*, 183, 101, 102.

25. Seward to Dayton, Mar. 3, 1862, quoted in Owsley, *King Cotton Diplomacy*, 510.

26. Dayton to Seward, Mar. 31, 1862, and Thouvenel to Mercier, March 7, 27, 1862, both cited in Owsley, *King Cotton Diplomacy*, 511.

27. Seward to Dayton, Mar. 31, 1862, Dayton to Seward, Apr. 22, 1862, both quoted in Owsley, *King Cotton Diplomacy*, 511–12.

28. Owsley, *King Cotton Diplomacy*, 513–14.

29. *Economist* (London), July 5, Aug. 2, 1862, quoted in Owsley, *King Cotton Diplomacy*, 137; see also 137–38, 142.

30. Owsley, *King Cotton Diplomacy*, 152; Case and Spencer, *U.S. and France*, 159, 162, 164–66, 319–23.

31. Hanna and Hanna, *Napoleon III and Mexico*, xiii-xiv, 4, 19, 79, 199, 303; Napoleon quoted on 78.

32. Case and Spencer, *U.S. and France*, 300–301; Slidell's memorandum of conversation with Napoleon in Slidell to Secretary of State Judah P. Benjamin, July 25, 1862, *ORN*, 2d ser., 3:479.

33. Slidell's memorandum of conversation with Napoleon in Slidell to Benjamin, July 25, 1862, *ORN*, 2d ser., 3:479; Case and Spencer, *U.S. and France*, 145–48, 301–3.

34. Slidell's memorandum of conversation with Napoleon in Slidell to Benjamin, July 25, 1862, *ORN*, 2d ser., 3:479; Case and Spencer, *U.S. and France*, 301–3.

35. Slidell's memorandum of conversation with Napoleon in Slidell to Benjamin, July 25, 1862, ORN, 2d ser., 3:479; Case and Spencer, *U.S. and France*, 302–3.

36. Slidell's memorandum of conversation with Napoleon in Slidell to Benjamin, July 25, 1862, ORN, 2d ser., 3:479; Case and Spencer, *U.S. and France*, 303–4.

37. Slidell's memorandum of conversation with Napoleon in Slidell to Benjamin, July 25, 1862, ORN, 2d ser., 3:479; Case and Spencer, *U.S. and France*, 304.

38. Slidell's memorandum of conversation with Napoleon in Slidell to Benjamin, July 25, 1862, ORN, 2d ser., 3:479; Case and Spencer, *U.S. and France*, 304–5.

39. Slidell's memorandum of conversation with Napoleon in Slidell to Benjamin, July 25, 1862, ORN, 2d ser., 3:479; Case and Spencer, *U.S. and France*, 305.

40. Slidell's memorandum of conversation with Napoleon in Slidell to Benjamin, July 25, 1862, ORN, 2d ser., 3:479; Case and Spencer, *U.S. and France*, 305.

41. Napoleon and Thouvenel quoted in Case and Spencer, *U.S. and France*, 307, 308.

42. Gorchakov quoted in Case and Spencer, *U.S. and France*, 309.

43. Slidell to Benjamin, July 25, 1862, ORN, 2d ser., 3:479–81.

44. Case and Spencer, *U.S. and France*, 311–12; Thouvenel quoted in Case and Spencer, *U.S. and France*, 312; Mason to Benjamin, July 30-Aug. 4, 1862, with enclosures, ORN, 2d ser., 3:490–504; Adams, *G.B. and Civil War*, 2:25–29.

45. Thouvenel quoted in Case and Spencer, *U.S. and France*, 313, 314.

46. CFA diary, July 14, 17, 1862; CFA to Seward, July 17, 1862, no. 189, FRUS *1862*, 139–40; *Parliamentary Debates*, 168:569–73 (Commons, July 18, 1862); H. C. G. Matthew, ed., *The Gladstone Diaries*, 9 vols. (Oxford: Clarendon, 1978), 6:136 (July 18, 1862); Mason to Slidell, July 11, 13, 1862, Mason Papers.

47. *Parliamentary Debates*, 168:511–22 (July 18, 1862); Sarah A. Wallace and Frances E. Gillespie, eds., *The Journal of Benjamin Moran, 1857–1865*, 2 vols. (Chicago: University of Chicago Press, 1949), 2:1041 n.13; Moran diary, July 19, 1862; CFA diary, July 18, 1862; Graebner, "Northern Diplomacy and European Neutrality," 67.

48. *Parliamentary Debates*, 168:522–27 (Taylor, Commons, July 18), 527–34 (Vane-Tempest, Commons, July 18), 534–38 (Forster, Commons, July 18); Adams, *G.B. and Civil War*, 2:22.

49. *Parliamentary Debates*, 168:569–73 (Commons, July 18, 1862).

50. Moran diary, July 19, 1862; Graebner, "Northern Diplomacy and European Neutrality," 67.

51. CFA diary, July 19, 1862; CFA to Seward, July 10, 1862, CFA letterbook; CFA to Seward, July 31, 1862, no. 197, FRUS *1862*, 159–60; Jones, *Union in Peril*, 136–37; CFA to Seward, July 24, 1862, no. 193, Disp., GB, NA; Louis B.

Schmidt, "The Influence of Wheat and Cotton on Anglo-American Relations during the Civil War," *Iowa Journal of History and Politics* 16 (July 1918): 431, 437, 439; Amos Khasigian, "Economic Factors and British Neutrality, 1861–1865," *Historian* 25 (Aug. 1963): 451–65; Eli Ginzberg, "The Economics of British Neutrality during the American Civil War," *Agricultural History* 10 (Oct. 1936): 151, 155; Robert H. Jones, "Long Live the King?" *Agricultural History* 37 (July 1963): 167–69; Adams, *G.B. and Civil War*, 2:13–14 n.2.

4. EMANCIPATION BY THE SWORD?

1. Stuart to Russell, July 21, 29, Aug. 4, 1862, Russell Papers, PRO 30/22/36; Stuart to Russell, July 21, 1862, *BFSP, 1864–1865*, 55:519.

2. Russell to Stuart, July 25, 1862, Russell Papers, PRO 30/22/96; Russell to Stuart, Aug. 7, 1862, *BPP: Civil War*, 17:29; Stuart to Seward, Aug. 30, 1862, with enclosure: Russell to Stuart, July 28, 1862, NFBL NA; Brauer, "Slavery Problem," 450.

3. Seward to CFA, July 28, 1862, no. 308, *FRUS 1862*, 156–58.

4. Beale, ed., *Diary of Welles*, 1:70–71 (July 13, 1862); "Emancipation Proclamation – First Draft," July 22, 1862, *CWL*, 5:336–37; Thomas and Hyman, *Stanton*, 238–40; Donald, *Lincoln*, 365; Simpson, *America's Civil War*, 77.

5. Blair to Lincoln, July 23, 1862, *CWL*, 5:337 n.1; David Donald, ed., *Inside Lincoln's Cabinet: The Civil War Diaries of Salmon P. Chase* (New York: Longmans, Green, 1954), 99–100; Lincoln's "Remarks to Deputation of Western Gentlemen," Aug. 4, 1862, *CWL*, 5:357; William H. Seward, *Autobiography of William H. Seward from 1801 to 1834, with a Memoir of His Life, and Selections from His Letters from 1831 to 1846*, ed. Frederick W. Seward, 3 vols. (New York: D. Appleton, 1877), 3:74; Brauer, "Slavery Problem," 452; McPherson, *Battle Cry of Freedom*, 505; Van Deusen, *Seward*, 328–29.

6. Lincoln to Reverdy Johnson, July 26, 1862, *CWL*, 5:343; Lincoln to Belmont, July 31, 1862, *CWL*, 5:350.

7. Belmont to Lincoln, Aug. 10, 1862, *CWL*, 5:351 n.1; Lincoln to Cuthbert Bullitt (Union advocate), July 28, 1862, *CWL*, 5:344–45; James G. Randall, *Constitutional Problems under Lincoln*, rev. ed. (Urbana: University of Illinois Press, 1951), 377–78; Irving Katz, *August Belmont: A Political Biography* (New York: Columbia University Press, 1968), 110–11.

8. Henry Adams to CFA Jr., Sept. 5, 1862, J. C. Levenson et al., eds., *The Letters of Henry Adams*, 6 vols. (Cambridge MA: Harvard University Press, 1982–88), 1:309–10.

9. Pease and Randall, eds., *Diary of Browning*, 1:562 (July 24, 1862); Adams, *G.B. and Civil War*, 2:87; Gasparin to Lincoln, July 18, 1862, *CWL*, 5:355 n.1; Lincoln to Gasparin, Aug. 4, 1862, *CWL*, 5:355–56 n.1.

10. Grant and Grenville Dodge (officer) quoted in McPherson, *Battle Cry of Freedom*, 502.

11. Act quoted in James G. Randall and David H. Donald, *The Civil War and Reconstruction* (Lexington MA: D. C. Heath, 1969), 373; Randall, *Constitutional Problems under Lincoln*, 357–64; McClellan to Lincoln, July 7, 1862, quoted in Trefousse, *Lincoln's Decision for Emancipation*, 76; see also 32; Lincoln to Senate and House of Representatives, July 17, 1862, *CWL*, 5:329; Pease and Randall, eds., *Diary of Browning*, 1:555; Donald, *Lincoln*, 364–65; Paludan, *Presidency of Lincoln*, 145–46.

12. Paludan, *Presidency of Lincoln*, 145–46.

13. Paludan, *Presidency of Lincoln*, 146–47, 153–54; Militia Act quoted in McPherson, *Battle Cry of Freedom*, 500; Randall, *Constitutional Problems under Lincoln*, 357–64.

14. McPherson, *Battle Cry of Freedom*, 506–8.

15. Lincoln's Annual Message to Congress, Dec. 1, 1862, *CWL*, 5:534.

16. Paludan, *Presidency of Lincoln*, 130–33; Gabor S. Boritt, "The Voyage to the Colony of Linconia: The Sixteenth President, Black Colonization, and the Defense Mechanism of Avoidance," *Historian* 37 (Aug. 1975): 622–23; Fredrickson, "A Man but Not a Brother," 56–57; Lincoln's "Address on Colonization to a Deputation of Negroes," Aug. 14, 1862, *CWL*, 5:371–72.

17. Black Philadelphian in *New York Tribune*, Sept. 20, 1862, and Douglass in *Douglass' Monthly*, Sept. 1862, both quoted in McPherson, *Battle Cry of Freedom*, 509.

18. Donald, *Lincoln*, 368; Cox, *Lincoln and Black Freedom*, 5, 14; Fehrenbacher, "Only His Stepchildren," 293–310; Fredrickson, "A Man but Not a Brother," 53; Stephen B. Oates, *With Malice Toward None: The Life of Abraham Lincoln* (New York: Harper & Row, 1977), 41; Oates, "'Man of Our Redemption,'" 15–16, 19–20; Randall, *Constitutional Problems under Lincoln*, 370.

19. Greeley to Lincoln, Aug. 19, 1862, *CWL*, 5:389 n.1; Lincoln to Greeley, Aug. 22, 1862, *CWL*, 5:388.

20. Lincoln to Greeley, Aug. 22, 1862, *CWL*, 5:388–89; Donald, *Lincoln*, 368–69.

21. Stuart to Russell, Aug. 22, 1862, Russell Papers, PRO 30/22/36; Argyll to Gladstone, Aug. 26, 1862, Gladstone Papers, Brit. Lib., Add. Mss., 44,099, vol. 14; Argyll to Palmerston, Sept. 2, 1862, GC/AR/25/1, Palmerston Papers, University of Southampton.

22. Stuart to Russell, Aug. 26, 1862, Russell Papers, PRO 30/22/36; Hammond to Sir Austen Henry Layard, Aug. 28, 1862, Layard Papers, Brit. Lib., Add. Mss., 38,951, vol. 21; Slidell to State Department in Richmond, Aug. 24, 1862, in Graebner, "Northern Diplomacy and European Neutrality," 69–70.

23. Gladstone to Argyll, Aug. 29, 1862, Gladstone Papers, and Gladstone to Russell, Aug. 30, 1862, Letter-Book, 1862–63, Brit. Lib., Add. Mss., 44,533, vol. 448; Owsley, *King Cotton Diplomacy*, 137; McPherson, *Battle Cry of Freedom*, 548.

24. Gladstone to Argyll, Sept. 8, 1862, Gladstone Papers, Letter-Book, 1862–63, Brit. Lib., Add. Mss., 44,533, vol. 448.

25. British industrial figures and British shipping figures in Brian R. Mitchell, comp., *European Historical Statistics, 1750–1970* (New York: Columbia University Press, 1975), 355, 618; Owsley, *King Cotton Diplomacy*, 137, 140; McPherson, *Battle Cry of Freedom*, 386, 549–51, 620–25, 710; Hotze to Benjamin, Dec. 20, 1862, ORN, 2d ser., 3:632–33; Hotze quoted in Clement Eaton, *A History of the Southern Confederacy* (New York: Free Press, 1954), 75–76; Frenise A. Logan, "India – Britain's Substitute for American Cotton, 1861–1865," *Journal of Southern History* 24 (Nov. 1958): 475–76; Edward M. Earle, "Egyptian Cotton and the American Civil War," *Political Science Quarterly* 41 (Dec. 1926): 527.

26. Jenkins, *Britain and the War for the Union*, 1:214; Lincoln, "Message to Congress in Special Session," July 4, 1861, CWL, 4:438; Marx quoted in McPherson, *Battle Cry of Freedom*, 550.

27. Henry Adams to CFA Jr., Feb. 13, 1863, Ford, ed., *Cycle of Adams Letters*, 1:253; Argyll to Gladstone, Sept. 2, 1862, Gladstone Papers, Brit. Lib., Add. Mss., 44,099, vol. 14.

28. Mitchell, comp., *European Historical Statistics*, 355, 618; Thouvenel quoted in Case and Spencer, *U.S. and France*, 289–90; Owsley, *King Cotton Diplomacy*, 152.

29. Stuart to Russell, Sept. 1, 1862, Russell Papers, PRO 30/22/36.

30. Bigelow quoted in Case and Spencer, *U.S. and France*, 333.

31. Stuart to Russell, Sept. 9, 1862, Russell Papers, PRO 30/33/36.

32. Stuart to Russell, Sept. 9, 1862, Russell Papers, PRO 30/33/36.

33. CFA diary, Sept. 14, 1862; Bates quoted in CWL, 5:404 n.1 (top), 486 n.1 (top); McPherson, *Battle Cry of Freedom*, 528; Lincoln quoted in McPherson, *Battle Cry of Freedom*, 533.

34. Russell to Cowley, Sept. 13, 1862, Russell Papers, PRO 30/22/105; Palmerston to Russell, Sept. 14, 1862, Russell Papers, PRO 30/22/14; Russell to Palmerston, Sept. 17, 1862, Russell Papers, PRO 30/22/14; Walpole, *Life of Russell*, 2:349; Duberman, *Charles Francis Adams*, 294; McPherson, *Battle Cry of Freedom*, 555–56; Kinley J. Brauer, "British Mediation and the American Civil War: A Reconsideration," *Journal of Southern History* 38 (Feb. 1972): 57; Adams, *G.B. and Civil War*, 2:38, 41.

35. *Moniteur*, Sept. 10, 1862, cited in Case and Spencer, *U.S. and France*, 335; Thouvenel quoted in Dayton to Seward, Sept. 17, 1862, Case and Spencer, *U.S. and France*, 336.

36. Thouvenel to Mercier, Sept. 11, 1862, Thouvenel to Mercier, Sept. 18,

1862, Cowley to Russell, Sept. 18, 1862, all cited in Case and Spencer, *U.S. and France*, 336, 337–38; Adams, *G.B. and Civil War*, 2:38–39.

37. Thouvenel cited in McPherson, *Battle Cry of Freedom*, 554; Jones, *Union in Peril*, 160.

38. CFA diary, Sept. 21, 1862; Seward quote in Mercier to Thouvenel, Sept. 9, 1862, Seward to Dayton, Sept. 8, 1862, quoted in Owsley, *King Cotton Diplomacy*, 330–31.

39. *Times* (London), Sept. 16, 1862, p. 6; *Morning Post* and *Morning Herald*, both dated Sept. 16, 1862, and quoted in Jenkins, *Britain and the War for the Union*, 2:151, see also 167; McPherson, *Battle Cry of Freedom*, 534–35.

40. Palmerston to Russell, Sept. 14, 1862, Russell Papers, PRO 30/22/14D; Russell to Palmerston, Sept. 17, 1862, GC/RU/728, Palmerston Papers.

41. Palmerston to Russell, Sept. 22, 1862, Russell Papers, PRO 30/22/14D; Russell to Palmerston, Sept. 22, 1862, GC/RU/729, Palmerston Papers. Stuart's letter was dated September 9, 1862.

42. Palmerston to Russell, Sept. 23, 1862, Russell Papers, PRO 30/22/14D; Benjamin P. Thomas, *Russo-American Relations, 1815–1867* (Baltimore: Johns Hopkins Press, 1930), chap. 8.

43. Palmerston to Russell, Sept. 23, 1862, Russell Papers, PRO 30/22/14D.

44. Palmerston to Gladstone, Sept. 24, 1862, John Morley, *The Life of William Ewart Gladstone*, 3 vols. (London: Macmillan, 1903), 2:76; Russell to Gladstone, Sept. 26, 1862, Gladstone Papers, Brit. Lib., Add. Mss., 44,292, vol. 207; Russell to Cowley, Sept. 26, 1862, Russell Papers, PRO 30/22/105.

45. Gladstone to Palmerston, Sept. 25, 1862, Gladstone Papers, Brit. Lib., Add. Mss., 44,272, vol. 187.

46. Russell to Gladstone, Sept. 26, 1862, Gladstone Papers, Brit. Lib., Add. Mss. 44,292, vol. 207.

47. Jones, *Union in Peril*, 166.

48. McPherson, *Battle Cry of Freedom*, 545; James V. Murfin, *The Gleam of Bayonets: The Battle of Antietam and the Maryland Campaign of 1862* (New York: Thomas Yoseloff, 1965); Stephen W. Sears, *Landscape Turned Red: The Battle of Antietam* (New York: Ticknor and Fields, 1983).

49. Stuart to Russell, Sept. 29, 1862, Russell Papers, PRO 30/22/36.

50. Palmerston to Russell, Sept. 30, 1862, Russell Papers, PRO 30/22/14D.

51. Stuart to Russell, Sept. 23, 1862, Russell Papers, PRO 30/22/36; Case and Spencer, *U.S. and France*, 326–28, 338.

52. Gladstone to Argyll, Sept. 29, 1862, Gladstone Papers, Brit. Lib., Add. Mss., 44,533, vol. 448.

53. Argyll to Gladstone, Sept. 23, 1862, Gladstone Papers, Brit. Lib., 44,099, vol. 14; Granville to Russell, Sept. 27, 1862, Lord Edmond Fitzmaurice, *The Life of Granville George Leveson Gower, Second Earl Granville, 1815–1891*, 2 vols. (Lon-

don: Longmans, Green, 1905), 1:443–44; Granville to Russell, Sept. 29, 1862, Russell Papers, PRO 30/22/25.

54. Slidell to Benjamin, Sept. 29, 1862, *ORN*, 2d ser., 3:546, and Slidell to Benjamin, Oct. 9, 1862, *ORN*, 2d ser., 3:551; CFA to Everett, May 2, 1862, CFA letterbook; Brauer, "British Mediation and Civil War," 50–51.

55. CFA to Seward, no. 229, Oct. 3, 1862, *FRUS 1862*, 205; Seward to CFA, no. 372, Oct. 18, 1862, *FRUS 1862*, 212–13; Jones, *Union in Peril*, 171–72.

5. "DAYS OF GRACE"

1. Lincoln's, "Reply to Emancipation Memorial Presented by Chicago Christians of All Denominations," Sept. 13, 1862, *CWL*, 5:421–23.

2. Lincoln, "Reply to Emancipation Memorial Presented by Chicago Christians of All Denominations," Sept. 13, 1862, *CWL*, 5:419–21, 423; *Chicago Tribune*, Sept. 23, 1862, and *National Intelligencer* (Washington DC), Sept. 26, 1862, both cited in *CWL*, 5:419 n.1.

3. Seward to CFA, no. 336, Sept. 8, 1862, *FRUS 1862*, 188; Seward to CFA, circular, Sept. 22, 1862, *FRUS 1862*, 195; Donald, ed., *Inside Lincoln's Cabinet*, 149–51 (Sept. 22, 1862); "Preliminary Emancipation Proclamation," Sept. 22, 1862, *CWL*, 5:434.

4. Jones, *Union in Peril*, 173–74; Jenkins, *Britain and the War for the Union*, 2:153; John Hope Franklin, *The Emancipation Proclamation* (Garden City NY: Doubleday, 1963), 129–40; McPherson, *Battle Cry of Freedom*, 510, 557–58; Oates, "Man of Our Redemption," 17, 19–20; McPherson, *Lincoln and the Second American Revolution*, 34–35; Harris, *With Charity for All*, 56.

5. Brauer, "Slavery Problem," 467; Van Deusen, *Seward*, 333; Roland C. McConnell, "From Preliminary to Final Emancipation Proclamation: The First Hundred Days," *Journal of Negro History* 48 (Oct. 1963): 275.

6. McClellan to Mary Ellen (wife), Sept. 25, 1862, Stephen W. Sears, ed., *The Civil War Papers of George B. McClellan: Selected Correspondence, 1860–1865* (New York: Ticknor and Fields, 1989), 481; McClellan quoted in Donald, *Lincoln*, 319.

7. Dennett, ed., *Diaries and Letters of Hay*, 50 (Sept. 26, 1862); George S. Denison (internal revenue collector for Louisiana after Lincoln lifted the blockade) to Chase, Oct. 8, 1862, American Historical Association, *Annual Report of the American Historical Association for the Year 1902*, vol. 2, *Sixth Report of Historical Manuscripts Commission: With Diary and Correspondence of Salmon P. Chase* (Washington DC: U. S. Government Printing Office, 1903), 319.

8. Lincoln quoted in T. J. Barnett to Samuel L. M. Barlow, Sept. 25, 1862, in McPherson, *Battle Cry of Freedom*, 558; Donald, *Lincoln*, 398.

9. Stuart to Russell, Sept. 23, 26, Oct. 7, 10, 1862, Russell Papers, PRO 30/22/36.

10. Richard A. Heckman, "British Press Reaction to the Emancipation Proclamation," *Lincoln Herald* 71 (winter 1969): 150–53; *Times* (London), Oct. 7, 1862, p. 8, Oct. 21, 1862, p. 9; *Spectator* (London), n.d., quoted in Arnold Whitridge, "British Liberals and the American Civil War," *History Today* 12 (Oct. 1962): 694; *Bee-Hive* (London), Oct. 11, 1862, quoted in Kevin J. Logan, "The *Bee-Hive* Newspaper and British Working-Class Attitudes Toward the American Civil War," *Civil War History* 22 (Dec. 1976): 341; "The Crisis of the American War," *Blackwood's Edinburgh Magazine* 92 (Nov. 1862): 636–46, quote on 636.

11. *Times* (London), Oct. 7, 1862, p. 8.

12. Hammond to Layard, Oct. 6, 1862, Layard Papers, Brit. Lib., Add. Mss., 38,051, vol. 21; Cobden to Bright, Oct. 6, 1862, Cobden Papers, Brit. Lib., Add. Mss., 43,652, vol. 6; Adams, *G.B. and Civil War*, 2:103 n.5.

13. Mercier to Thouvenel, Sept. 23, 25, 30 (two letters), 1862, cited in Case and Spencer, *U.S. and France*, 327–28; Thouvenel quoted in Dayton to Seward, Oct. 2, 1862, Case and Spencer, *U.S. and France*, 341–42.

14. Granville to Lord Stanley, Oct. 1, 1862, Fitzmaurice, *Life of Granville*, 1:442.

15. Thouvenel to Mercier, Oct. 2, 1862, cited in Case and Spencer, *U.S. and France*, 342–43.

16. Bigelow diary, Oct. 5, 1862, and Bigelow to Seward, Oct. 7, 10, 1862, Sanford to Seward, Oct. 10, 1862, Orleanist *Revue*, Oct. 15, 1862, all cited in Case and Spencer, *U.S. and France*, 329–30, 331; Seward's circular, Sept. 22, 1862, *FRUS 1862*, 195.

17. Dayton to Seward, Oct. 14, 1862, *FRUS 1862*, 394; French newspapers cited in Case and Spencer, *U.S. and France*, 330–31.

18. Palmerston to Russell, Oct. 2, 3, 1862, Russell Papers, PRO 30/22/14D; Jenkins, *Britain and the War for the Union*, 2:170; Merli, *Great Britain and the Confederate Navy*, 118, 257, 259.

19. Adams, *G.B. and Civil War*, 2:45 n.2; Russell to Palmerston, Oct. 2, 4, 6, 1862, GC/RU/731–33, Palmerston Papers.

20. Jones, *Union in Peril*, 178–79.

21. Matthew, ed., *Gladstone Diaries*, 6:152 n.6; *Times* (London), Oct. 8, 1862, p. 7, Oct. 9, 1862, pp. 7–8; Jasper Ridley, *Lord Palmerston* (New York: E. P. Dutton, 1971), 558.

22. Mann to Benjamin, Oct. 7, 1862, ORN, 2d ser., 3:551; Lawley to Gladstone, Dec. 23, 1862, Gladstone Papers, Brit. Lib., Add. Mss., 44,399, vol. 314; Charles Francis Adams Jr., "The Crisis of Foreign Intervention in the War of Secession, September–November, 1862," *Massachusetts Historical Society Proceedings* 47 (1914): 32–33; CFA diary, Oct. 8, 9, 12, 1862; CFA to Seward, Oct. 10, 1862, no. 237, *FRUS 1862*, 209; Martin Crawford, *The Anglo-American Crisis of the Mid-Nineteenth Century: The Times and America, 1850–1862* (Athens: Uni-

versity of Georgia Press, 1987), 132, 172 n.8; Brian Jenkins, "Frank Lawley and the Confederacy," *Civil War History* 23 (June 1977): 144–60; Jenkins, *Britain and the War for the Union*, 2:47–50.

23. H. C. G. Matthew, *Gladstone, 1809–1874* (New York: Oxford University Press, 1986), 133–34, 186; Gladstone to Arthur Gordon (the correspondent), Sept. 22, 1862, Matthew, *Gladstone*, 134; Jenkins, *Britain and the War for the Union*, 2:22–23; Gladstone to Russell, Oct. 17, 1862, Gladstone Papers, Brit. Lib., Add. Mss., 44,292, vol. 207; Robert L. Reid, ed., "William E. Gladstone's 'Insincere Neutrality' during the Civil War," *Civil War History* 15 (Dec. 1969): 293–307; Frank J. Merli and Theodore A. Wilson, "The British Cabinet and the Confederacy," *Maryland Historical Magazine* 65 (fall 1970): 239–62; Merli, *Great Britain and Confederate Navy*, 100, 107–8; Jones, *Union in Peril*, 182–86.

24. Palmerston to Russell, Oct. 12, 1862, Russell Papers, PRO 30/22/22; Palmerston to Russell, Oct. 17, Dec. 17, 1862, Russell Papers, PRO 30/33/14D; Russell to Gladstone, Oct. 20, 26, 1862, Gladstone Papers, Brit. Lib., Add. Mss., 44,292, vol. 207.

25. CFA diary, Oct. 8, 9, 23, 1862; Morley, *Life of Gladstone*, 2:80; Moran diary Oct. 9, 24, 1862; CFA to Seward, Oct. 24, 1862, no. 248, *FRUS 1862*, 224.

26. Vattel, *Law of Nations*, bk. 3, secs. 295, 296; Russell, "Memorandum" for Foreign Office, Oct. 13, 1862, Gladstone Papers, Brit. Lib., Add. Mss., 44,595, vol. 510; Russell to Cowley, Oct. 11, 1862, Russell Papers, PRO 30/22/105.

27. Eugene D. Genovese, *From Rebellion to Revolution: Afro-American Slave Revolts in the Making of the New World* (Baton Rouge: Louisiana State University Press, 1979), 19–38, 55–70, 101–5; Alfred N. Hunt, *Haiti's Influence on Antebellum America: Slumbering Volcano in the Caribbean* (Baton Rouge: Louisiana State University Press, 1988), 20–29.

28. Russell, "Memorandum" for Foreign Office, Oct. 13, 1862, Gladstone Papers, Brit. Lib., Add. Mss., 44,595, vol. 510; Adams, *G.B. and Civil War*, 2:49–50; Russell to Cowley, Oct. 11, 1862, Russell Papers, PRO 30/22/105.

29. Palmerston to Russell, Oct. 8, 1862, Russell Papers, PRO 30/22/14D; Jones, *Union in Peril*, 186, 189–91.

6. AUTUMN OF DISCONTENT

1. Jones, *Union in Peril*, 177–78, 181–82; CFA Jr., "Crisis of Foreign Intervention," 24; Jenkins, *Britain and the War for the Union*, 2:33, 63–64, 71; Kinley J. Brauer, "British Mediation and the American Civil War: A Reconsideration," *Journal of Southern History* 38 (Feb. 1972): 49–64; Norman A. Graebner, "European Interventionism and the Crisis of 1862," *Journal of the Illinois State Historical*

Society 69 (Feb. 1976): 33–45; Howard Jones, "History and Mythology: The Crisis over British Intervention in the Civil War," in *The Union, the Confederacy, and the Atlantic Rim*, ed. Robert E. May (West Lafayette IN: Purdue University Press, 1995), 29–67.

2. Palmerston to Russell, Oct. 20, 21, 22, 1862, Russell Papers, PRO 30/22/14D; Lewis, "Memorandum on the American Question," Oct. 17, 1862, Gladstone Papers, Brit. Lib., Add. Mss., 44,595, vol. 510; Jones, *Union in Peril*, 190–91.

3. Palmerston to Russell, Oct. 22, 1862, Russell Papers, PRO 30/22/14.

4. Palmerston to Russell, Oct. 26, 1862, Russell Papers, PRO 30/22/14D.

5. Palmerston to Russell, Oct. 23, 1862, Russell Papers, PRO 30/22/14; Russell's memo for Foreign Office, Oct. 23, 1862, and Gladstone's memo "The War in America," Oct. 24, 1862, Gladstone Papers, Brit. Lib., Add. Mss., 44,595, vol. 510; Russell to Palmerston, Oct. 24, 1862, GC/RU/736, Palmerston Papers.

6. Case and Spencer, *U.S. and France*, 17, 27, 31, 38–39, 40–42, 337; quote on 42.

7. Stuart to Russell, Oct. 17, 24, 26, 1862, Russell Papers, PRO 30/22/36; Case and Spencer, *U.S. and France*, 346–47, 353, 355–60; Drouyn quoted in Case and Spencer, *U.S. and France*, 359–60, 371.

8. Memo of Slidell interview with Napoleon on Oct. 28, 1862, enclosure B in Slidell to Benjamin, Oct. 28, 1862, ORN, 2d ser., 3:574–77; Case and Spencer, *U.S. and France*, 356–57; Owsley, *King Cotton Diplomacy*, 333–36.

9. Memo of Slidell interview with Napoleon, Oct. 29, 1862, in Slidell to Mason, Oct. 29, 1862, Mason Papers (Library of Congress).

10. Benjamin to Mason, Oct. 31, 1862, ORN, 2d ser., 3:584–88; Benjamin to Mason, Dec. 11, 1862, Mason Papers; Case and Spencer, *U.S. and France*, 356–57, 364; Benjamin to Mason, Jan. 15, 1863, ORN, 2d ser., 3:656; Mason to Benjamin, Nov. 6, 1862, Richardson, ed., *Messages and Papers of the Confederacy*, 2:359.

11. Palmerston to Russell, Nov. 2, 1862, Russell Papers, PRO 30/22/14D; Mason to Benjamin, Nov. 6, 1862, Richardson, ed., *Messages and Papers of the Confederacy*, 2:359; Benjamin to Mason, Oct. 28, 31, 1862, Mason Papers; Russell to Lyons, Nov. 1, 1862, Russell Papers, PRO 30/22/96; Russell to Cowley, Nov. 1, 1862, Russell Papers, PRO 30/22/105; Jones, *Union in Peril*, 202–4.

12. Stuart to Russell, Nov. 7, 1862, Russell Papers, PRO 30/22/36; McPherson, *Battle Cry of Freedom*, 561–62; Jones, *Union in Peril*, 206–7; Graebner, "Northern Diplomacy and European Neutrality," 55–78; Brauer, "British Mediation and Civil War"; Stuart to Russell, Nov. 4, 1862, Russell Papers, PRO 30/22/36; Russell to Grey, Oct. 28, 1862, G. P. Gooch, ed., *The Later Correspondence of Lord John Russell, 1840–1878*, 2 vols. (London: Longmans, Green, 1925), 2:332.

13. Lyons to Russell, Nov. 11, 1862, Russell Papers, PRO 30/22/36.

14. Lyons to Russell, Nov. 14, 1862, Russell Papers, PRO 30/22/36.

15. Lyons to Russell, Nov. 17, 1862, *BFSP 1864–1865*, 55:534–39; Lyons to Russell, Nov. 14, 1862, Russell Papers, PRO 30/22/36.

16. Lyons to Russell, Nov. 14, 1862, Russell Papers, PRO 30/22/36; Lyons to Russell, Nov. 17, 1862, *BFSP 1864–1865*, 55:534; Lyons to Russell, Nov. 18, 24, 1862, Russell Papers, PRO 30/22/36; Lyons to Russell, Nov. 18, 1862 (confidential), no. 438, FO 5/838, PRO.

17. Newton, *Lyons*, 1:89–90.

18. A. G. Gardiner, *The Life of Sir William Harcourt*, 2 vols. (New York: George H. Doran, 1923), 1:125, 127, 132–37; Jenkins, *Britain and the War for the Union*, 2:179–80; Crook, *The North, the South, and the Powers*, 241; Merli, *Great Britain and the Confederate Navy*, 114–15; Historicus letter dated Nov. 4, 1862, *Times* (London), Nov. 7, 1862, pp. 6–7; letter reprinted in *Letters by Historicus on Some Questions of International Law* (London: Macmillan, 1863), 3–15 (quotes on 8, 9–10); Historicus, "Neutrality or Intervention," *Letters*, 41–51 (quotes on 42, 43, 46, 47, 48, 49–50, 51); letter in *Times* of London, Nov. 17, 1862, p. 9.

19. Lewis, "Recognition of the Independence of the Southern States of the North American Union," Nov. 7, 1862, Gladstone Papers, Brit. Lib., Add. Mss., 44,595, vol. 510 (original draft, though incomplete, in Lewis Papers, War Office and India, 3509, 3510, and 3514, National Library of Wales, Aberystwyth). Lewis cited in John Austin, *The Province of Jurisprudence Determined* (London: Weidenfield and Nicolson, 1832), 214, in support of his argument on recognition. Other specialists in international law he consulted were Vattel, *Law of Nations*, bk. 3, sec. 295, and Wheaton, *Elements of International Law* (1836), pt. 1, sec. 26. See also Jones, *Union in Peril*, 210–15.

20. Lewis, "Recognition of Independence."

21. Lewis, "Recognition of Independence"; Jones, *Union in Peril*, 216–17.

22. Lord Napier (British ambassador in St. Petersburg) to Russell, Nov. 8, 1862, cited in Adams, *G.B. and Civil War*, 2:63, 66; Lewis to Clarendon, Nov. 11, 1862, Maxwell, *Life and Letters of Clarendon*, 2:268; Jenkins, *Britain and the War for the Union*, 2:180; Gladstone to wife, Nov. 12, 13, 1862, Morley, *Gladstone*, 2:85; Jones, *Union in Peril*, 217–20.

23. Russell to Cowley, Nov. 13, 1862, Cowley Papers, FO 146/1046; Cowley to Russell, Nov. 18, 1862, cited in Case and Spencer, *U.S. and France*, 363; Gladstone to wife, Nov. 12, 1862, Morley, *Gladstone*, 2:85.

24. Drouyn quoted in Case and Spencer, *U.S. and France*, 359 (first quote), 360–61 (second quote), 361 (third quote).

25. Case and Spencer, *U.S. and France*, 366–67.

26. Case and Spencer, *U.S. and France*, 367–69; Dayton quoted on 368, 369; Drouyn quoted on 368.

27. Drouyn to Mercier, Nov. 18, 1862, cited in Owsley, *King Cotton Diplomacy*, 359.

28. *Times* (London), Nov. 13, 1862, p. 8.

29. Seward to Dayton, Nov. 30, 1862, BFSP *1864–1865*, 55:435–36; Seward to CFA, Dec. 8, 1862, no. 418, U.S. Department of State, *Papers Relating to Foreign Affairs, Accompanying the Annual Message of the President to the First Session of the Thirty-Eighth Congress* (Washington DC: U.S. Government Printing Office, 1864), *1863*, 12–13 (hereafter cited as FRUS *1863*); Seward to Bayard Taylor, Dec. 7, 1862, no. 9, U. S., Department of State, Diplomatic Instructions of the Department of State, 1801–1906, Russia, National Archives, Washington DC.

30. Slidell to Mason, Nov. 16, 1862, and Lindsay to Mason, Nov. 20, 1862, Mason Papers; Bigelow to Seward, Nov. 21, 1862, quoted in John Bigelow, *Retrospections of an Active Life*, 5 vols. (New York: Baker and Taylor, 1909–13), 1:574; Slidell to Benjamin, Nov. 21, 29, 1862, ORN, 2d ser., 3:612–13.

31. Jones, *Union in Peril*, 219–20, 223; Lincoln's first quote on 221; Lincoln's second quote in Annual Message to Congress, Dec. 1, 1862, CWL, 5:518, 519.

32. Lincoln's Annual Message to Congress, Dec. 1, 1862, CWL, 5:530; Donald, *Lincoln*, 396.

33. Donald, *Lincoln*, 396–98.

34. Lincoln's Annual Message to Congress, Dec. 1, 1862, CWL, 5:537.

7. THE EMANCIPATION PROCLAMATION

1. James M. McPherson, "'The Whole Family of Man': Lincoln and the Last Best Hope Abroad," in *The Union, the Confederacy, and the Atlantic Rim*, ed. May, 131–32.

2. Emerson quoted in Nevins, *Statesmanship of the Civil War*, 131; McPherson, *Lincoln and the Second American Revolution*, 34, 85; Paludan, *Presidency of Lincoln*, xiv–xv.

3. Adams, *G.B. and Civil War*, 2:98.

4. R. J. M. Blackett, "Pressure from Without: African Americans, British Public Opinion, and Civil War Diplomacy," in *The Union, the Confederacy, and the Atlantic Rim*, ed. May, 77–81, 87–90; Owsley, *King Cotton Diplomacy*, 177; Russell to Lyons, Feb. 14, 1863, quoted in Adams, *G.B. and Civil War*, 2:155; Gregory to Mason, Mar. 18, 1863, Mason Papers.

5. Adams, *G.B. and Civil War*, 2:153, 155; Hanna and Hanna, *Napoleon III and Mexico*, 58–60; Sanford to Seward, Aug. 13, Sept. 2, 1862, Jan. 20, 1863, cited in Hanna and Hanna, *Napoleon III and Mexico*, 81.

6. Mann to Benjamin, Sept. 1, 1862, Jan. 29, May 8, 1863, cited in Hanna and Hanna, *Napoleon III and Mexico*, 117–18; Benjamin to Slidell, Oct. 17, 1862, ORN, 2d ser., 3:556–58.

7. Adam Gurowski, *Diary, from March 4, 1861 to November 12, 1862* (Boston:

Lee & Shepard, 1862), 278; Emancipation Proclamation, Jan. 1, 1863, *CWL*, 6:30; Franklin, *Emancipation Proclamation*, 86–87.

8. Marx quoted in Paludan, *Presidency of Lincoln*, 187–88; Preliminary Emancipation Proclamation, Sept. 22, 1862, *CWL*, 5:433–34.

9. "Proclamation Appointing a National Fast Day," Mar. 30, 1863, *CWL*, 6:156.

10. Lincoln's Inaugural Address, Mar. 4, 1861, *CWL*, 4:268.

11. Lincoln to Chase, Sept. 2, 1863, *CWL*, 6:428–29; Cox, *Lincoln and Black Freedom*, 15; Jones, "To Preserve a Nation," 174–75.

12. McPherson, *Lincoln and the Second American Revolution*, 35; Lincoln to Andrew Johnson, Mar. 26, 1863, *CWL*, 6:149–50; Lincoln to James C. Conkling, Aug. 26, 1863, *CWL*, 6:408–9; Paludan, *Presidency of Lincoln*, xv; James M. McPherson, *The Negro's Civil War: How American Negroes Felt and Acted during the War for the Union* (New York: Knopf, 1965), 158.

13. Pennsylvania and New York soldiers quoted in McPherson, *What They Fought For*, 62; others in James M. McPherson, *For Cause and Comrades: Why Men Fought in the Civil War* (New York: Oxford University Press, 1997), 19, 121–22, 128, 172.

14. McPherson, *What They Fought For*, 63–69.

15. Iowa and Minnesota privates quoted in McPherson, *For Cause and Comrades*, 118; all others in McPherson, *What They Fought For*, 6, 46, 56.

16. McPherson, *What They Fought For*, 49–50, 51.

17. Volunteer, South Carolinian, soldier, and slaveholding officer quoted in McPherson, *For Cause and Comrades*, 20, 21.

18. *Morning Star* (London), Oct. 6, 1862, quoted in Nevins, *War Becomes Revolution*, 270.

19. Bright to Cobden, Dec. 24, 1862, Bright Papers, Brit. Lib., Add. Mss., 43,384, vol. 2; Henry Adams to CFA Jr., Jan. 27, 1863, and CFA to CFA Jr., Dec. 25, 1862, Ford, ed., *Cycle of Adams Letters*, 1:243–45, 220–21; CFA Diary, Jan. 2, 13, 16, 17, Feb. 27, 1863; CFA to Seward, Jan. 2, 1863, no. 289, Disp., GB, NA; Blackett, "Pressure from Without," 71–74, 90–91; Donaldson Jordan and Edwin J. Pratt, *Europe and the American Civil War* (Boston: Houghton Mifflin, 1931), 145–63; Adams, *G.B. and Civil War*, 2:152.

20. Lincoln to Workingmen of Manchester, England, Jan. 19, 1863, *CWL*, 6:64; Lincoln to Workingmen of London, Feb. 2, 1863, *CWL*, 6:88–89; Donald, *Lincoln*, 415.

21. Lincoln's Resolution on Slavery, Apr. 15, 1863, *CWL*, 6:176; Donald, *Lincoln*, 415.

22. Jones, *Union in Peril*, 225–26.

23. Case and Spencer, *U.S. and France*, 332, 347, 352, 358–59, 375–78.

24. Case and Spencer, *U.S. and France*, 385.

25. Case and Spencer, *U.S. and France*, 386–88; Drouyn to Mercier, Jan. 9, 1863, quoted in Case and Spencer, *U.S. and France*, 387.

26. Drouyn quoted in Dayton to Seward, Jan. 15, 1863, and Dayton to Seward, Jan. 15, 1863, cited in Case and Spencer, *U.S. and France*, 389–90.

27. Dayton to Seward, Jan. 27, 1863, cited in Case and Spencer, *U.S. and France*, 391.

28. Napoleon's Annual Address to National Assembly, Jan. 15, 1863, cited in Case and Spencer, *U.S. and France*, 392; see also 393.

29. Donald, *Lincoln*, 416–18; Vallandigham quoted in *Congressional Globe*, 37th Cong., 3d sess., 314, appendix, 52–60.

30. Donald, *Lincoln*, 414–15; Case and Spencer, *U.S. and France*, 393–94; Warren F. Spencer, "The Jewett-Greeley Affair: A Private Scheme for French Mediation in the American Civil War," *New York History* 5 (1970): 238–67.

31. *New York Tribune*, Jan. 28, 29, 1863, quoted in Case and Spencer, *U.S. and France*, 394.

32. Carroll, *Mercier*, 251–57; Donald, *Sumner*, 103; Donald, *Lincoln*, 414.

33. Case and Spencer, *U.S. and France*, 393–95; Donald, *Lincoln*, 414–15.

34. Donald, *Lincoln*, 415.

35. Case and Spencer, *U.S. and France*, 396.

8. THE FINAL IMPACT OF SLAVERY

1. Thomas Schoonover, "Napoleon Is Coming! Maximilian Is Coming? The International History of the Civil War in the Caribbean Basin," in *The Union, the Confederacy, and the Atlantic Rim*, ed. May, 107, 112–14, 121; Henry Blumenthal, *A Reappraisal of Franco-American Relations, 1830–1871* (Chapel Hill: University of North Carolina Press, 1959), 172.

2. Hotze to Benjamin, June 6, 1863, ORN, 2d ser., 3:783–86; Carlyle quoted in Bigelow, *Retrospections*, 2:26; Henry Adams to CFA Jr., June 25, 1863, Ford., ed., *Cycle of Adams Letters*, 2:40; Case and Spencer, *U.S. and France*, 398.

3. McPherson, *Battle Cry of Freedom*, 683–84; Sanford to Seward, May 19, 1863, cited in Hanna and Hanna, *Napoleon III and Mexico*, 90.

4. McPherson, *Battle Cry of Freedom*, 683–84.

5. Drouyn quoted in Dayton to Seward, Apr. 9, 1863, cited in Hanna and Hanna, *Napoleon III and Mexico*, 117; Dayton to Seward, Apr. 24, 1863, cited in Owsley, *King Cotton Diplomacy*, 514. Charles Maurice de Talleyrand-Périgord was French foreign minister during the late eighteenth and early nineteenth centuries.

6. Case and Spencer, *U.S. and France*, 399–401; Owsley, *King Cotton Diplomacy*, 441, 513–14; Crook, *The North, the South, and the Powers*, 264–65, 335–

36; Kathryn A. Hanna, "The Roles of the South in the French Intervention in Mexico," *Journal of Southern History* 20 (Feb. 1954): 9–10; Hanna and Hanna, *Napoleon III and Mexico*, 90.

7. Crook, *The North, the South, and the Powers*, 336.

8. Case and Spencer, *U.S. and France*, 401–2; Paul to Drouyn, Mar. 15, 1863, cited in Case and Spencer, *U.S. and France*, 401.

9. Napoleon quoted in Cowley to Russell, Apr. 10, 1863, cited in Case and Spencer, *U.S. and France*, 402; see also 402, 408.

10. Case and Spencer, *U.S. and France*, 408.

11. Case and Spencer, *U.S. and France*, 409.

12. Slidell memorandum, ORN, 2d ser., 3:812–14; Case and Spencer, *U.S. and France*, 409.

13. Slidell memorandum, ORN, 2d ser., 3:812–14; Case and Spencer, *U.S. and France*, 409; Slidell to Mason, June 29, 1863, Mason Papers.

14. Slidell memorandum, ORN, 2d ser., 3:812–14; Case and Spencer, *U.S. and France*, 409.

15. Slidell to Benjamin, June 21, 1863, ORN, 2d ser., 3:810–12; Case and Spencer, *U.S. and France*, 409–10.

16. Case and Spencer, *U.S. and France*, 410–11; Drouyn quoted in Slidell to Benjamin, June 21, 1863, cited in Case and Spencer, *U.S. and France*, 411.

17. Slidell to Benjamin, June 21, 1863, ORN, 2d ser., 3:811; Case and Spencer, *U.S. and France*, 411.

18. Lindsay's account in Owsley, *King Cotton Diplomacy*, 449.

19. Case and Spencer, *U.S. and France*, 412–16; Napoleon to Drouyn, July 14, 1863, cited in Case and Spencer, *U.S. and France*, 415–16.

20. Case and Spencer, *U.S. and France*, 331, 403; *La France* quoted in Case and Spencer, *U.S. and France*, 420; Dayton to Seward, May 29, 1863, cited in Case and Spencer, *U.S. and France*, 420; Crook, *The North, the South, and the Powers*, 315.

21. Drouyn quoted in Dayton to Seward, June 25, 1863, and Dayton quoted in Case and Spencer, *U.S. and France*, 420.

22. Roebuck quoted in Owsley, *King Cotton Diplomacy*, 452.

23. Roebuck quoted in Owsley, *King Cotton Diplomacy*, 452; see also 452–53.

24. Owsley, *King Cotton Diplomacy*, 453–56; Crook, *The North, the South, and the Powers*, 313–14.

25. Owsley, *King Cotton Diplomacy*, 453–56; Crook, *The North, the South, and the Powers*, 313–14.

26. Hotze to Benjamin, July 11, 1863, ORN, 2d ser., 3:839–41; Mason to Slidell, July 1, 1863, Mason Papers; Case and Spencer, *U.S. and France*, 413.

27. Case and Spencer, *U.S. and France*, 420–21; Drouyn quoted in Dayton to Seward, July 2, 1863, cited in Case and Spencer, *U.S. and France*, 421.

28. Dayton to Seward, July 2, 10, 1863, cited in Case and Spencer, *U.S. and France*, 421; 421–22.

29. Case and Spencer, *U.S. and France*, 422–23; Seward to Dayton, July 8, 1863, cited in Case and Spencer, *U.S. and France* 422–23.

30. Seward to Dayton, July 10, 1863, cited in Case and Spencer, *U.S. and France*, 423; Seward to Dayton, July 29, 1863, quoted in Owsley, *King Cotton Diplomacy*, 464.

31. Slidell to Benjamin, Sept. 22, 1863, *ORN*, 2d ser., 3:905–10; Case and Spencer, *U.S. and France*, 423–24; Dayton to Seward, July 30, 1863, and Paul to Drouyn, Aug. 24, 1863, cited in Case and Spencer, *U.S. and France*, 424.

32. Owsley, *King Cotton Diplomacy*, 357.

33. Napoleon to Drouyn, July 14, 1863, cited in Case and Spencer, *U.S. and France*, 416.

34. Napoleon to Drouyn, June 22, 1863, Drouyn to Gros, June 23, 1863, and Gros to Drouyn, July 1, 1863, all cited in Case and Spencer, *U.S. and France*, 417, 418.

35. Case and Spencer, *U.S. and France*, 417–18.

36. Napoleon quoted in Case and Spencer, *U.S. and France*, 416.

37. Benjamin to Mason, Aug. 4, 1863, Mason to Russell, Sept. 21, 1863, and Russell to Mason, Sept. 25, 1863, both enclosed in Mason to Benjamin, Oct. 19, 1863, and Benjamin to Mason, Nov. 13, 1863, all in *ORN*, 2d ser., 3:852–53, 934–35, 950–51; Owsley, *King Cotton Diplomacy*, 465–66.

38. *Charleston Courier*, Feb. 28, 1862, *Montgomery Advertiser*, Mar. 15, 1863, both quoted in Owsley, *King Cotton Diplomacy*, 468, 469; see also 467–70.

39. *Richmond Whig*, Dec. 29, 1862, *Richmond Enquirer*, Feb. 7, April 1, 1863, both quoted in Owsley, *King Cotton Diplomacy*, 470, 471, 472; Benjamin to Slidell, June 10, 1863, *ORN*, 2d ser., 3:792–96; Benjamin quoted in Owsley, *King Cotton Diplomacy*, 492.

40. Owsley, *King Cotton Diplomacy*, 508.

41. Owsley, *King Cotton Diplomacy*, 507–8.

42. Dayton to Seward, Sept. 7, 1863, Owsley, *King Cotton Diplomacy*, 514–15; Fred H. Harrington, *Fighting Politician: Major General N. P. Banks* (Philadelphia: University of Pennsylvania Press, 1948), 128, 130–31.

43. *Moniteur* and *Documents diplomatiques*, *New York Times*, Sept. 25, 1863, and tract, all cited in Hanna and Hanna, *Napoleon III and Mexico*, 58, 60.

44. Hanna and Hanna, *Napoleon III and Mexico*, 66–68.

45. Hanna and Hanna, *Napoleon III and Mexico*, 60–64; Schoonover, "Napoleon Is Coming!", 106.

46. Hanna and Hanna, *Napoleon III and Mexico*, 64–66.

47. Napoleon to Gen. Achille François Bazaine (commander), Sept. 12, 1863, cited in Hanna and Hanna, *Napoleon III and Mexico*, 169; see also 170–71;

Thomas Schoonover, *Dollars over Dominion: The Triumph of Liberalism in Mexican–United States Relations, 1861–1867* (Baton Rouge: Louisiana State University Press, 1978), chap. 6.

48. Motley to Oliver Wendell Holmes, Sept. 22, 1863, quoted in Hanna and Hanna, *Napoleon and Mexico*, 130.

49. Seward to Dayton, Sept. 21, 1863, Owsley, *King Cotton Diplomacy*, 515; Seward to Dayton, Feb. 14, 1864, cited in Owsley, *King Cotton Diplomacy*, 517.

50. Maximilian to Slidell, Nov. 7, 1863, enclosed in Slidell to Benjamin, Dec. 3, 1863, contact reported, and Mann to Benjamin, Mar. 11, 1864, all in ORN, 2d ser., 3:968–70, 1057–59; Crook, *The North, the South, and the Powers*, 335, 339–41; Owsley, *King Cotton Diplomacy*, 521.

51. Slidell's conversation with aide in Slidell to Mason, Mar. 22, 1864, Mason Papers; Slidell to Benjamin, Mar. 16, 1864, Benjamin to Slidell, June 23, 1864, both in ORN, 2d ser., 3:1063–65, 1156–57; Owsley, *King Cotton Diplomacy*, 524–25.

52. Owsley, *King Cotton Diplomacy*, 525–26; Napoleon quoted in Hanna and Hanna, *Napoleon III and Mexico*, 122.

53. Owsley, *King Cotton Diplomacy*, 525–26; Hanna and Hanna, *Napoleon III and Mexico*, 125.

54. Slidell to Benjamin, Mar. 16, 1864, ORN, 2d ser., 3:1063–65; Dayton to Seward, Mar. 21, 1864, cited in Owsley, *King Cotton Diplomacy*, 527; see also 526–28; Slidell to Benjamin, Apr. 7, 1864, and Slidell to Mason, May 2, 1864, ORN, 2d ser., 3:1077–79, 1107–11.

55. Benjamin to Slidell, June 23, 1864, ORN, 2d ser., 3:1156–57.

56. Elbert B. Smith, *Francis Preston Blair* (New York: Free Press, 1980), 363–68; McPherson, *Battle Cry of Freedom*, 822–24.

57. Hanna and Hanna, *Napoleon III and Mexico*, 300.

58. Lincoln's Response to a Serenade, Feb. 1, 1865, CWL, 8:254–55. 1864, ORN, 2d ser., 3:1156–57.

EPILOGUE

1. Lincoln's Second Inaugural Address, Mar. 4, 1865, CWL, 8:333; McPherson, *Lincoln and the Second American Revolution*, 37.

2. Benjamin to Mason and Slidell, Dec. 27, 1864, Hotze to Benjamin, Sept. 26, 1863, Slidell to Mason, Mar. 6, 1865, in Mason to Benjamin, Mar. 31, 1865, all in ORN, 2d ser., 3:1253–57, 914–18, 1270–71; Owsley, *King Cotton Diplomacy*, 535–41.

3. Duberman, *Charles Francis Adams*, 293–304; Crook, *The North, the South, and the Powers*, 258–62; Adams, *G.B. and Civil War*, 2:119–31; Jones, "To Preserve a Nation," 182.

4. Frederick Douglass, *Life and Times of Frederick Douglass: His Early Life as a*

Slave, His Escape from Bondage, and His Complete History (1892; rpt. New York: Collier, 1962), 488–89.

5. Lincoln's speech at Springfield IL, June 26, 1857, *CWL*, 2:406–7.

6. Webster's speech, Jan. 27, 1830, Charles M. Wiltse, ed., *The Papers of Daniel Webster: Speeches and Formal Writings*, 2 vols. (Hanover NH: University Press of New England, 1986), 1:347–48; Lincoln to Hodges, Apr. 4, 1864, *CWL*, 7:281.

7. Lincoln's first quote in speech at Edwardsville IL, Sept. 11, 1858, *CWL*, 3:95; second quote in Lincoln to Henry L. Pierce and others, Apr. 6, 1859, *CWL*, 3:376; third quote in McPherson, *Drawn with the Sword*, 203; last quote in Lincoln's Annual Address to Congress, Dec. 1, 1862, *CWL*, 5:537.

8. First quote in Lincoln's Annual Message to Congress, Dec. 3, 1861, *CWL*, 5:53; second quote in Lincoln to Congress, July 4, 1861, *CWL*, 4:426; third quote in Gettysburg Address, Nov. 19, 1863, *CWL*, 7:23.

Bibliographical Essay

The starting place for any research on Lincoln is his published papers, edited by Roy P. Basler et al. and entitled *The Collected Works of Abraham Lincoln*, 9 vols. (New Brunswick: Rutgers University Press, 1953–55), *Supplements* (1973, 1991). Lincoln's ideas receive careful, sympathetic consideration in James M. McPherson, *Abraham Lincoln and the Second American Revolution* (New York: Oxford University Press, 1991). Garry Wills examines Lincoln's republicanism in *Lincoln at Gettysburg: The Words That Remade America* (New York: Simon and Schuster, 1992). The British interventionist threat and related issues involving slavery receive special attention in Howard Jones, *Union in Peril: The Crisis over British Intervention in the Civil War* (Chapel Hill: University of North Carolina Press, 1992).

Lincoln's policies toward slavery and the Union have drawn attention, although not enough on their interrelationship. LaWanda Cox offers a close and favorable analysis in *Lincoln and Black Freedom: A Study in Presidential Leadership* (Columbia: University of South Carolina Press, 1981). For a critical view, see Robert W. Johannsen, *Lincoln, the South, and Slavery: The Political Dimension* (Baton Rouge: Louisiana State University Press, 1991). See also Don E. Fehrenbacher, "Only His Stepchildren: Lincoln and the Negro," *Civil War History* 20 (December 1974); George M. Fredrickson, "A Man but Not a Brother: Abraham Lincoln and Racial Equality," *Journal of Southern History* 41 (February 1975); and Howard Jones, "To Preserve a Nation: Abraham Lincoln and Franklin D. Roosevelt as Wartime Diplomatists," in *War Comes Again: Comparative Vistas on the Civil War and World War II*, ed. Gabor S. Boritt (New York: Oxford University Press, 1995), 167–95. For the classic account of Lincoln's move against slavery, see John Hope Franklin, *The Emancipation Proclamation* (Garden City NY: Doubleday, 1963).

The most useful broad studies of America's relations with Europe during the Civil War are Ephraim D. Adams, *Great Britain and the American Civil War*, 2 vols. (New York: Longmans, Green, 1925); Lynn M. Case and Warren F. Spencer, *The United States and France: Civil War Diplomacy* (Philadelphia: University of Pennsylvania Press, 1970); and Brian Jenkins, *Britain and the War for the Union,* 2 vols. (Montreal: McGill-Queen's University Press, 1974, 1980). For the economics of the South's diplomacy, see Frank L. Owsley, *King Cotton Diplomacy: Foreign Relations of the Confederate States of America* (Chicago: University of Chicago Press, 1959). The most thorough analysis of Napoleon III's policies toward Mexico and the Confederacy is Alfred J. Hanna and Kathryn A. Hanna, *Napoleon III and Mexico: American Triumph over Monarchy* (Chapel Hill: University of North Carolina Press, 1971).

Index

abolition: and Britain, 129; and colonization, 91; and dissolution of the Union, 50; and the Emancipation Proclamation, 145; and equal rights for blacks, 38; and evangelical Christianity, 14; and gradual emancipation, 65; opposed by northerners, 38; and the purpose of the Civil War, 15, 83; viewed by Clay, 27; viewed by Lincoln, 14, 22, 23, 38, 83, 149, 150, 151, 187; without compensation, 14, 21, 38, 90

abolitionists: Emancipation Proclamation criticized by, 115–16; Lincoln viewed by, 189; viewed by Napoleon III, 180–81

Adams, Charles Francis: and British intervention, 70, 82, 108, 125, 137; and diplomatic recognition of the Confederacy, 46, 64, 124, 125; and emancipation, 39, 64; mentioned, 54, 63, 66, 67, 81, 85, 88, 177; and the sanctity of the Union, 38; and the Second Battle of Bull Run, 98; and slavery, 38, 39, 49, 50, 64, 80, 82

Adams, Charles Francis, Jr., 8, 88

Adams, Henry, 88, 165

Alabama, 163

Alexandra, 163

American Colonization Society, 22

American Revolution. *See* Revolutionary War

Antietam, Battle of, 105–6; and foreign intervention, 4, 84, 106, 108–9, 110, 116, 156; and Lincoln, 108, 113–14; mentioned, 107, 111, 112, 118, 122; and Union victory in the war, 120

Anti-Slavery Society, 63

Appomattox Courthouse, 17

Argyll, Duke of: and diplomatic recognition of the Confederacy, 48; and intervention in the American Civil War, 57, 92, 94–95, 129; and mediation, 107; slavery opposed by, 95, 154

Arizona, 24

Army of the Potomac, 4, 117

Austria, 70, 165; and diplomatic recognition of the Confederacy, 98, 181; and intervention in the American Civil War, 3, 102; and mediation, 130

Banks, Nathaniel, 179

Bates, Edward, 98

Belgium, 148, 165, 182

Belmont, August, 88

Benjamin, Judah P., 44, 79, 133, 143, 148; and French diplomatic recognition of the Confederacy, 184; and the French presence in Mexico, 182–83;

4, 33; and foreign intervention, 1–2,
4–5, 10, 11, 15, 16–17, 18; as ideological conflict, 6; international impact of,
93, 110; purpose of, 14, 15, 187, 189;
viewed by Lincoln, 14–15, 33, 189–
90

Clay, Henry: and slavery, 22, 23, 26–
27; Union regarded by, 14, 21, 27, 30

Cobden, Richard, 70, 117, 154

colonization: and Lincoln, 68, 90–91,
113, 144, 145; opposition to, 91; voluntary, 22, 26–27, 30, 90

Compromise of 1850, 13

Confederacy: and an armistice, 157; cotton interests utilized by, 7–8, 52, 85,
178, 184; diplomatic recognition
sought by, 2, 3, 7, 8, 10, 37, 44, 45,
46, 48, 49, 51, 54, 60, 63, 67, 75–76,
77–78, 86, 97–98, 100, 108, 123–24,
136–37, 142, 171, 173–74, 177–78,
179, 184, 187–88; emancipation offered by, in exchange for diplomatic
recognition, 64, 187–88; and foreign
affairs, 2, 184; and the French presence in Mexico, 164, 166, 170, 171,
175, 177, 178; independence of, 41–
43, 50, 52, 53, 55, 81, 84, 93, 97–98,
101, 103, 107, 108, 122, 126, 130, 139,
142, 178, 185; and mediation, 76–77,
104–5, 120; and nationhood status,
96, 100; and northern oppression,
114; relations with Britain, 46–48,
178; relations with France, 75, 178,
183; and slavery, 35, 36

Confederate Congress, 8–9, 111, 115

Confederate Constitution, 34, 41

Confederate States of America. *See* Confederacy

Confiscation Acts, 64–65, 73, 112, 126;
Second, 86, 88–89, 90, 92

Congress of the United States, 134, 159,
190; and the Confiscation Acts, 64–
65; and emancipation, 64, 66, 86,
89–90; and slavery, 23, 27, 29, 68,
185

Congress of Vienna, 2

Conservative party, 50, 53

Constitution: and emancipation, 89,
149, 153; Fifth Amendment to, 113;
interpreted by the Union and Confederacy, 6–7; and Lincoln, 12, 13, 18,
19, 38, 69, 111, 190; and property
rights, 25–26; and racial equality,
150; racial views of colonial period reflected in, 26; and secession, 135; and
slavery, 19, 21, 25–26, 29, 31, 38;
Thirteenth Amendment to, 11, 185;
and the Union, 15; war powers under,
33

Constitutional Union party, 52

Copperheads. *See* Peace Democrats

cotton, 7–8, 49, 79; and the argument
for slavery, 21; British interests in, 8,
39, 44–45, 48, 52, 53, 70, 72–73, 77,
81, 85, 93–94, 104, 107, 108, 110,
118, 121, 129, 164, 172, 187; French
interests in, 8, 52, 54, 60, 67, 73, 78,
95, 97, 99, 110, 118, 119, 128, 136,
137, 141, 148, 157, 187, 188; shortages of, 70, 72–73, 93, 110, 124, 130,
133, 155; surplus of, 8, 52

Cowley, Lord, 99, 167

Crimean War, 79, 93, 103, 129, 165

Crittenden Compromise, 31–32

Cuba, 32, 171, 180

Cutting, Francis B., 86

Davis, Garrett, 62

Davis, Jefferson: and the British attitude
toward slavery, 44, 45; and British
diplomatic recognition, 177; cotton as